Heritage after Conflict

The year 2018 marks the twentieth anniversary of the signing of the Belfast Agreement that initiated an uneasy peace in Northern Ireland after the forty years of the Troubles. The last twenty years, however, has still not been sufficient time to satisfactorily resolve the issue of how to deal with the events of the conflict and the dissonant heritages that both gave rise to it and were, in turn, fuelled by it. With contributions from across the UK and Europe, *Heritage after Conflict* brings together a range of expertise to examine the work to which heritage is currently being put within Northern Ireland.

Questions about the contemporary application of remembering infiltrate every aspect of heritage studies, including built heritages, urban regeneration and planning, tourism, museum provision and intangible cultural heritages. These represent challenges for heritage professionals, who must carefully consider how they might curate and conserve dissonant heritages without exacerbating political tensions that might spark violence. Through a lens of critical heritage studies, contributors to this book locate their work within the wider contexts of post-conflict societies, divided cities and dissonant heritages.

Heritage after Conflict should be essential reading for academics, researchers and postgraduate students engaged in the study of the social sciences, history, peace studies, economics, cultural geography, museum heritage and cultural policy, and the creative arts. It should also be of great interest to heritage professionals.

Elizabeth Crooke is the Professor of Heritage and Museum Studies at the University of Ulster, Northern Ireland.

Tom Maguire is a Senior Lecturer in Theatre Studies at the University of Ulster, Northern Ireland.

Routledge Studies in Heritage

https://www.routledge.com/Routledge-Studies-in-Heritage/book-series/
RSIHER

Heritage after Conflict
Northern Ireland

Edited by
Elizabeth Crooke and Tom Maguire

Routledge
Taylor & Francis Group

LONDON AND NEW YORK

First published 2018
by Routledge
2 Park Square, Milton Park, Abingdon, Oxon OX14 4RN

and by Routledge
711 Third Avenue, New York, NY 10017

Routledge is an imprint of the Taylor & Francis Group, an informa business

British Library Cataloguing-in-Publication Data
A catalogue record for this book is available from the British Library

Library of Congress Cataloging-in-Publication Data
A catalog record has been requested for this book

ISBN: 978-0-8153-8636-0 (hbk)
ISBN: 978-1-351-16432-0 (ebk)

Typeset in Sabon
by codeMantra

Printed and bound in Great Britain by
TJ International Ltd, Padstow, Cornwall

Contents

List of figures

List of contributors

Henriette Bertram is a Lecturer in Social Sciences at the University of Göttingen, Germany. She holds a degree in cultural sciences from the European University Viadrina in Frankfurt (Oder) and a PhD from the Department of Architecture Town Planning and Landscape Planning at the University of Kassel. Her research focusses on urban development and regeneration after political and societal change, urban memory cultures and the ways in which post-conflict societies deal with unagreed elements of heritage.

Karine Bigand lectures in Irish Studies in Aix-Marseille Université in France. She holds a PhD on the representations and political uses of the 1641 Catholic rising in Ireland from Université Sorbonne-Nouvelle, Paris. Her research focusses on the relations between history, memory, politics and identity in Ireland. She has published several articles and book chapters on the representations and political uses of history in Ireland in various media – historiography, photography and museums. Following further training in Cultural Heritage and Museums Studies from Ulster University, her research now focusses on public history and museums, particularly in post-conflict Northern Ireland. She is a member and former intern of Healing Through Remembering.

David Coyles is a Lecturer in Architecture at the School of Architecture and the Built Environment at Ulster University. He is principal investigator of the AHRC-funded Cartographies of Conflict research project (www.cartographiesofconflict.com). His research investigates the political use of architecture, with particular focus on military and paramilitary contexts. He writes on urban planning in relation to the management of conflict in Northern Ireland and how the legacy of conflict continues to be evident in the city space, and has published in *The Journal of Architecture, Environment and Planning D: Society & Space* and *City*.

Elizabeth Crooke is the Professor of Heritage and Museum Studies at Ulster University. She writes in the areas of museum studies, community, material culture studies and memory. She is co-investigator in the

AHRC-funded First World War Engagement Centre, Living Legacies (www.livinglegacies1914-18.ac.uk). She has published in *International Journal of Heritage Studies*, *Memory Studies* and *Irish Political Studies*. Her work can also be found in *Museum Practice: Critical Debates in the Contemporary Museum* (Wiley-Blackwell 2015) and *Making 1916* (Liverpool University Press, 2015). She has published *Museums and Community: Ideas, Issues and Challenges* (Routledge 2007) and *Politics, Archaeology and the Creation of a National Museum of Ireland* (Irish Academic Press 2000).

Tom Maguire is Head of School of Arts and Humanities, Ulster University. He researches and teaches in the areas of contemporary British and Irish drama and theatre, and in heritage and performance. He has published *Making Theatre in Northern Ireland: Through and Beyond the Troubles* (2006) and *Performing Story on the Contemporary Stage* (2015). His essays have been published in a number of edited collections and in a range of international journals including the *Journal of Contemporary Drama in English*, *International Journal of Scottish Theatre and Screen*, *Postcolonial Text* and *Performance Research*. He is a member of the Arts and Humanities Research Council Peer Review College and of the Editorial Panel of the journal *About Performance*. He is the Chair of the Board of Big Telly Theatre Company, Northern Ireland.

Katie Markham has recently graduated with her PhD in Sociology from the University of Leeds. Her thesis, titled '"The person inside it has to be part of it": Empathy, Post-Conflict Heritage and "Troubles Tourism" in Northern Ireland', engaged with the limits of empathy in relation to Belfast's black cab tours and paramilitary museums. She lectures in the Department of Media, Culture and Heritage at Newcastle University, and she is the author of 'Two-dimensional engagements: photography, empathy and interpretation at District Six Museum' and a book chapter, 'Touring the post-conflict city: negotiating affects during Belfast's black cab mural tours', which is out soon as part of Routledge's *Key Issues in Cultural Heritage* series.

Laura McAtackney is an Associate Professor in the School of Archaeology and Heritage at Aarhus University, Denmark. An archaeologist by training, her current research explores a number of areas, including the dark heritage of political imprisonment in Ireland (with a focus on Long Kesh/Maze and Kilmainham Gaol), material segregation and the proliferation of walls and the historic Irish diaspora in the Caribbean. She is currently the secretary of CHAT (Contemporary & Historical Archaeology in Theory group) and is a co-assistant editor of Post Medieval Archaeology.

Philip McDermott is a Lecturer in Sociology at Ulster University. His research focusses on the relationship between the state and minority groups.

He has a specific interest in diversity in the public space, the ways that government and communities deal with such diversity, and the manner in which institutions deal with new policy expectations. He has published a book and several peer-reviewed articles on these themes. The British Academy and the Arts and Humanities Research Council have also funded his research on migrant communities and their engagement with the heritage sector. In addition, he has also acted as an expert research evaluator for the European Commission. From 2015–2016, he was the holder of a prestigious Charlemont Scholarship from the Royal Irish Academy.

Paul Mullan is the Head of The Heritage Lottery Fund in Northern Ireland and a PhD Researcher at Ulster University, looking at the challenge of commemoration in a divided society. He has worked in the field of heritage for the last three decades, setting up a number of major heritage projects, and spent time as Acting Regional Director of the National Trust. He has written, lectured and broadcasted on heritage. He Chairs the Decade of Centenaries Roundtable.

Louise Purbrick is a Principal Lecturer in the History of Art and Design at the University of Brighton (http://arts.brighton.ac.uk/staff/louise-purbrick). She has published a number of works on sites of exploitation and imprisonment. She is an editor, with Jim Aulich and Graham Dawson, of *Contested Spaces: Sites, Histories and Representations* (Palgrave, 2007) and, with John Schofield and Axel Klausmeier, of *Re-Mapping the Field: New Approaches in Conflict Archaeology* (Berlin-Bonn: Westkreuz-Verlag, 2006). Of a series of essays and articles on Long Kesh/Maze, 'The Architecture of Containment' in Donovan Wylie's *The Maze* (Granta, 2004) is the most frequently cited. Louise is currently working with photographers Xavier Ribas and Ignacio Acosta on the Arts and Humanities Research Council-funded project *Traces of Nitrate* (http://www.tracesof nitrate.org/), which examines the political legacies of nitrate mining in the Atacama Desert of northern Chile.

Chris Reynolds is an Associate Professor of Contemporary French and European Studies at Nottingham Trent University. His main research interests are in relation to the events of 1968. Having initially focussed on the French events of Mai 68, he has widened his analysis to examine the period from a European perspective. He has published a number of articles on the French events, and his first monograph, *Memories of May '68: France's Convenient Consensus* (University of Wales Press), on the subject was published in 2011. He has also been involved in research on the events of 1968 in Northern Ireland, and in 2015 he published his second monograph, titled *Sous les pavés...The Troubles: Northern Ireland, France and the European Collective Memory of 1968*, with Peter Lang. He is currently leading a significant project with the Ulster Museum on the question of Northern Ireland's 1968.

Acknowledgements

In June 2016 the editors of this volume were both part of the Association of Critical Heritage Studies biannual conference, held at Université du Québec à Montréal (UQAM) in partnership with Concordia University. Perhaps the inspiring academic debate during and between conference sessions made us think afresh about the meaning and manipulation of heritage. Maybe the distance from home encouraged us to explore the synergies between scholars who share our interest in how we engage the past for social, cultural or political purpose. We are sure it was a combination of both that convinced us, in an airport departure lounge in Montreal, to bring together some of the best new work in the field to consider the creation, interpretation and communication of heritage in Northern Ireland in recent decades. In late 2016 our invitation to the contributors in this volume to be involved in a book project was graciously accepted. This was followed by the seminar *Post-Conflict Heritages: Northern Ireland Twenty Years after the Belfast Agreement*, held at Ulster University in April 2017. We would like to thank the Arts and Humanities Research Institute for the administrative and financial support for that event. We would like to thank our colleagues at Ulster University who have encouraged us in the completion of this book.

We are indebted to the wider research community in heritage studies at Ulster University, particularly the doctoral researchers and postgraduate students (past and present) on the MA Cultural Heritage and Museum Studies, who constantly remind us of the importance of the ideas captured in this volume. Of course, this book was only possible because of the scholarship, energy and commitment of the contributors. We would like to thank the contributors for accepting our invitation, submitting their articles in a timely fashion and responding to our queries. We would also like to thank the anonymous reviewers who both supported the production of this volume and suggested further directions that enhanced the writing. It was a pleasure to work with Routledge/Taylor & Francis in the production of this book. We would like to offer our thanks to Heidi Lowther, Editor for Museum & Heritage Studies and Library & Information Science, and Marc

Stratton, Editorial Assistant in the same division. The editors would also like to thank Erin Arata (copyeditor) for her help in preparing the manuscript for publication.

Professor Elizabeth Crooke
Dr Tom Maguire
Ulster University
February 2018

1 Negotiating heritage after conflict

Perspectives from Northern Ireland

Elizabeth Crooke and Tom Maguire

On 10 April 1998, then British Prime Minister, Tony Blair, marked the signing of the Belfast Agreement by announcing to the world's press, 'Today I hope that the burden of history can at long last start to be lifted from our shoulders'. Since then, that 'burden of history' has been engaged by the heritage and memory industries in Northern Ireland. The methods and consequences of this engagement are the subject of this volume.

Whilst the burden Blair referred to can be traced back to centuries of conflict on the island of Ireland, the Agreement sought to end the decades of violence in Northern Ireland, known as 'The Troubles', that erupted in 1968. That period of violent conflict between Irish republican paramilitaries and British unionism (both state forces and loyalist paramilitaries) had its roots in the partition of Ireland into two states in the 1920s. The Government of Ireland Act of 1920 responded to the Irish War of Independence by proposing an extended form of Home Rule on the island. This would provide for 'harmonious action' between a Parliament of Northern Ireland (constituted by the six counties with a majority Protestant population) and a Parliament of Southern Ireland (governing the rest of the island). Although the Northern Ireland Parliament met for the first time in June 1921, the refusal of Irish republicans to accept partition saw the continuation of the conflict. When the Anglo-Irish Treaty of 1922 created the Irish Free State, Northern Ireland's Parliament exercised its right to remain in the UK, and the unified Council of Ireland, envisaged by the original act, was never realised. With revisions to the constitution of the Free State in 1937 to remove remnants of British imperial control and the establishment of the Irish Republic in 1949, replacing the British monarch with the office of the President of the Republic as Head of State, the division of the island was completed. Until 1998, the Irish Republic insisted on its claim to the whole island, whilst Northern unionists maintained the project of constructing a Protestant state for the majority Protestant population (Brewer and Higgins 1998). This institutionalised sectarianism conflated religious affiliation and political allegiance: Protestant meant unionist or loyalist; Catholic meant Irish nationalist or republican. The asymmetrical dispensation of the resources of the state to these identity blocs continued until it was challenged in the 1960s by campaigns for an end to discrimination against the Catholic minority. The violent response of the Northern Irish state to the demands for reform made by the Civil Rights movement led to violence that would cost thousands of lives at the hands of paramilitaries and state security forces, creating further legacies of dark heritage.

With the signing of the Belfast Agreement, it was anticipated that a Northern Irish society would find ways to manage peacefully conflicts of identity and the legacies of the past. Much of the work of political institutions and civil society over the past two decades has been concerned with addressing the insistent outworking of history in the present. This is not surprising since, as Ashworth, Graham and Tunbridge contend, 'heritage is a primary instrument in the discovery or creation and subsequent nurturing of a national identity' (2005: 27). Heritage is thus a potent mechanism for making or contesting claims on territory and resources for that identity. Frequently, heritage is used as a resource in the present, often as a continuation of the contestation of the past. The deployment of the imagined heritages of the dominant identity blocs (Shirlow and McGovern 1997) has been a recurrent political strategy in Northern Ireland. Legacy issues and the different claims of separate cultural identities continue to threaten the political stability of the devolved Northern Ireland Assembly, once again suspended at the time of writing in early 2018. As editors we are acutely aware that factors and processes evident here can be discerned too across a range of international contexts. Northern Ireland's issues and the uses of heritage within them are distinctive but not necessarily unique, and any understanding of them must be informed by engagement with the wider fields of contested heritages in other divided societies. The constitutional crisis between Catalunya and Spain (Breen et al. 2016), the legacy of the war in former Yugoslavia and initiatives in Rwanda and Uganda (Giblin 2014) or Cambodia (Winter 2008) all point to commonalities of experience when societies in conflict or emerging from conflict make use of the past. This collection provides a series of case studies that examine where heritage practices in Northern Ireland are now, twenty years after the Agreement; what work they have been put to (Harrison 2013b); and how they might provide models and insights that can be adapted to other societies emerging from conflict.

Whilst much has been made of the importance of tangible heritage in its function of marking territorial exclusivity and identity, the potency of intangible cultural heritage is evidenced in the discussion of language and naming conventions. One of the reasons for the collapse of the power-sharing Executive in January 2017 was the inability of politicians to resolve the issue of an Irish Language Act and the relative status of Ulster-Scots, for example. Yet even in the use of English, dissonance is obvious. Whilst some may refer to the 'North of Ireland' to contest the legitimacy of the state, or 'Ulster' to emphasise separateness from the rest of the island, we deliberately use 'Northern Ireland' as a means of focussing the discussion on the relationships between public policy, institutional practices and lived experience. Less straightforward is the naming of the second city as Derry or Londonderry, as was the case when it was awarded the title of UK City of Culture, Derry-Londonderry. The use of such names may be taken to mark alignment with one or other of the two main identity blocs, though even here naming is problematic. Whilst Catholic-Nationalist-Republican and Protestant-Unionist-Loyalist are widely used, their effect is to homogenise a very diverse range of people to conflate religion, ethnicity and political grouping, masking asymmetries, internal contradictions and other taxonomies of identity.

We do not subscribe to any account that suggests that the violence of the Troubles was between only these two blocs or monolithic communities. Even with the historical document that marks the beginning of the period under consideration, some refer to it as the Belfast Agreement, while others refer to it as the Good Friday Agreement or both interchangeably. We have not sought to impose uniformity on our contributors about any such naming practices since they bring a wide range of perspectives to bear. They were invited together for a one-day symposium at Ulster University's Belfast campus in 2017, organised through the University's Engaging the Past research group, which we lead. Our personal backgrounds and experiences are very different, and, although we both teach on the same Heritage and Museum Studies postgraduate programme, our discipline orientations and research interests are very different as well. The chapters here span different discipline backgrounds, often working across and between disciplines; they work in a range of institutional settings, are produced by academics at different stages of their careers and together provide international perspectives due to these backgrounds and the critical frameworks they deploy.

Heritage and political change in Northern Ireland

The heritage landscape is a past curated for the present, involving selective remembering and deliberate concealing in equal measure. In every case, that heritage is bound in present-day concerns and shaped by the power of memory, identity and belonging. Scanning the century since the formation of Northern Ireland, and considering the buildings, sites and landscapes deemed as heritage; the artefacts and artworks considered worthy of museum attention; the practices established and then defended as 'heritage'; and emerging recognition of intangible cultural heritage (such as language, folklore and music), we see trends through the years that reflect the current social and political mood. This was clearly demonstrated by two commemorative events in 1998: first, the bicentenary of the 1798 Rebellion, an insurrection against British rule; second, the opening of the Peace Park in Belgium, a cross-community initiative that marked the contribution of men from Ireland, north and south, to the First World War. The bicentenary events were marked by two major exhibitions, one in the National Museum of Ireland and the other in the Ulster Museum. As the peace process was gathering pace, historians reframed the rebellion as less divisive and more 'open, inclusive and dynamic', with the author of the Dublin exhibition suggesting we 'use the 1790s as a vision and inspiration for the 1990s' (Whelan 1996, cited by Howe 1999: 227). In a similar spirit of revisionism, standing at the Peace Tower in Belgium, built to mimic a medieval Irish round tower, the then President of the Republic of Ireland, Mary McAleese, asked us to remember the past differently (Crooke 2000: 159–162; see also Poulter 2017). Both the bicentenary events and the opening of the Peace Park are examples of conscious and active reshaping of the meaning of past events – a reshaping that is motivated by the concerns of the time – such as the Belfast Agreement (more commonly referred to as the Good Friday Agreement) and later the referendums held in Northern Ireland and the Republic of Ireland on 22 May 1998, which resulted in its ratification.

Providing a context for the focus of this book, which is heritage after 1998, this Introduction provides a brief account of the political history of the region, divided into three phases. Within each we focus on moments of what might be termed heritage construction: first, the consolidation of unionist identity through monumental buildings; second, the growing confidence of nationalist and republican communities expressed through remembrance and murals; and later (in the phase which is the time period of this book) the dual uses of heritage to, on the one hand, continue a legacy of the Troubles and, on the other, as a medium through which to explore conflict transformation, reconciliation and resolution. It is impossible in this short Introduction to cover every example of heritage that could be deemed relevant to each period. Instead, we have chosen key activities in each that we believe epitomise the various ways in which heritage has been employed – choosing each for the characteristics it demonstrates of how the past is engaged in identity concretion, challenge and reconstruction (Assmann and Czaplicka 1995). Between this Introduction as the starting point and the chapters as deeper exploration, we demonstrate how the creation and manipulation of the heritage landscape is reflected in the changing confidence and aspirations of political communities through time. Each phase, in turn, has contributed its own heritage legacies, which continue to work in relation to each other in the present as they continue to be reworked and revisited.

Consolidation phase, 1920–1968

In the first decades of the new Northern Ireland, unionist identity was consolidated around the creation of buildings for governance, statues and rituals. The reference points for these were largely the contemporary and recent history, rather than any more distant past, demarcating a territory for the present and constructing a heritage for the future. The new Parliament Buildings at Stormont, 'a grand stage for unionists' (McIntosh 2000: 97), agreed upon in 1922 and completed in 1931, are an example of 'monumental architecture' that not only 'reflected the determination of the dominant Ulster Unionists to carve out a distinctive political identity' but also demonstrated the 'permanence and status of Northern Ireland to the wider world', becoming an 'icon for the new régime' (Greer 1999: 374–375). Consolidation was furthered by ceremonial festivals honouring the Unionist leader Edward Carson: the opening of Stormont parliament, the unveiling of the Carson statue in 1933, his funeral in 1935 and the plaque erected in his memory in 1938 (McIntosh 2000). These are 'marking devices' laced with political propaganda and enacted in 'rituals which spoke primarily, although not exclusively, to a unionist audience' (McIntosh 2000: 95; see also Loughlin 2007). The aim was to consolidate a hegemonic unionist identity that erased markers of class, faith and gender to silence internal dissent within the majority population. To the extent that such marking devices spoke to the Irish nationalist minority, they articulated the exclusion and estrangement of that section of the population from the emergent state.

The declaration of the Irish Republic in 1948 was a provocation for the government of Northern Ireland to turn to heritage assets as a source of a distinctive and separate *national* identity. Contributing to this, the extension of the scope of the Belfast Museum and Art Gallery, to become the Ulster Museum, was motivated by a 'fear of Ulster being included in the Southern project, thereby losing its specificity' (Bigand 2011: online). It was made a national museum under the 1961 Museum Act (Northern Ireland), and, as Bigand observes, 'from its creation the museum had to deal with the reputation of being strongly Protestant/Unionist-biased' (2011: online). During the same period, but under a different primary impetus, the development of a distinctive Ulster folklore movement was underway, spearheaded by E. Estyn Evans, in line with wider movements in folklore across the UK. By 1954 Evans had gathered a committee to establish a folk museum, and in 1958 the legislation to bring it about was passed, with the current site at Cultra being purchased in 1961 (Ó Giolláin 2000: 57). It might be seen that in each of these instances an example of a type of British regional museum was elevated to a national status just as the Northern Irish state needed to identify and justify its separate identity from its southern neighbour. One might see also in these strategies of heritage separation a further denial of the heritage of Northern Ireland's Catholic nationalist citizens and their claims to a place in the state.

Challenge phase, 1968–1998

Whilst Irish republicans contested the state's power sporadically through campaigns of violence by the Irish Republican Army (IRA) in the 1940s and in a Border Campaign from the 1950s, the state remained relatively stable, and its unionist hegemony remained unchecked until the 1960s. By this time the political climate was changing in the region. Rolston describes nationalist opposition to the unionist state as ranging from 'sullen participation' to 'armed rebellion against the state' (1987: 8). At this time nationalist culture was more contained than that of its unionist neighbours: 'it was anything but triumphalist, but was instead clandestine ... safely hidden from unionist view ... relegated to the margins of civil society' (Rolston 1987: 8). From 1964 the Campaign for Social Justice in Northern Ireland was bringing discrimination against Catholics to wider attention. In 1966 the Northern Ireland Government tolerated the republican celebrations of the fiftieth anniversary of the Easter Rising. Counterdemonstrations were led by Ian Paisley (later founder of the Democratic Unionist Party) in Belfast, including a 'thanksgiving service' to commemorate the defeat of the 1916 rebels, held in the Ulster Hall 16 April 1966 (O'Callaghan and O'Donnell 2006). Furthermore, it is thought that the Ulster Volunteer Force was re-established in 1966 in anticipation of the fiftieth anniversary of the rising (Higgins 2012). By August 1968 an increasingly uneasy peace between hegemonic unionism and the Catholic nationalist minority was shattered as a non-violent campaign for civil rights gave way to widespread civil disorder. British troops were dispatched in 1969 to restore order. As paramilitary violence between armed groups of republicans, loyalists and state security forces increased the British government suspended the Northern Irish parliament and imposed direct rule in 1972.

In the early Troubles period, as unionism was derailed, and loyalism sought new symbols, 'nationalist culture thrived in its ghettoes' (Rolston 1987: 13), reflected in increased commitment to the Irish language, history and folk music. Here the recourse to Irish heritage was used to underpin political claims by nationalists and republicans to legitimate a separate identity and the rights attendant to it. Later, the death of the hunger striker Bobby Sands saw the first wave of highly politicised republican murals (Rolston 1987). Rolston sees this period as one that is marked by increasing confidence amongst nationalist and republican communities, and a crisis of identity amongst unionists and loyalists. Brian Graham argues that the latter was, in part, fuelled by a lack of belonging invested in the cultural landscape, giving Protestants little authority over their territory (Graham 1997). By the end of this period we see rival communities of identity repeatedly justified by competing understandings of the past expressed in largely separate heritages (Graham and Nash 2006; Beiner 2007). The forty years of conflict only further increased the polarisation of community identity, and appeals to separate heritages were reinforced by the heritage of the violence itself, leading to a complex relationship with how seminal periods during the Troubles are remembered (see Reynolds this volume; Crooke 2010). Crucially, whilst these polarised identities competed for political power, they had also to suppress many of the distinctions within their own communities to maintain their hegemony. This meant ignoring or recuperating very different forms of heritage or insisting on the primacy of specific interpretations of the past within their own communities, producing what O'Dowd and Komarova have termed 'antagonistic, fixed ideas of place and territory' (2011: 2013).

Conflict transformation phase, 1998–2018

In 1998 the Good Friday Agreement brought the Troubles to an end (although violence and sectarianism continue unabated, if diminished). In the time since, the deployment of heritage has been primarily twofold: on the one hand it has been put to work to continue the conflict through other means (McDowell and Braniff 2014), and, on the other, it has been used in the service of conflict resolution and conflict transformation (see Mullan this volume). Regarding the former, since the signing of the Agreement there has been a significant increase in the number of new murals, plaques and other memorials mounted in loyalist and republican areas (Viggiani 2014), and the continuing use of memorials to 'promote one-sided and deliberately partial memories of the conflict that reflect the longstanding and ongoing segregation' (McAtackney 2015: 116; see Coyles this volume; and Bertram this volume). In this climate, new largely single-identity heritage spaces have emerged (such as the Museum of Free Derry and the Siege Heroes Museum, both in Derry/Londonderry), and political campaigns have continued to recognise the value of the artefact and display as a means of sharing their message and shaping public opinion (see Crooke 2016).

In the same period, existing in parallel, are cross-community projects co-produced with academic and museum professionals, working to enhance engagement and understanding (Bouchard 2009). Post Agreement, 'border studies' emerged and flourished, with a rush in photographic and oral history projects connected with the border area (Nash and Reid 2010). The Decade of Centenaries, marking the First World War and the events that led to the partition of Ireland, has been commemorated at local sites and in national institutions in ways that have revised many of the dominant mythologies that have fed divisions across the island. Indeed the 2016 centenaries of the Battle of the Somme and the Easter Rising were marked without any of the violence that had erupted at their fiftieth anniversaries (Dixon 2001: 78). Since 2013 the Heritage Lottery Fund (see Mullan this volume) has supported heritage landscape partnerships to protect rural landscapes in an unprecedented way, for example. In the city of Derry/Londonderry, once the crucible of the violence, and in 2013 the first UK City of Culture, historic public spaces are being regenerated and repurposed as cultural facilities open to all. New conceptions of heritage in Northern Ireland are being developed too. Hillsborough Castle, once a landmark expression of British sovereignty and itself the setting for some of the most intensive negotiations around the peace process, has become a heritage site; since 2014 it has come under the auspices of Historic Royal Palaces. Much work has been done to promote other formations of heritage identity beyond the dominant identity blocs, including through work with minority ethnic groups and refugees (see McDermott this volume), garnering cross-community participation in heritage projects, and reconceiving existing heritage assets.

Alongside the initiatives just listed, state and public institutions have struggled to come to terms with what McDowell has termed the 'tangible and intangible heritage of division and hurt' (2008: 405). Continuing disagreement within the Northern Ireland Executive concerning budget implementation, welfare reform, the Irish language and dealing with the past have resulted in repeated periods of stalemate and the current collapse of devolved government. This lack of progress is replicated in heritage-based projects that have never gotten off the ground. The idea of a Living Memorial Museum, so thoughtfully explored by Healing Through Remembering (Purbrick 2007), seems a long way off. The Peace Building and Conflict Resolution Centre, planned for the Maze/Long Kesh site and granted £18 million of financial support, came to a halt due to fear amongst some unionist communities that the site would become an IRA shrine (see Purbrick, this volume). On the legacy issue the Stormont House Agreement (2014) recommended the creation of an Oral History Archive, described as a central place for people to 'share experiences and narratives related to the Troubles' (Northern Ireland Office 2014: 5). Despite the many community-based Oral History Archive projects, both prior to and since this recommendation, an official manifestation is yet to come to pass for reasons explored by Hamber and Kelly (2016). Instead remembrance of the Troubles period is found in a complex heritage landscape that is a mix of state-funded initiatives hosted by arm's-length bodies, such as National Museums Northern Ireland or the Arts Council, Northern Ireland; projects supported and funded by groups in receipt of public money by other means, such as the Heritage Lottery Fund (see Mullan this volume); and independent developments, such as the new community-based museums (see chapters by Markham and Bigand this volume).

Looking at the museum and heritage landscape of 2016, our national and local museums have been co-opted into official, state-sanctioned programmes of national commemorations. In the *Together: Building a United Community* (2013) strategy, the Office of the First Minister and Deputy First Minister described partnerships between museums and communities as playing 'a vital role in understanding our shared history, heritage and culture'. In this document museums are also presented as 'valuable in building a culture of respect, tolerance and reconciliation'. At the opening of the Decade of Centenaries the principles for commemorative activity were forged to promote an education focus; encourage reflection and inclusivity; and promote tolerance, respect and responsibility: 'The decade of commemoration presents an opportunity to celebrate our shared differences in a way which will position Northern Ireland as a powerful example in conflict resolution and transformation on the world stage' (OFMDFM 2013: 94). In late 2014 National Museums Northern Ireland reopened their Modern History Gallery with a new interpretation of the past 500 years. In the creation of the gallery, the official approach to the Decade of Centenaries is apparent. What is also clear is that the rhetoric of politicians does not abate. Reflecting on the gallery, the then Department for Culture Arts and Leisure Minister Carál Ní Chuilín saw an initiative that was 'helping to lead innovative and inclusive approaches to remembering our shared past' (Creative Centenaries 2014). No matter how worthy we might consider the sentiment, it is evidence that commemoration is 'fused to the politics of the present' and plays a crucial role in the 'negotiation of identity, power and place' (Bodnar 1992: 13). Like memorial museums discussed in this volume (Bigand; Markham), the commemorative exhibition will select 'certain memories (and not others)' to spin into 'a coherent story, which legitimises and de-legitimises certain actions' (Selimovic 2013: 336, see also Crooke 2017). Ultimately such exhibitions become places where 'intellectuals, media, politicians and pressure groups participate in a struggle to define the past' (Selimovic 2013: 336). An understanding of the function of museums and heritage sites as places where conflicts over the past might be channelled as a way of handling dissonance without recourse to violence is beginning to emerge (Maguire 2017).

A further strand of this use of heritage for conflict transformation is in its relationship with regeneration projects and the associated re-imaging of space and place. For example, Titanic Belfast was opened in 2012 as the signature project for the redevelopment of part of the former Harland and Wolff shipyard site that has been designated the Titanic Quarter. Spread over six floors, the building hosts nine interactive and interpretive galleries that explore the histories of the ship and the city in which it was built. Privately owned and managed – the cost of its construction was co-funded by the Northern Ireland Tourist Board, Belfast City Council and the private developer – Titanic Belfast quickly became a key tourist destination and in 2016 was named as 'World's Leading Tourist Attraction' in the World Travel Awards. The displays gloss over the sectarian history of the former shipyard, creating a much more anodyne version of this industrial heritage to allow it to be marketed as experience tourism. Whilst the success of this project as a tourist icon is indisputable, other attempts to reuse heritage sites have proven more controversial, including the Crumlin Road Gaol and the former Girdwood army barracks in Belfast (see Bertram this volume).

Format of this book

In 2003 Mary McAleese confidently suggested that the heritage landscape on this island has been transformed. Rhetorically, she asked, 'Who could ever have imagined that an Irish Government would purchase the site of the Battle of the Boyne and develop there a heritage site for all the people of the island of Ireland?' (McAleese 2003). Present-day actions are bound in the duty we feel towards past generations, the obligations we feel towards the present and the aspirations we hold for the future. McAleese suggests that 'the old vanities of history are disappearing'; she tells us that the 'carefully hidden stories of the Irish who died in the First World War are coming out of the shoeboxes in the attic and into daylight'. These new stories are impacting the present: 'We are making new friends we are influencing new people, we are learning new things about ourselves, we are being changed' (McAleese 2003). The evidence for these transformations, not always as smooth and wholly welcome as our political elite may suggest, are explored in this volume.

A critical awareness of the active manipulation of heritage, by those with the power and agency to do so, is the focus of critical heritage studies (Smith 2012; Winter 2013) and the underpinning inspiration for this book. Whilst the activities of state-run heritage institutions prior to the Troubles as instruments of nation-building can be accounted for within the broader conception of Authorised Heritage Discourse, the democratisation of heritage urged by critical heritage studies (Smith 2012) is not unproblematic in the context of Northern Ireland. It is all too obvious here how 'heritage' is the outcome of processes and practices of representing the past, conditioned by the ideological structures and power relationships of the present moment. It is in the operation of these antagonistic power relationships, between dominant, emergent and residual ideologies and constituencies, that heritage dissonance arises and is maintained. In this context, opening up the field of heritage construction may well contribute to ongoing social divisions and violence – a continuation of the conflict by proxy. Anxieties around this have led to the principles for remembering in public space discussed in Mullan's chapter in this volume. However, communities and non-specialists are not always willing to conform to the rules set by others, as the examples in this volume demonstrate (see the chapters by Markham and Bigand, for example). Populist commemoration and its associated heritage remain unruly features of the cultures of representation in Northern Ireland, often serving as a means of advocacy for groups who feel they would otherwise be silenced or ignored. However, it is possible to reframe this unruliness and develop a further function for museums and heritage institutions. Rather than avoiding contentious topics and aspects of dissonant heritage, they may well have a more positive role in allowing dissonance to be articulated in a safe and controlled way. Doing so may facilitate public discussion to allow disagreements to be discussed within a discursive framework of civility rather than threat (Bishop 2004, cited in Maguire 2017: 79).

One of the advantages of a multi-authored volume such as this is that it allows a range of perspectives to emerge. Whilst contributors were invited because of our prior knowledge of their work, we did not prescribe their focus or approach. The responses to our invitation answered that clarion call of the original 2012 manifesto of the Association of Critical Heritage Studies to integrate 'heritage and museum studies with studies of memory, public history, community, tourism, planning and development'. Together the chapters here address a range of examples to create a multidisciplinary perspective that illuminates the intersections of policy, practice and the lived experiences of heritage in Northern Ireland. Memory is recognised as critical in both its personal and social domains. Chris Reynolds's discussion of how the events of 1968 in Northern Ireland are remembered contributes to an understanding of how discourses of exceptionalism have conditioned and are conditioned by dominant narratives of insularity that present Northern Ireland as exceptional. Paul Mullan's chapter deals with the adoption of principles of ethical remembering by the Heritage Lottery Fund to allow the Decade of Centenaries to be commemorated in ways that disrupted dominant narratives of identity. Two central chapters by Katie Markham and Karine Bigand explore the experience of examples of paramilitary commemoration from very different perspectives on the narratives they construct. Markham identifies how they articulate a discourse of innocent victimhood that exonerates the former paramilitaries of the atrocities they committed; Bigand identifies in them signs of hope that these same paramilitaries are engaged in some form of reflective criticism. These differing perspectives can be seen to be writ large in the debates about the development of the site of the former Her Majesty's Prison (HMP) Maze discussed by Louise Purbrick. Responding to the impasse over the use of the site, Purbrick proposes that participation in the site as a form of meaning-making through art practice may open it up as a site of potential rather than referring only to its contested past. This relationship between built heritage and the experience of space and place is central to the two chapters that follow. Henriette Bertram examines the ways in which discourses of conflict transformation have intersected with planning policies pursuing strategies of urban regeneration in two adjacent sites in North Belfast, the Crumlin Road Gaol and Girdwood Park, under the logic of normalisation. David Coyles's chapter traces the legacy of the intersection of security and planning policy in the late 1970s, where built heritage actively reinforces the ethno-religious segregation that normalises it as part of everyday life. The relationship between place or territory and identity that underpins the dominant identity blocs in Northern Ireland is confounded in many respects by the experiences of new migrant communities. Philip McDermott's chapter explores how the heritage sector has sought to recognise the rights of these new citizens in developing inclusive practices that go beyond the binary oppositions of the conflict. Finally, Laura McAtackney's account of memorialisation in contemporary Belfast identifies recurrent tropes in the ways in which the representation of women's experience is used in place-making processes that still marginalise them within an urban landscape that is resolutely androcentric.

Of course, there are many gaps that we have not been able to fill here. There are many other communities of identity whose heritage has not been addressed. Queer heritage and the experiences of the lesbian, gay, bisexual, transgender (LGBT) communities are one obvious example. None of our contributions address the many forms of intangible heritage that distinguish the experience of living in or visiting Northern Ireland. The rich food and drink heritage here is enjoying a resurgence as part of the region's rebranding as a tourist destination that has seen accelerated growth in artisanal produce, food tours and festivals. The absence of any critical attention to this here also means that we have paid only passing attention to the relationship between heritage and many forms of experience tourism outwith those concerned with the conflict. We have also found our contributors focussing largely on examples from Belfast. Whilst the city functions metonymically for the whole of Northern Ireland for many people who come here from outside, for those living in other towns and cities or in rural communities, the intersections of heritage, identity and the Troubles may be experienced very differently from Belfast and from other apparently similar settings. The network of county museums alongside big houses (privately owned or run by the National Trust) and the introduction of Landscape Partnerships by the Heritage Lottery Fund, for example, mean that the experience of heritage at local levels outside Belfast may be very specific to each place and community. Moreover, many heritages and the practices associated with them may have been conditioned by the conflict here without ever having directly engaged with the Troubles. The popularity of rallies by vintage automobile and tractor clubs, for example, seems to have endured throughout the period, a form of grass-roots community heritage about which little has been written. We identify these areas for future development in writing about the heritage of this place.

The outcome of these chapters is not a simple guidebook for how other societies emerging out of conflict might engage with their heritage. Much of the difficulty in dealing with heritage in Northern Ireland is tied to the specificities of its place and time. The contributors have developed the depth of their discussion by focussing precisely on these specificities. However, we are convinced that this volume can speak to other contexts for two principle reasons. The first is to do with the objects of study. Here, the work that heritage does for a society emerging from conflict in building or resisting political consensus or negotiating and contesting political and symbolic power is located across a range of areas, from the built environment to local politically curated exhibitions and conflict transformation initiatives. The complex interaction between remembering and forgetting more characteristic of a wider crisis in the accumulation of the past (Harrison 2013a) is made evident in the examples under consideration in individual chapters. The treatment of commemorative practices around contested living histories opens fields of inquiry that may be useful in other contexts. The second concerns the approaches and methodologies deployed here. Adopting a critical heritage studies perspective has allowed the writers to articulate the experience of heritage so that the work that heritage has been put to might be understood both in terms of what the principal actors have intended and how that intention has been registered in the experience of the visitor. This responds to Harrison's proposition that we think of heritage as 'relational and emergent in the dialogue between people, objects, places and practices' (Harrison 2013b: 226), where the critic is placed within that relationship explicitly. The methodologies here model ways in which a dialogic engagement can reveal ways of doing heritage that are both attentive and respectful, that are subjective but without losing a critical perspective (Winter 2013). Thus, the contributions here manifest a kind of civility in their critique in ways that might benefit both heritage professionals and the wider Northern Irish society if adopted. Recognising the ways in which knowledge production is a process that draws different stakeholders into relationships allows a more complete dialogue to begin.

Bibliography

Ashworth, J., Graham, B., Tunbridge, J.E. (2005). *Heritage, Museums and Galleries*. Abingdon: Routledge.

Assmann, J. and Czaplicka, J. (1995). Collective Memory and Cultural Identity. *New German Critique*, 65, pp. 125–133.

Beiner, G. (2007). Between Trauma and Triumphalism: The Easter Rising, the Somme, and the Crux of Deep Memory in Modern Ireland. *Journal of British Studies*, 46(2), pp. 366–389.

Bigand, K. (2011). How Is Ulster's History Represented in Northern Ireland's Museums? The Cases of the Ulster Folk Museum and the Ulster Museum. *E-rea* 8.3 [online]. Available at: http://erea.revues.org/1769 [Accessed 26 November 2015].

Bodnar, J. (1992). *Remaking America: Public Memory, Commemoration and Patriotism in the Twentieth Century*. Princeton, NJ: Princeton University Press.

Bouchard, D. (2009). Museums, Cultural Heritage and Dialogue in Northern Ireland: Strategies for Divided Societies. *Heritage and Beyond*. Strasbourg: Council of Europe, pp. 91–100.

Breen, C., McDowell, S., Reid, G. and Forsythe, W. (2016). Heritage and separatism in Barcelona: the case of El Born Cultural Centre. *International Journal of Heritage Studies*, 22(6), pp. 434–445.

Brewer, J.D. and Higgins, G.I. (1998). *Anti-Catholicism in Northern Ireland, 1600–1998: The Mote and the Beam*. Basingstoke: MacMillan.

Creative Centenaries (2014). *Ulster Museum launch Modern History Gallery*. [online] Available at: www.creativecentenaries.org/post/ulster-museum-launch-modern-history-gallery [Accessed 26 January 2018].

Crooke, E. (2000). *Politics, Archaeology and the Creation of a National Museum of Ireland. An Expression of National Life*. Dublin: Irish Academic Press.

Crooke, E. (2010). The Politics of Community Heritage: Motivations, Authority and Control. *International Journal of Heritage Studies*, 16(1–2), pp. 16–29.

Crooke, E. (2016). Artefacts as Agents for Change: Commemoration and Exchange via Material Culture. *Irish Political Studies*, 31(1), pp. 86–100.

Crooke, E. (2017) Memory Politics and Material Culture: Display in the Memorial Museum. *Memory Studies*, OnlineFirst.

Dixon, P. (2001). *Northern Ireland: The Politics of War and Peace*. Basingstoke: Palgrave Macmillan.

Giblin, J.D. (2014). Post-conflict Heritage: Symbolic Healing and Cultural Renewal. *International Journal of Heritage Studies*, 20(5), pp. 500–518.

Graham, B. (1996). The Contested Interpretation of Heritage Landscapes in Northern Ireland. *International Journal of Heritage Studies*, 2(1–2), pp. 10–22.

Graham, B. (1997) Ulster: A Representation of Place yet to Be Imagined. In: Shirlow, P. and McGovern, M. eds. *Who Are "the People"?: Unionism, Protestantism and Loyalism in Northern Ireland.* London: Pluto Press, pp. 34–54.

Graham, B. and Nash, C. (2006). A Shared Future: Territoriality, Pluralism and Public Policy in Northern Ireland. *Political Geography*, 25(3), pp. 253–278.

Greer, A. (1999). Sir James Craig and the Construction of Parliament Buildings at Stormont. *Irish Historical Studies*, 31(123), pp. 373–388.

Hamber, B. and Kelly, G. (2016). Practice, Power and Inertia: Personal Narrative, Archives and Dealing with the Past in Northern Ireland. *Journal of Human Rights Practice*, 8(1), 25–44.

Harrison, R. (2013a) Forgetting to Remember, Remembering to Forget: Late Modern Heritage Practices, Sustainability and the 'Crisis' of Accumulation of the Past. *International Journal of Heritage Studies*, 19(6), pp. 579–595.

Harrison, R. (2013b). *Heritage: Critical Approaches.* Abingdon: Routledge.

Higgins, R. (2012). *Transforming 1916. Meaning, Memory and the Fiftieth Anniversary of the Easter Rising.* Cork: Cork University Press.

Howe, S. (1999). Speaking of '98: History, Politics and Memory in the Bicentenary of the 1798 United Irish Uprising. *History Workshop Journal*, 47, pp. 222–239.

Loughlin J. (2007). Creating 'a Social and Geographical Fact': Regional Identity and the Ulster Question 1880s–1920s. *Past and Present*, 195(1), pp. 159–196.

Maguire, T. (2017). Curating Hatred: The Joe McWilliams's Controversy at the Ulster Museum. *Journal of Hate Studies*, 13(1), pp. 61–83.

McAleese, M. (2003). Speech by the President of Ireland, Mary McAleese, at the 'Re-Imagining Ireland' conference, Charlottesville, Virginia, 7 May 2003 [online] Available at: www.president.ie/en/media-library/speeches/speech-by-the-president-of-ireland-mary-mcaleese-at-the-re-imagining-irelan [Accessed 26 January 2018]

McAtackney, L. (2015). Memorials and Marching: Archaeological Insights into Segregation in Contemporary Northern Ireland. *Historical Archaeology*, 49(3), pp. 110–125.

McDowell, S. (2008). Selling Conflict Heritage through Tourism in Peacetime Northern Ireland: Transforming Conflict or Exacerbating Difference? *International Journal of Heritage Studies*, 14(5), pp. 405–421.

McDowell, S. and Braniff, M. (2014). *Commemoration as Conflict: Space, Memory and Identity in Peace Processes.* Basingstoke: Palgrave.

McDowell, S., Braniff, M. and Murphy, J. (2015). Spacing Commemorative-Related Violence in Northern Ireland: Assessing the Implications for a Society in Transition. *Space and Polity*, 19(3), pp. 231–243.

McIntosh, G. (1999). *The Force of Culture, Unionist Identities in Twentieth-Century Ireland* Cork: Cork University Press.

McIntosh, G. (2000). Symbolic Mirrors: Commemorations of Edward Carson in the 1930s. *Irish Historical Studies*, 32(125), pp. 93–112.

McKittrick, D. and McVea, D. (2001). *Making Sense of the Troubles.* Revised. London: Penguin.

Nash, C. and Reid, B. (2010). Border Crossings: New Approaches to the Irish Border. *Irish Studies Review*, 18(3), pp. 265–284.

Northern Ireland Office (2014). The Stormont House Agreement. An Agreement on Key Issues that Opens the Way to a More Prosperous, Stable and Secure Future for Northern Ireland. [online] Available at: www.gov.uk/government/uploads/system/uploads/attachment_data/file/390672/Stormont_House_Agreement.pdf [Accessed 26 January 2018].

O'Callaghan, M. and O'Donnell, C. (2006). The Northern Ireland Government, the 'Paisleyite Movement' and Ulster Unionism in 1966. *Irish Political Studies*, 21(2), pp. 203–222.

O'Dowd, L. and Komarova, M. (2011). Contesting Territorial Fixity? A Case Study of Regeneration in Belfast. *Urban Studies*, 48(10), pp. 2013–2028.

OFMDFM (2013). *Together Building a United Community Strategy.* [online] Available at: www.ofmdfmni.gov.uk/articles/together-building-united-community [Accessed 5 February 2016].

Ó Giolláin, D. (2000). *Locating Irish Folklore: Tradition, Modernity, Identity.* Cork: Cork University Press.

Poulter, J. (2017). The Discursive Reconstruction of Memory and National Identity: The Anti-war Memorial the Island of Ireland Peace Park. *Memory Studies*, 11(2), pp. 1–18.

Purbrick, L. (2007). *Without Walls: A Report on Healing through Remembering's Open Call for Ideas for a Living Memorial Museum of the Conflict in and about Northern Ireland.* Belfast: Healing Through Remembering.

Rolston, B. (1987). Politics, Painting and Popular Culture: The Political Wall Murals of Northern Ireland. *Media, Culture and Society*, 9(1), pp. 5–28.

Selimovic, J.M. (2013). Making Peace, Making Memory: Peacebuilding and Politics of Remembrance at Memorials of Mass Atrocities. *Peacebuilding*, 1(3), pp. 334–348.

Shirlow, P. and McGovern, M., eds. (1997). *Who Are 'The People'? Unionism, Protestantism and Loyalism in Northern Ireland.* London: Pluto.

Smith, L.J. (2012) Editorial: A *critical* in heritage studies. *International Journal of Heritage Studies* 18(6) 533–540.

Viggiani, E. (2014). *Talking Stones: The Politics of Memorialization in Post-conflict Northern Ireland.* New York: Berghahn Books.

Winter, T. (2008). Post-conflict Heritage and Tourism in Cambodia: The Burden of Angkor. *International Journal of Heritage Studies*, 14(6), pp. 524–539.

Winter, T. (2013). Clarifying the Critical in Critical Heritage Studies. *International Journal of Heritage Studies*, 19(6), pp. 532–545.

2   Enduring insularity and the memory of Northern Ireland's 1968

Chris Reynolds

The post-Troubles context since 1998 offers up opportunities to reconsider key moments in Northern Ireland's past and, in some instances, to question accepted ideas surrounding them. In the case of 1968, the first real opportunity to do so came in 2008, on the fortieth anniversary of the events. In 2011, the author of this chapter entered into a collaboration with the Ulster Museum with the aim of overhauling the section of the Museum's permanent exhibition dedicated to the 1968 period. One of the underpinning objectives of this project was to widen the scope to include much more prominently broader international circumstances and the influence these had on what happened in Northern Ireland. This chapter sets out this international dimension before identifying the different perspectives that were incorporated into that exhibition, making explicit the dissonant heritages that govern the commemoration of the period. This broadening of perspective might be a strategy for any society emerging from conflict to be adopted as a form of critical heritage practice. What might be experienced as a peculiarly local situation might be better framed as part of a wider phenomenon to release new ways of thinking about it and its heritages.

The 1968 Zeitgeist

That 1968 was a period of global revolt is today widely accepted. As the years since this seminal time have passed, it has become increasingly clear that there existed very strong connections between the areas of the world that experienced the upheavals that have come to typify this era. Such similarities can be found in the make-up of those involved, the forms of actions employed or the influences and inspirations that drove people all around the world to rebel. This has enabled the term 'Zeitgeist' to become commonplace when discussing how there was something in the air, globally, that united (in particular) young people in a common struggle to challenge the status quo of their time. Recognition of the transnationality of this period was evident at the time and has been building ever since (Jameson 1984; Katsiaficas 1987; Caute 1988; Fraser 1988). The fortieth anniversary events commemorating 1968 in 2008 saw quite a strong tendency to focus on the transnational aspect and helped consolidate recognition that a true understanding of any nation's '1968' was predicated on an appreciation of the very specific and exceptional international context (Crane and Muellner 2008; de Groot 2008; Førland 2008). Equally noteworthy has been the seemingly exponential proliferation of nations joining the roster of those having experienced a 1968-style revolt. In the early days, it was indeed the events of France, Germany and Italy that dominated European perspectives, whilst any widening of the optic on the global scale would see attentions focussed on China or the US. However, as the years have passed the number of nations that have become incorporated into the international narrative has grown and shows no sign of stopping. From a European perspective, the connections of Eastern nations to what was happening in the West have been particularly fruitful trends (Frei 2008; Gassert and Klimke 2009; Tismaneanu 2011; von der Goltz 2011; Gildea, Mark, and Warring 2013). On the global scale, ventures into peripheral regions and former colonies of nations such as France go to show that there remain some fertile areas for future research projects (Farik 2008; Førland 2008; Klimke and Scharloth 2008; Dramé and Lamarre 2009; Gildea, Mark, and Warring 2013; Zancarini-Fournel 2016: 778–865).

Whilst the transnationalism of 1968 has been expanded and consolidated, it has been very interesting to note the continued absence of Northern Ireland from such perspectives. One only has to scan the plethora of material that covers the question of the global/European nature of 1968 to see that only a very small number of works include reference to Northern Ireland as having experienced a set of events comparable to those experienced in so many other countries in and around the same time (Caute 1988; Fink et al. 1998; Dreyfus-Armand 2008; Cornilis and Waters 2010). It would be no exaggeration to argue that Northern Ireland has largely been forgotten or, at best, pushed to the periphery of how this period is considered transnationally. Without any knowledge of recent Irish history, one would be forgiven for thinking that the absence of Northern Ireland is simply the consequence of the fact that nothing of any significance must have happened. However, 1968 is arguably one of the most pivotal times in terms of the period that was to follow and what would characterise Northern Ireland and perspectives on it both from within and without. Even more interesting, however, is the fact that when one looks closely at what took place, there is a very strong argument to be made for including Northern Ireland alongside those nations so commonly associated with the events of this year. As demonstrated in more detail elsewhere, whether it is in terms of the make-up of those involved, the context from which the events emerged, the forms of action employed or language used by protestors, it is not very difficult to build up a compelling case for Northern Ireland to be considered as part of this transnational period of revolt (Reynolds 2015). Like so many other countries, there was a context of relative stability and peace that paved the way for a new generation of people to ask very serious questions about the rules that governed their society and to do so through very innovative forms of actions and provocative language, all within the context of a recognition that something was happening on the international scene that they could and should be spurred on by. Northern Ireland was not, and simply could not have been, immune to what was going on elsewhere. There were, of course, some local specificities that set it apart from, say, Paris, Rome or Berlin, but the same could be as for any nation on the roster of those having experienced a '1968'. Therefore, the argument that Northern Ireland's 1968 was a case apart is simply insufficient in helping explain its absence.

This chapter argues that instead of looking at what actually happened to make sense of this absence, we need to look at how Northern Ireland's 1968 has been *perceived* to have fitted with what was happening elsewhere. It is important to consider this in three phases as this is central to understanding how this absence first emerged, was then consolidated and is now potentially challengeable. In each of the following three sections, the place of Northern Ireland alongside what was happening elsewhere in the world at the time must be considered both from within and without. This includes both how people in Northern Ireland viewed the events of 1968 as part of the international wave of revolt that was sweeping the globe and the extent to which there was interest beyond the borders of Northern Ireland in trying to draw connections. In the following sections, I draw on testimonies collected as part of the collaboration with the Ulster Museum.

Northern Ireland's 1968 as part of a transnational revolt: at the time

When one considers the timing of events in Belfast and Derry in 1968, it can hardly be of any surprise that movements from elsewhere took notice. It was indeed the spring of 1968 that saw some of the most interesting developments on the European continent, for example. In France, Germany and Italy, significant revolts took place that were unquestionably part of some sort of transnational desire for change. Therefore, with the beginning of significant protest in Derry on 5 October and the formation of the People's Democracy (PD) on 9 October, there were movements in France, Italy and Germany that looked upon what was happening as some sort of continuation or extension of their own revolt. There were even a number of groups from these countries that travelled to Belfast and Derry to experience the revolt and, in some instances, offer advice. As explained by a number of those present at the time: There were one or two Italians had come through and we discussed various things. So, there was a sort of wandering revolutionary vanguard going on in different sites in Europe, et cetera, spreading the message. (Interview with Paul Bew, conducted by CR, Bangor 6 June 2016).

> Some of the younger revolutionaries so-called, knew Ireland was starting to bubble and the Revolutionary Tourists started to arrive, and then the Italians as well, Lotta Continua, them boys started to land in late '68/69 were interested in the marches, wanted to go on some Civil Rights marches.
>
> (Interview with Joe Mulheron, conducted by CR, Derry 4 October 2008)

This 'revolutionary tourism' was commonplace at the time and may help explain why such strong commonalities can be found between different movements in different countries (Jobs 2009). This is not to say that everyone looking in on Northern Ireland saw what was happening there as a simple continuation of some sort of transnational revolt. The particular context was recognised, and, as the example of French press coverage demonstrates, there was a certain degree of division and even ignorance as to how the emergent Civil Rights movement should be understood and how it should be considered in light of what was happening internationally (Deslandes 2013: 25–29).

In terms of attitudes from within, one can ascertain early signs of a certain degree of insularism. This was obvious, for example, in the ways in which these 'revolutionary tourists' were greeted and how well their advice on how to proceed was received. As Dermie McClenaghan explained,

> [W]henever the whole thing broke out, there were students from France who came here to give their assistance and show them what they had done in France and that's what happened in Bogside, the battle of Bogside these French students showing them what they had done [...]. I think the first were a couple of minor celebrities but after that they got pissed off looking at them. Their credentials got a bit weak.
>
> (Interview with Dermie McClenaghan, conducted by CR, Derry 13 December 2008)

This is early evidence of a certain reticence, even amongst the most involved, to draw any connections between the situation in Northern Ireland and what was happening elsewhere. This can be explained perhaps by the fact that some elements perceived what was happening as much more serious and 'real' than what was happening on the streets of Paris, Rome or Berlin. This raises interesting questions about the ways in which such revolts were perceived within Northern Ireland and how the media coverage of them projected a certain banality in comparison to the very serious nature of the Northern Irish context.

Equally interesting to note is how, for different reasons, those opposed to the emerging Civil Rights movement questioned any connection to the international context. Gregory Campbell commented thus:

> So for many in the Unionist community, this was another example of the IRA, this time using methods that were then subsequently so in the likes of Paris and America with Martin Luther King et cetera. And then the Unionist community, they had determined, in my view with some just cause, that this was a recreation in a much more non-violent way, initially, of the IRA campaign to try and destabilise the State, rather than a demand for social justice.
>
> (Interview with Gregory Campbell, conducted by CR, Coleraine 7 October 2016)

Such a perspective was commonplace amongst those who perceived the events of 1968 as some sort of threat, with the possibility of connecting the struggle with what was happening elsewhere running the risk of legitimising what was happening. As Maurice Mills's testimony exemplifies,

> the students' movements raked throughout the world because there's a world trend [...] And there was obviously a follow-through and a copy of that here as far as our problems in Northern Ireland was concerning, of course, it was used...had its motive there and people here followed that through [...] I believed it was an obviously, imminent challenge because obviously there'll be issues involved with which certainly unionists could not agree. And it would be of great concern to unionists, as it did turn out to be. So we had then, as you're aware, the Civil Rights movement that seriously...and I mean seriously...set in motion steps designed to destabilise the Northern Ireland state and constitution and to unnerve this dormant regime.
>
> (Interview with Maurice Mills, conducted by CR, Ballymena 11 October 2016)

That some elements of those involved with the struggle as well as those opposed to it rejected any connection to the international served to heighten the insularism that would lay the foundations that help explain why Northern Ireland would go on to have such a marginal place in the transnational narrative of these events. However, it must equally be noted that there was strong recognition, particularly amongst the more radical elements, that what was happening was and should be considered as part of the international wave of protest. As Paul Bew reflected,

> These international influences were very important. It was a sense that there was a left-wing challenge to capitalism in mature capitalist societies like France. At the same time, the possibility or so Czechoslovakia

seemed to show a more humane sort of socialism in the east. So, it was the sense that the world was full of really quite good possibilities. This was all an illusion but that was there in our head and then of course the Civil Rights Movement in America was to a degree at least an influence.
(Interview with Paul Bew, conducted by CR, Bangor 6 June 2016)

At the time of the events in 1968 in Northern Ireland there was a clear division between those who believed that what was happening should be understood as part of something broader that extended beyond the borders of Northern Ireland and those who (for varying reasons) simply rejected that this was the case. As the next section explains, the onset of the Troubles would enhance the insular perspective and create the next stage in the marginalisation of Northern Ireland from the transnational collective memory of 1968.

Northern Ireland's 1968 as part of a transnational revolt: during the Troubles

In the thirty-year period following the transnational events of 1968, a dominant narrative around how these events should be understood was forged. Briefly, a consensus formed that 1968 marked a very positive turning point for those nations having experienced such a revolt (Reynolds 2015). For example, in the case of France, 1968 would progressively acquire the reputation as a very positive moment and one that should (and was and continues to be) celebrated (Reynolds 2011). Not everyone in France is of the opinion that 1968 should be considered positively. However, when, in 2007, Presidential candidate Nicolas Sarkozy attacked the legacy of 1968, claiming that it need to be liquidated from French society, the widespread rejection amongst the public demonstrated the extent to which this is perceived as a positive moment in recent French history. Former '68ers are periodically wheeled out, particular during anniversary periods, to regale anyone interested in the exploits of back in the day. There is a certain pride associated with these events, both for those who were involved and generally as part of the national history of France (Rioux 2008: 15). The context in Northern Ireland was, of course, very different. As the largely positive Doxa took hold transnationally, the province spiralled down into the nightmare that was the Troubles. It can hardly be a surprise that there was little or no place for Northern Ireland in the positive spin on the transnational 1968 and that what happened in the streets of Belfast and Derry was edged out and forgotten. Such sidelining from without, as a consequence of a very divergent afterlife, is perfectly understandable and important in the general marginalisation of Northern Ireland's 1968. However, perhaps even more important was the perspective from within.

When the Troubles took hold, the argument of those who never really saw any connection with the international situation was strengthened.

The thirty-year conflict was proof indeed that Northern Ireland was a case apart. Even more significant was the attitude of those who had previously seen connections with the international Zeitgeist. Whilst 68ers elsewhere quickly assumed a positive position and went about constructing a narrative of their experiences that was couched in largely upbeat terms, those involved in Northern Ireland went in a completely different direction. The onset and duration of the conflict, with all its horrendous consequences, meant that there was little in the way to celebrate for Northern Irish 68ers. Instead, the story and memory would be buried, forgotten, and this is for two specific reasons. In the initial stages, when the early years of violence took hold, there was little desire for anyone who was involved in the Civil Rights struggle, Northern Ireland Civil Rights Association (NICRA) or the People's Democracy to vaunt their exploits of 1968/69. In fact, as described by some, from the perspective of personal security, it was even in their interests to keep a very low profile.

> A job came up in a Protestant grammar school in Belfast and I applied and I was taken for a preliminary meeting with the headmaster [...] So I was given the job, [...] I was living in Donaghadee which was a very Protestant town. [...] And so I was travelling in to Belfast every day, through largely loyalist territory. One of the things I've always remembered was, it took me, the paper I was reading at the time was *Irish Times*, it took me I'm sure a month or longer to suss out what newspaper shop I could go into to buy an *Irish Times* and feel safe. You know you really, your antennae were working overtime all the time, and so I go in to this school [...] And here was I as a Catholic who had been involved in the Civil Rights movement, going in to the school and I had to establish my credentials fairly quickly. I had one advantage that was my name. My name was not a telling factor, it was neutral. The second advantage occurred really in the first or second day when the boys were testing me and asking me had I taught anywhere before, and I said yes I'd taught at Queens. So that put me up in their estimations but also Queens was a neutral space, so they couldn't identify it, are you with me. So, I had a brief enough period to establish my credentials before they did discover I was a Catholic. And I found that out when I went in to my class one day, and someone had taken a knife and scored on my desk, Arthur is a Taig.
>
> (Interview with Paul Arthur, conducted
> by CR, Bangor 13 February 2009)

Unlike in other countries, the early years of the construction of the narrative around 1968 saw little in the way of any desire amongst participants to discuss their involvement let alone talk up connections with what happened elsewhere. This insularism was enhanced by the second element related to the sense of guilt and responsibility felt by some of those involved. In no way did any of those involved intend to trigger the onset of the Troubles. However, as the magnitude of violence, death and destruction increased over the three decades of Troubles, it can hardly be of any surprise that instead of celebrating what they had done, some instead talk of certain degree of regret. For example,

> I do ask myself the question that had I known in '68 that actions I was going to take could lead to directly or indirectly to three thousand people losing their lives, would I have gone ahead? And of course, the answer is no, I wouldn't have.
>
> (Interview with Kevin Boyle, conducted by CR, Colchester 10 July 2009)

> Oh, there has to be a huge sense of regret. There has to be a huge sense of regret. I think that one of the most important books to come out of the Troubles is Lost Lives, the story of every man, woman and child who was killed in Troubles.
>
> (Interview with Paul Arthur, conducted by CR, Bangor 7 June 2016)

Compare such sentiments with those that dominated elsewhere, and one can get closer to understanding how the construction of the memory of this period was very different to other countries. The story of Northern Ireland's 1968 was effectively buried by because those people best placed to tell the story and situate it in its proper context were simply unable or unwilling to do so and thereby make connections to the international context. Thus, the Troubles only served to consolidate the insularism that was already evident during the events. Externally, the increasingly consensual positive spin attributed to these events meant that there was no place for Northern Ireland. The next section brings the discussion up to the current-day context and outlines just how in a post-Troubles context there may well be some possibility of righting the wrong that is this absence as well as identifying some of the ongoing challenges of doing so.

Northern Ireland's 1968 as part of a transnational revolt: in a post-Troubles context

Since the onset of peace in Northern Ireland it is clear that it is much more possible for academics and historians from elsewhere to take an interest in what happened and try to make sense of it. This has inevitably meant that the optic of understanding the past there has been widened somewhat. In terms of the period under investigation here, there has been some evidence of growing interest in how Northern Ireland fits into the transnational narrative (Prince 2007; McGrogan 2008; Dramé and Lamarre 2009).

However, despite this increase in attention, there remains some work to be done before Belfast and Derry can be talked of in the same breath as Paris, Rome and Berlin. Nevertheless, it would be fair to suggest that there has been evidence of mounting interest from without now that peace has come. However, what is crucial to ensuring that Northern Ireland finds its rightful place on the '68 roster is what comes from within. As discussed earlier, up until the conclusion of the Troubles there was little in the way of interest amongst those involved in telling their story of 1968. However, as with most things since the conclusion of the Troubles, this too has been subject to change.

In the case of 1968, the first real opportunity to reconsider it came in 2008, on the fortieth anniversary of the events. Prior to 2008, there had been little in the way of any effort to commemorate, celebrate or even mark this anniversary and this for the same reasons outlined earlier (one notable exception is Farrell 1988). Throughout the year, there was a whole series of events held to mark the anniversary (Reynolds 2015: 194–201). The 1968 period went from being something that was not discussed in any real detail to being a moment worthy of celebration and commemoration. This unquestionable surge in interest contained a number of noteworthy characteristics.

First, the onset of peace meant that for the first time, many of those who had been involved in these events now felt that it was possible and important to have their say and tell their story. So, in the wide range of events that took place, it was indeed the very participants that set the tone. Kevin Boyle commented thus on that nature of the fortieth anniversary and the role of former activists:

> I think that it was important that it happened and it was and there may have been some insights and reflections that came from some of the speeches that were made. [...] the events were of such a nature that they related more to the activists, the aging activists I should say but I suppose underlying it was a sense of pride that you know tempered with the sorrows of all those who have died but in a sense that it was a very important period an important period of Irish History to have been involved in whatever it unleashed and couldn't have foreseen.
>
> (Interview with Kevin Boyle, conducted by CR, Colchester 10 July 2009)

Second, such was the impact of the shift in context that a set of events that had hitherto remained very much under the radar became the subject of a political struggle. The two major Nationalist parties vied for ownership of the events of 1968, which, in turn, helps explain why there were so many events and perhaps a real determination on the part of some of those involved to ensure that the legacy of what had happened would not be hijacked (Reynolds 2015: 194–201). This tension was summed up by prominent Civil Rights activists Austin Currie:

> I very much felt that the people involved in the Commemorative committee had to do what they did. Otherwise others would have taken over. [...] So it had to be done. I mean the rewriting of history has to be combated.
>
> (Interview with Austin Currie, conducted by CR,
> Cultra, 10 June 2016)

Third, and perhaps most crucially for this chapter, one of the most interesting trends decipherable in the tone of the fortieth anniversary celebrations was the clear desire to try and set what had happened within a broader, international context. This was clear in terms of the themes covered in a number of the workshops and conferences as well as some of the media coverage (Reynolds 2015: 200–201). Such a broadening of the optic was welcomed by certain participants. For example: I think it's quite a good thing to do yes, [...] and I know in terms of what they've put out, the international perspective, was missing out a bit [...] So it's widened out a bit... (Interview with Brìd Ruddy, conducted by CR, Belfast 31 October 2008).

What 2008 demonstrated was that the onset of peace was a significant enough shift in context to enable a reconsideration of the 1968 events and this opportunity was seized upon. As a result, there was a surge in interest, a real desire by former participants to have their say and, importantly, a breakdown, from within, of the insularity that had until this point been a crucial factor in keeping Northern Ireland on the periphery of the transnational narrative of this period. A major project at the Ulster Museum is further evidence of this push to reconsider and broaden perspectives on this period.

In 2011, I entered into a collaboration with the Museum on this project to overhaul the section of its permanent exhibition dedicated to the 1968 period. As well as curating a number of important objects from the period, the most innovative departure of this new exhibition was the use of a series of video interviews with key protagonists from the time. Sections of these interviews were selected and compiled together to enable visitors to hear more about the context, the objects on display and the significance of this period. Before the new section was opened to the public it underwent a rigorous evaluation with a number of focus groups representing a cross section of Northern Irish society.[1] A further part of the public engagement strategy of the exhibition was the hosting of a study day for 15–16 year old students from both sides of the community. Having visited the gallery and attended a number of sessions where, amongst other issues, the need to consider the international context was emphasised, the participants were invited to provide feedback that contributed to the overall evaluation process. The testimonies of those who were present at the time as well as some of the results of the evaluation offer up interesting, current-day perspectives Northern Ireland's place in the transnational narrative.

Amongst the reflections of those who were present at the time, there were many who felt it important, correct and relevant for the international context to be given more prominence. For example, Bernadette McAliskey reflected,

> I think at that period of time yes, all...Northern Ireland did not exist in a bubble. It was often referred to as a stagnant backwater and that might not have been an inaccurate description. But we had television. We could see what was happening in the world. We had record shops and we could buy rock and roll music, we could read. And, so when you put those three things together, we could see what was happening.
>
> (Interview with Bernadette McAliskey, conducted by CR, Cultra 8 June 2017)

Such recognition of the context beyond the national paradigm was equally supported by some of the results and comments found in the evaluation process. Focus groups were shown a video clip introducing the international context and then asked to respond to the following question: 'We need to consider what was going on elsewhere in the world when we try to understand what was happening in Northern Ireland at this time'. Across the board, there was strong agreement, backed up with comments such as

> "It swept across Europe"; "Northern Ireland was heavily influenced by events in Europe and USA"; "It's good to know what happened in other countries during this period and compare to Northern Ireland."; "People saw what was happening across the world on TV. The conditions were here were ripe for change – the impetus came from USA."; "It's always better to know the bigger picture to help understand our own situation"; "It made people think that all people in NI needed rights too".
>
> (Social Research Centre 2016: 21–22)

Whilst this demonstrates clear evidence of a desire to emphasise the importance of the international context of the time in order to better understand what happened, it would be incorrect to state that this view was shared by everyone. In terms of both testimonies and evaluation results, it is very clear to see that there is a certain enduring insularity that offers up some interesting questions on the challenges facing the question of how the past is to be dealt with. A number of interviewees who would have been opposed back in 1968 to making connections to what was taking place elsewhere maintained this line. For example, Gregory Campbell rejected any connection with the international context, instead seeing this as an attempt by the

Republican movement at the time to jump on the bandwagon of international upheaval:

> Yes. I don't think we were aware of that at the time, but then as the... as the international movement started to get reported and to pick up speed, it became clear to us that...and our view was, this is Irish Nationalism seeing an international bandwagon that was on broadly similar lines which they could adapt for their own local purposes and which we saw as yet as another...is often called Trojan Horse, to try and succeed where the '56-'62 campaign had failed.
>
> (Interview with Gregory Campbell, conducted by CR, Coleraine 7 October 2016)

Such insularism was equally evident in the results of the evaluation. It must be noted that a reticence to align the events with the international context was not exclusive to one side of the community. For different reasons, in both Nationalist and Unionist responses, caution was voiced in making Northern Ireland part of some broader, international narrative.

The evaluation report details that some commentators were keen to emphasize that Northern Ireland 'was not just a mini version of unrest and rights movements' that exists across the world. Their point was that the reality of inequality in Northern Ireland 'should not be diminished', adding:

> "What was happening here was different"; "Literally people were rising up"; "There was an appetite (in Northern Ireland) already for something to happen"; "What was happening here was happening here (discrimination)"; "People had got to a point where they would have reacted anyway".
>
> (Social Research Centre 2016: 18)

It was apparent that these participants had some fear that their beliefs about inequality and injustice in Northern Ireland's 1968 might be diluted or diminished by placing Northern Ireland in a wider world context. This is reflected in the comment 'I don't think we need to look at international issues to understand Northern Ireland's issues' (Social Research Centre 2016: 21).

Overall then, the post-Troubles era has unquestionably provided the context for a shift in terms of how the 1968 events are understood in Northern Ireland. This is true from without but most importantly from within. There can be no doubt, as evidenced during fortieth anniversary celebrations and through the ongoing Ulster Museum project, that there has been a change. Importantly, this internal change has featured a concerted effort to focus more prominently on the international context and consolidate the argument that what happened at this time cannot and should not be disassociated from what was happening elsewhere. However, the testimonies of those involved and the results of the evaluation carried out for the Ulster Museum project have demonstrated that not everyone is convinced and there remains a certain reluctance to look beyond the borders of Northern Ireland when making sense of this period. The following section will attempt to explain this enduring insularity before concluding on what this case tells us about the challenges facing those having to deal with the legacy of Northern Ireland's divided past.

Explaining the enduring insularity

There are several, interrelated reasons that one can offer in order to explain the continued reticence to place Northern Ireland in the international context of the late 1960s. Such insularity is not exclusive to the events of 1968. In fact, the tendency to see Northern Ireland as a case apart is a long-standing feature of Irish history and identity (McCann 2009). This has only been consolidated as a consequence of the Troubles that very much set Northern Ireland apart and encouraged those both from within and without to consider what was happening there as specific and not related to anything beyond its borders. In terms of the 1968 events, as explained previously, the very divergent post-1968 trajectory of Northern Ireland goes a long way towards setting it up as a case apart and not to be compared to elsewhere. Such attitudes to Northern Ireland have only been enhanced by the response of the British government that had very much persisted with the line that what was happening there was very much a localised, tribal conflict that was beyond its control despite its efforts. This is known as the 'internal conflict interpretation' and has only served to further underscore the insularism that has prevented Northern Ireland from looking beyond its borders to make sense of its predicament (Reynolds 2015: 178–179). Insularism appears to be the norm, so it is no surprise that there is a reluctance to make international connections. However, there are other potential explanations.

From a collective memory perspective, whilst it is true that significant contextual changes can and do lead to the possibility of recalibrating particular memories, such memories are not going to be changed overnight (Olick 1999). In the case of Northern Ireland's 1968, the forty-year period following the events has seen a certain narrative of this period emerge, become consolidated and in fact be anchored in the collective memory. Understandings of this period have been framed by the dominant narrative that until this point paid little or no attention to the potential links to the international situation. The onset of peace may well have opened up possibilities for this narrative to be challenged, and in particular, for the international circumstances to become part of the way this story is told. However, this will take time. A well-anchored memory cannot and will not just be simply replaced overnight. Only through time can this new context start to have an impact on and even shape the dominant narrative of this period.

A further possible explanation relates to how the events of 1968 abroad are perceived from within Northern Ireland. There is somewhat of a consensus that Northern Ireland does not fit what was happening elsewhere because of the seriousness of the predicament in the troubled province. To a certain extent, one is left with the impression that connecting the events of Northern Ireland at the time with events in Paris, Rome or Berlin would somehow undermine the seriousness of the predicament there. This is perfectly understandable given the very different turn that Northern Ireland took in the aftermath. However, it somehow suggests that what was happening elsewhere is viewed as irresponsible or unimportant. This offers up some interesting questions as to the nature of how the 1968 events, particularly on the continent, were and continue to be viewed from within Northern Ireland. The strong tendency to posit 1968 as a positive moment has, in some instances, led to the overemphasis of a certain sugar-coated version of what happened, leading to the idea that it was a somewhat harmless bit of fun when a spoilt generation of young, educated, bourgeois students had a tantrum and eventually triggered some positive changes. One can see quite easily how the connection with Northern Ireland becomes very difficult in such instances.

One final and critically important trend in both the testimonies and in the results of the evaluation was the existence of a communal divide in terms of how the events of Northern Ireland's 1968 should be considered alongside what was happening internationally. In crude terms, it becomes clear that there is quite a strong tendency within the Catholic/Nationalist community to accept, endorse and encourage connections between what happened in Northern Ireland and the international situation. So, for example, in the testimonies it is easy to find reflections such as that of Anne Devlin, who emphasised the centrality of the international context in her experience:

> The European thing impacts on you because you suddenly start seeing, as I'm going to the Young Socialists, I'm seeing things going on in France. And you're saying, "Wow, look at that." There are... and that's a young generation. That's a generation where you're looking at what's happening in Britain, and thinking, that's not happening in Britain. That's happening there. It's happening in Germany. You're looking at young, the young. You're looking at the counter culture. And you're looking at America and you're thinking, wow. Look at those demonstrations.
>
> (Interview with Anne Devlin, interviewed by CR, Cultra 8 June 2017)

When one considers the results of the Museum project evaluation, there was a more positive inclination from within the Catholic/Nationalist community regarding the international perspective. For example, when the Nationalist focus group were asked the following question: 'We need to consider what was going on elsewhere in the world when we try to understand what was happening in Northern Ireland at this time', there was a strong tendency to positively acknowledge the international perspective (Social Research Centre, 2016: 19).

On the flip side, the evidence of the interviews and the evaluation suggests that there is a heightened degree of insularism from within the Protest/Unionist community regarding connections between the events of 1968 in Northern Ireland and what took place elsewhere. Reflections such as the following from Hubert Nichol exemplify this trend. Asked if he thought the international context was important:

> No. Because in those days, totally different from now. Something happens within minutes; you see it in the TV or you see it in Facebook. But those times where something happened in France and happened in United States, it was probably two or three days before it reached. We happen to, we only had a radio. You turn on the radio and you heard it. It doesn't really concern you. I mean that was far away from here. It's not like today, you can be Bronson an hour and a half now. You can be in America in six hours. In those days 50 years ago, that was a world away. So it didn't really concern you. It's something that you didn't get involved in.
>
> (Interview with Hubert Nichol, conducted by CR, Cultra 24 March 2017)

Furthermore, there was less agreement amongst the Protestant/Unionist focus group with the statement 'We need to consider what was going on elsewhere in the world when we try to understand what was happening in Northern Ireland at this time' (Social Research Centre, 2016: 19). Together, this suggests greater insularism within the Protestant/Unionist community.

Overall then, the continued reticence to widen the optic of Northern Ireland's 1968 from within is due to a combination of the aforementioned factors. Insularism is the norm, and this will always be a challenge to overcome, particularly given the very specific recent history of conflict. This has meant that in relation to 1968 a certain understanding of how this period played out has very much taken root. Inflected by the very divergent afterlife that was the Troubles, the inherent insularism has only been further consolidated and any contextual change (such as the onset of peace) will bring changes, but only over time. Slowing this process is a particular understanding of what happened internationally that posits many of the revolts as largely irresponsible, almost joyous moments only serving to further widen the gap between what happened in Northern Ireland and elsewhere. Finally, and perhaps most importantly, is the continuation of a communal divide, present at the time that sees the same events viewed very differently across the two communities. The evidence is clear that with the Catholic/Nationalist community is much more sympathetic to the international perspective whilst the Protestant/Unionist community remains reticent. This lack of consensus is a significant hurdle in the process to recalibrate how Northern Ireland's 1968 is remembered and understood.

Conclusions

Despite the progress over the twenty years since the Good Friday Agreement, many deeply problematic issues still require attention. One of the most difficult of such issues is how the past should be dealt with. All too often, the past only serves to further entrench divisions between the communities of Northern Ireland. The events of 1968 are a potent example of how a critically important period in the past can undergo a recalibration with positive consequences. During the Troubles, Northern Ireland's 1968 was rarely associated with the wave of revolt that swept the globe at the same time. This marginalisation has come both from within and without. Whilst the latter is clearly very important, it has been the reluctance from within that lies at the crux of Northern Ireland's absence from the transnational narrative of this period. The evidence from this exhibition is that by taking on a broader perspective, better understanding of such periods offers the possibility of building a degree of mutual understanding of how Northern Ireland got to where it is today. Key to this is breaking through the insularism that too frequently has presented the province as a specific case destined for a troubled fate. This is reflected in anonymous feedback from a school student, following the GCSE study '1968: An opportunity missed?' hosted at the Ulster Museum, 24 March 2016:

> I think it was good that international protest was brought up because it gives you a better insight into what the world was like back then. It gives people a better understanding of why the civil rights came out. These [activities] have shown me that they were important and did have an impact on Northern Ireland ... By hearing other people's stories, it helped me understand better.
>
> (NMNI 2016b)

Note

1 Evaluation carried out by *Social Research Centre*. Data used taken from National Museums Northern Ireland (2016a).

Bibliography

Caute, D. (1988). *Sixty-Eight: The Year of the Barricades. A Journey through 1968*. London: Harper and Row.

Cornilis, I. and Waters, S. (2010). *Memories of 1968. International Perspectives*. Bern: Peter Lang.

Crane, C. and Muellner, N. (2008). *Episodes of Culture in Contest*. Cambridge: Cambridge Scholar Publishing.

de Groot, G. (2008). *The Sixties Unplugged*. London: Pan Books.

Deslandes, K. (2013). *Regards français sur le conflit nord-irlandais*. Bern: Peter Lang.

Dramé, P. and Lamarre, J. (2009). *1968. Des sociétés en crise: une perspective globale/ Societies in Crisis: A Global Perspective*. Laval: Les Presses de l'Université de Laval.

Dreyfus-Armand, G. (2008). *Les Années 68. Un monde en mouvement. Nouveaux regards sur une histoire plurielle*. Paris: Syllepse.

Farik, N. (2008). *1968 Revisited. 40 Years of Protest Movements*. Brussels: Heinrich Boll Foundation.

Farrell, M. (1988). *Twenty Years On*. Dingle: Brandon.

Fink, C., Gassert, P. and Junker, D., eds. (1998). *1968: The World Transformed*. Washington: Cambridge University Press.

Førland, E. (2008). Introduction to the Special issue on 1968. *Scandinavian Journal of History*, 33(4), pp. 317–502.

Fraser, R. (1988). *1968: A Student Generation in Revolt*. New York: Pantheon.

Frei, N. (2008). *1968. Jugendrevolte und globaler Protest*. Munich: Deutscher Taschenbuch Verlag.

Gassert, P. and Klimke, M., eds. (2009). *1968 – Memories and Legacies of a Global Revolt*. Washington: German Historical Institute.

Gildea, R., Mark, J. and Warring, A. (2013). *Europe's 1968. Voices of Revolt*. Oxford: Oxford University Press.

Jameson, F. (1984). Periodizing the '60s. *Social Text*, 9/10, Spring Summer, pp. 178–209.

Jobs, R.I. (2009). Youth Movements: Travel, Protest and Europe in 1968. *The American Historical Review*, 114(2), pp. 376–404.

Katsiaficas, G. (1987) *The Imagination of the New Left: A Global Analysis of 1968*. Boston: South End Press.

Klimke, M. and Scharloth, J. (2008). *1968 in Europe. A History of Protest and Activism*. New York: Palgrave Macmillan.

McCann, E. (2009). Civil Rights in an International Context. In: McClenaghan, P., ed. *Spirit of '68: Beyond the Barricades*. Derry: Guildhall Press. pp. 20–21.

McGrogan, M. (2008). Art on the Street. *History Today*. May pp. 34–36.

National Museums Northern Ireland. (2016a). Evaluation of 1968 research and interpretation for Collecting the Troubles and Beyond at the Ulster Museum. NMNI.

National Museums Northern Ireland (2016b) Anonymous Student Feedback Submitted Following GCSE Study '1968: An Opportunity Missed?' hosted at the Ulster Museum, 24 March 2016.

Olick, J.K. (1999). Genre Memories and Memory Genres: A Dialogical Analysis of May 8, 1945 Commemorations in the Federal Republic of Germany. *American Sociological Review*, 64(3), pp. 381–402.

Prince, S. (2007). *Northern Ireland's 68. Civil Rights, Global Revolt and the Origins of the Troubles*. Dublin: Irish Academic Press.

Reynolds, C. (2011). *Memories of May '68. France's Convenient Consensus*. Cardiff: University of Wales Press.

Reynolds, C. (2015). *Sous les pavés…the Troubles. Northern Ireland, France and the European Collective Memory of 1968*. Bern: Peter Lang.

Rioux, J.-P. (2008). L'événement-mémoire. Quarante ans de commémorations. *Le Débat*, 149(March–April), pp. 4–19.

Social Research Centre (2016). *Evaluation of 1968 Research and Interpretation Re: Collecting the Troubles and Beyond at the Ulster Museum*. Belfast: National Museums Northern Ireland.

Tismaneanu, V., ed. (2011). *Promises of 1968: Crisis, Illusion and Utopia*. Budapest: Central European Press.

von der Goltz, A. (2011). *'Talkin' 'bout My Generation': Conflicts of Generation Building and Europe's 1968*. Gottingen: Wallstein Verlag.

Zancarini-Fournel, M. (2016). *Les lutes et les rêves. Une histoire populaire de la France. De 1685 à nos jours*. Paris: Zones.

3 The Decade of Centenaries and a methodology for engaging with 'difficult heritage'

Paul Mullan

In Northern Ireland commemoration is seemingly inescapable, particularly as the region moves towards the fiftieth anniversary of the start of the Troubles and the centenary of the partition of Ireland. Both periods continue to cast dominant shadows over Northern Ireland's politics and society. Twenty years on from the Good Friday Agreement, and its resetting of relationships between communities, the region is addressing whether commemoration can be actualised without deepening societal and community division. This chapter explores how the Heritage Lottery Fund (HLF) and its partners approached the contested nature of heritage in Northern Ireland through the funding of community-based heritage projects. The discussion focuses upon HLF's strategic and practical engagement with the Decade of Centenaries (sometimes called the Decade of Commemoration), which marks the period between 1912 and 1923 that includes the centenaries of the Easter Rising, First World War and Partition of Ireland. Drawing on the theoretical landscape of Heritage Studies, this chapter explores how heritage is produced and the forces that help shape its construction. The example of commemoration emphasises the challenges that heritage poses when put to use, and this becomes evident in the practical outworking of the work of the HLF and Community Relations Council (CRC) around commemoration.

Heritage: concepts and uses

Harrison asks us to think 'of heritage as a creative engagement with the past in the present [that] focuses our attention on our ability to take an active and informed role in the production of our own future' (Harrison 2013: 229). Heritage is a product of modernity, a response to a time of great change and uncertainty, shaped by a desire to hold onto those aspects of the past that are seen to be worth preserving (Hewison 1987; Lowenthal 1998). Stuart Hall described heritage as being everywhere and under constant construction (Hall 2008). If, then, heritage is created when the past is put to contemporary use, it is important to ask to what use and to whose purpose? Where once heritage was used to create the idea of a singular national heritage, as the ties of social order have loosened other versions of the past have emerged (Hobsbawm and Ranger 1992). Tunbridge and Ashworth see heritage as a process because it emerges from the choices that are made about what should be inherited and passed on. Implicit in those choices is deciding what will be remembered and what will be forgotten (Tunbridge and Ashworth 1996). The heritage that is created is inevitably 'imagined heritage' insofar as it represents the picture of the past that most fits the needs of those doing the remembering. Given that the past is being edited for its current purpose, this inevitably leads to injustices and inequalities. Stuart Hall, for example, argues for the need to 'rewrite the margins into the centre, the outside into the inside' (Hall 2008: 225), and in so doing open heritage up to all manner of manifestations and uses. Tunbridge and Ashworth recognise that the creation of an imagined past can hold people back from finding solutions for present-day issues by continuing to reinforce the status quo. So, for them, a thoughtful heritage is a key part of the heritage process. They use the term 'dissonant heritage' to describe the tensions that are created through the production of heritage built on 'the idea of discrepancy and incongruity' (Tunbridge and Ashworth 1996: 20).

Sharon Macdonald recognises the disruptive potential of heritage, which she conceptualises as difficult heritage. Difficult heritage is where 'a past is recognised as meaningful in the present but that is also contested' (Macdonald 2009: 11). Macdonald's interest is in how heritage is 'assembled and negotiated', and in particular how difficult history is often ignored, in the main, by state-sponsored museums and memorials. When it comes to difficult heritage the starting point should be the place where it is recognised to be difficult. One of the great concerns is the potential for the use of heritage, particularly by nations and groups, to rewrite their past and bend it to their purpose. David Lowenthal identifies heritage as being always about the conflict between 'us' and 'them' (Lowenthal 2015). It is here that heritage links very directly into identity and can be at its most powerful, harnessing the tools of nationalism, ethnicity, language, religion and narratives of belonging through a discourse of inclusion or exclusion. Equally 'heritage can also function as a form of resistance to such hegemonic discourses (ethno-nationalism) and a marker of plurality in multicultural societies' (Ashworth et al. 2007: 4).

Given that heritage is a process, and as such can be used to create different narratives, there is, for the French philosopher Paul Ricoeur, a requirement for an ethics of responsibility to the past: 'the debt we owe the dead' (Kearney 1995: 184). The goal of this would be the creation of a discourse where heritage and the past are remembered. To achieve this Ricoeur suggested a model of memory exchange: as Kearney phrases it, 'It is through stories revolving around others and around ourselves that we articulate and shape our own temporality' (Kearney 1996: 6). Kearney suggests that Ricoeur makes an ethical plea that identifies the importance of 'taking responsibility, in imagination and in sympathy, for the story of the other, through the life narratives which concern that other' (Kearney 1996: 6). In this, Ricoeur recognises that, given that there can be a number of interpretations and narratives about any aspect of the past, there should be a conscious plurality of reading about those actions and an openness to reinterpretation and reappraisal of the narratives of the past (Kearney 1996: 6–7).

Within the broader field of Heritage Studies, Laurajane Smith has led the reappraisal of narratives of the past through her critique of Authorised Heritage Discourse (AHD) and has endeavoured to show how heritage has been shaped by the social and political context of society: 'Discourses can have a persuasive power in maintaining and legitimising hierarchies of social relations' (Smith 2006: 16). AHD, Smith explains, is driven by a Western and expert view, and has dominated the production of heritage, thinking about the past and deciding what is important. Smith's critique begins to reveal the driving forces behind the production of heritage by seeking to identify what constitutes expertise, who decides and the levels at which expertise is exercised (local, regional or national). Expertise might be dependent on the specific heritage site, issue or material, and might be drawn from whatever source can shed light on the heritage under consideration. Whatever grand narratives are at play the local and vernacular can have profound importance, and, in this way, heritage can contribute greatly to place-making and local identity, constituting and giving meaning to communities.

Such heritage is important then since community is where members of a group have something in common which distinguishes them from others, 'where one learns and continues to practice how to "be social" … where one acquires culture' (Cohen 1989: 15). Sennett sees community as resistance against the real world (Sennett 1993). For Crooke 'community is a multi-layered and politically charged concept that, with a change in context, alters in meaning and consequence' (Crooke 2010: 16). What might be presented as definitional imprecision Crooke describes as 'malleability', a characteristic useful when combined with heritage constructed from the building blocks of customs, language, landscapes, history, artefacts and monuments. Once forged this has the potential to contribute to identity at both a community and national level. Thus, community, identity and heritage become interwoven in how they contribute meaning to each other when they engage with the local specificities, actors and contingencies (Macdonald 2009).

To explain how heritage can contribute to community identity formation, one can refer to how heritage and heritage spaces provide for the creation of social and cultural capital. Robert Putnam, in his analysis of the decline of community life in America during the 1990s, considered the role of local networks and associations in building social capital and their role in strengthening or weakening cohesion within society (Putnam 2000). It has been recognised that certain activities, whilst being good for the engaged group, may have external effects which are darker (de Souza Briggs 1998), leading to negative consequences such as deepening sectarianism, ethnic bigotry and simple corruption. Considering this dichotomy,

Putnam made the distinction between the creation of bridging and bonding capital – bridging capital being inclusive, outward looking and able to 'encompass people across diverse social cleavages' and bonding capital, on the other hand, being exclusive and inward looking, and having the potential to 'reinforce exclusive identities and homogeneous groups' – whilst recognising that 'bonding social capital is good for undergoing specific reciprocity and mobilising society', such as helping others at a time of need (Putnam 2000: 22). So clearly there are choices in approach to be made by groups, depending on their desired outcomes. The use of heritage raises questions in societies where there are contested views of the past: where the idea of a singular national story is disputed and where community engagement with the past is rooted in division. It is therefore not surprising that in Northern Ireland the narratives of both the Nationalist and Unionist communities are populated with radically divergent interpretations of the past. In this way heritage presents very particular challenges and difficulties.

The Heritage Lottery Fund and difficult heritage

HLF is the UK's biggest investor in the preservation of and engagement with heritage. Since funds were first awarded in 1994 over £7 billion has been spent on over 40,000 heritage projects. In Northern Ireland over £220 million has been spent on 1,300 projects, much of which has been spent on major heritage infrastructure projects, such as museums, cathedrals, landscapes and broader natural heritage. A major focus has been on encouraging communities to look at heritage that is important to them. This has ranged from local buildings to community projects, which can often involve a rediscovery of hidden or forgotten heritage. To facilitate this work HLF has a range of programmes through which groups can apply for funding, for example: Heritage Grants, for larger capital and activity projects; Landscape Partnership, for landscape scale projects which link people and landscape; and Your Heritage and Shared Heritage, for community-based projects.

Due to the contested nature of society in Northern Ireland, initially HLF had been wary about engaging in projects rooted in community identity. The prospect of funding projects that could be presented as forming part of a contemporary political project had been a concern. That wariness was to change in 2006, building on existing HLF policy to put communities at the heart of projects and embracing the wider themes of heritage. The establishment of a new power-sharing Northern Ireland Executive in May 2007 provided an opportunity for HLF to support projects that reflected more closely Northern Ireland's history and society. This new policy direction was launched at a one-day conference in Belfast in November 2007, *Digging Deeper: Sharing our Past, Sharing Our Future*, one of a series of events across the UK. The stated objective of the event was to help to navigate the space around how the past was used in Northern Ireland. The conference theme echoed *A Shared Future,* a key governmental policy framework for good relations (Community Relations Unit 2005) which sought to set the policy context of relations between the main communities in Northern Ireland. With a focus on heritage and identity the conference endeavoured to put these issues at the heart of the debate on Northern Ireland's future. Whilst similar themes were explored in Scotland and Wales the direct relevance to contemporary issues was most evident here because the contested nature of Northern Ireland society had identity issues at its core.

Issues of identity were well demonstrated in a presentation from the Holywell Trust focussing upon the Diamond War Memorial Project in Derry/Londonderry. The project had been given a modest HLF grant in 2006 to explore the backgrounds of the 756 names of the war dead commemorated on the monument. For the majority of the Nationalist community, war memorials had hitherto been an anathema, regarded as symbols of the British Army and of little relevance to the Nationalist story. The first public signs of Nationalist engagement with commemoration of the First World War had come with the joint opening, by the Queen and the Irish President, of the Irish Peace Park at Messines in 1998 (Butler 1998). Further interest from the Nationalist community was evident in 2002 when then Sinn Féin Mayor of Belfast and former member of the Irish Republican Army (IRA), Alex Maskey, officiated a Remembrance Sunday event at Belfast's cenotaph (McDonald 2003). The significance of what the researchers in Derry found was both profound and, yet in many ways, obvious. In Derry familial connections with the British Army had been very deliberately forgotten by Nationalists – post partition these men were seen as traitors to the independence campaign twinned with the still raw memories of the British Army's role in Bloody Sunday in 1972. It was found that nearly 50% of the names recorded on the memorial were of people from a Nationalist background (Hocking, 2014). From this recuperation of knowledge about the Diamond War Memorial came a noticeable shift in the perceptions in Derry/Londonderry of a site seen as a solely Unionist space to one which was more shared, where Unionists and Nationalists felt equally comfortable. The Diamond War Memorial showed that Nationalist re-engagement with the First World War was possible when demonstrable historical facts, such as Nationalist involvement in the First World War, were allowed to challenge existing narratives that had been forged around the needs of later generations. In so doing the narrative around those events has been complicated and reshaped, echoing Ricoeur's idea of recounting differently (Ricoeur 1995). The idea of complicating or reshaping the narrative might at first seem counter-intuitive in terms of understanding the past. However, in a society with oversimplified accounts of past events, editing out those stories or events that did not fit contemporary narratives, a thoughtful and informed complication could be seen as desirable. For HLF it became clear that heritage, whilst being true to itself, was also a tool that could be used for the purposes of reconciliation in a divided society like

Northern Ireland. This was not a search for a singular or shared history but recognition of the plurality of narratives that often became entwined. The Diamond War Memorial Project had given a glimpse of this possibility and exemplified an approach that became all the more important as HLF moved towards the Decade of Commemorations.

Engaging with the decade – the development of a set of principles for remembering

One of the first public mentions of the Decade of Commemorations was in May 2010 in a speech given by the then Taoiseach (Prime Minister) of the Republic of Ireland, Mr Brian Cowen (Cowen 2011). North of the border, the Department of Culture Arts and Leisure established a steering group on Centenaries. The 'Decade' referred to commemorative activity that focussed on the many 1911–1923 events significant and formative in the period that led up to the setting up of the two different states on the island of Ireland. Amongst these were the Third Home Rule Bill; the signing of the Ulster Covenant in 1912; the First World War, particularly the Somme; the Easter Rising; the 1918 Election; the War of Independence; the Belfast/Lisburn burnings; Partition and Civil War. Other key events were identified that would add richness to commemoration, such as women's emancipation in 1918. However, it was the events where commemoration could be seen as disruptive in fortifying divisive community narratives that were perceived to be the key challenge for this period. The Taoiseach, speaking at University College Dublin, presented a vision for the Decade as one of opportunities. In his address he explored how an entwined narrative could emerge from the 'separate histories – British and Irish, orange and green, republican, nationalist, unionist, (and) loyalist'. Cowen identified his desire for 'the process of commemoration to recognise the totality of history of the period, and all of the diversity that it encompasses' (Cowen 2011).

Against this backdrop, in the Autumn/Winter of 2010, HLF and the Northern Ireland CRC began to explore the challenge of the 'Decade'. For CRC, the motivation was the potential impact that the 'Decade' could have on community relations. For HLF, the concern was about being asked to fund inward looking single-identity projects. Where these were concerned with creating or reinforcing narratives lacking in wider historical context, there would be the potential to inflame community tensions, projects which were heavy on bonding and light on bridging capital (Putnam 2000: 22). However, given HLF's outlook on community-driven projects, and preparedness to fund the heritage important for those communities, this presented a dilemma. HLF conceptualised its response to this dilemma in this way: a community identity project should never be about a community talking exclusively to themselves about themselves; rather the dialogue should be framed in a way that it could be understood and engaged with by others outside of that community. Therefore the language used in the project should be open and engaging, rather than closed and excluding, allowing for a plurality of reading (Ricoeur 1995). Another important concern was one of truth. Todorov has written, 'Commemorative discourse obviously makes use of material supplied by historians and witnesses, but it does not respect the test of truth that these latter forms must pass' (Todorov 2003: 132). Commemoration clearly has the potential for significant misuse.

Both CRC and HLF were concerned about the long-term disruptive potential for fifty-year anniversaries of the Troubles. In many ways the Centenary events began to be seen as creating a potential template for handling the challenge of events that were still in living memory. It was not the desire, nor would it have been appropriate, for CRC or HLF to lead commemorative activity. Nonetheless, each accepted that there was a role for them in helping shape how commemoration could be actualised in public space. Each recognised that that could be done best through engaging with organisations who could have an influencing and context setting role: museums, libraries, archives, broadcast media, universities and remembering projects. A first step was to bring interested parties together, and an initial discussion was convened in late November 2010. The group, which now includes many other organisations, has continued to meet as the Decade Roundtable on an approximately quarterly basis to this day. In late 2010 a CRC/HLF discussion paper was produced for the round-table group that started to sketch out potential approaches to commemoration. One of the key initial outcomes was the creation of a set of principles about commemoration in public, with the view to announcing them at a conference in March 2011. The principles for remembering in public space which were ultimately agreed were to be seen in the context of an 'inclusive and accepting society' where the imperative would be to (1) start from the historical facts, (2) recognise the implications and consequences of what happened, (3) understand that different perceptions and interpretations exist and (4) show how events and activities can deepen understanding of the period (CRC, 2017). The principles drew on existing HLF guidance focussing on the importance of historically based research that could be interrogated and did not rely overly on reminiscence. They also underlined the importance of placing a commemorative event into wider cultural and historical contexts, so that it is not presented as a one-off isolated event. This is to encourage thoughtful and illuminating commemorative practices that would perhaps even address the silences and gaps within community memory. It was hoped that the period of 'Decade' commemoration could be turned into an opportunity creating a better understanding of the past in the face of selective and partial remembering.

Another aspect of the principles development was recognising the impact of the language used when remembering. Attention was focussed upon the need to make a clear distinction between the words 'celebrating' and 'commemorating'. Any casual use of the term 'celebrating' could be seen as triumphalist, where one community is talking to itself to the clear exclusion of the 'other', in the manner suggested by Putnam (2000). It was therefore important to frame the space within which commemoration could be interrogated. Todorov has written about the construction of meaning in memory work and the need for a sense of shared humanity (2003), and Arendt has identified the need for 'liberation from one's own private interests' (2006: 220) in order to take responsibility for how the past is remembered. In the context of Eliade's 'terror of history', Ricoeur stresses the necessity of 'imagining the suffering of others before re-examining one's own' (Kearney 1996: 9). The principles created an enabling space within which thoughtful commemoration could be actualised.

The importance of engaging key groups and people with the ethical principles has continued to underpin work in the region. Increasingly, the ideas of public spaces were pitched as 'places for exploration, learning and challenge instead of simple propaganda or banal neutrality' (Morrow and Mullan 2012: 8). A conference *Remembering the Future* convened in Belfast City Hall in March 2011 brought community, political and civic society representatives into discussion with historians and other commentators. As well as promoting the 'principles', the conference set out to outline the complexity and challenge that lay ahead in the Decade. Amongst the contributions the *Irish Times* journalist and commentator, Fintan O'Toole, cautioned against 'equal opportunities mythologising'; Professor Marianne Elliott identified the challenge of a 'communal memory' based on exclusion; politicians Tom Hartley, from Sinn Féin, and Nelson McCausland, from the Democratic Unionist Party (DUP), called for an open and ongoing dialogue which embraced the complexity of the past, and Ulster Unionist Councillor Ian Adamson saw the opportunity for a cultural consensus to emerge around a united Ulster (MacBride 2012).

At a Northern Ireland Executive level, agreement had been given for the, by now Sinn Féin controlled, Department of Culture, Arts and Leisure (DCAL) to work alongside with the DUP-controlled, Department of Enterprise Trade and Investment. They would produce jointly the Executive's response to the Decade. Whilst tweaking the CRC/HLF Principles they endorsed the work that was being done by CRC and HLF, and the various stakeholders at the round table. To help the sharing of resources, and to underpin the need for an expert 'historical' approach to the Decade, in conjunction with CRC/HLF, the Northern Ireland DCAL Minister and Republic of Ireland's Minister for Arts Heritage and the Gaeltacht launched a series of lectures on the Decade at the Ulster Museum. The Museum had, in support of the initiative, displayed the Ulster Covenant and the 1916 Proclamation side by side: both these documents regarded as deeply symbolic by the two main traditions in Northern Ireland. This juxtaposition of these two key documents was to invite comparison, provoke a desire for deeper understanding of each and to challenge the viewer to look beyond each individual document. In addition, a supportive programme, organised by Libraries NI, and with involvement of the Public Records Office of Northern Ireland

(PRONI), sought to get the maximum exposure for this material, and all the lectures at the Ulster Museum were recorded and put on YouTube. This work created a template for much of what followed: the development and dissemination of intellectual resources to communities, the identification of expert and authoritative help, encouragement of the use of the CRC/ HLF Principles, thoughtful engagement by public bodies and the provision of financial resources so that commemorative work could be realised. At a community level various potentially acrimonious centenary events of 2012, such as The Balmoral Review (commemorating the foundation of the Ulster Volunteer Force) and the Ulster Covenant commemoration, passed off peacefully.

1916 and 2016 and the use of the principles for remembering

When the early work on the Decade of Centenaries was being developed, the 1916 centenaries were being viewed as amongst the most problematic of the whole period. The two key events of 1916, the Battle of the Somme and the Easter Rising, have been long seen as foundation myths for the two dominant ethno-religious communities in Northern Ireland. CRC, HLF and the Roundtable approached 2016 in a similar way to 2012 and endeavoured to build on what had been learned. Consequently, a conference was organised in 2013 to consider the two key events of 1916. Further resource materials were produced that helped local groups to access expert support and knowledge. Other key resources came from public bodies, including the Public Records Office, a critical resource base throughout the Decade, programming many events and activities to support individual and community engagement. Two other HLF-funded projects are worth emphasising from this community resource perspective. The first is the Ulster Museum's new history gallery. The second is the project 'On the Brink', a collaboration between Mid Antrim Museum Service and the Causeway Museum Service.

The Ulster Museum started to work on revitalising its modern history gallery supported by HLF funding. From HLF's perspective this was an opportunity for a major public institution to contextualise and help to set the scene for the history that led up to the 'decade' in a challenging and engaging way. Then Curator of Modern History William Blair described the approach to remembering as shaped by the policy framework of the Decade of Remembering, with an emphasis on tolerance and a 'shared history' approach (Blair 2016: 192; see also MacBride 2014). Blair was mindful of the implications of following such an agenda, adding 'For the Museum, the current emphasis on "shared history" and "shared future" presents a potential tension in the presentation of history – that is the risk of shaping narratives to fit these aspirational agendas' (Blair 2016: 193). However, working with colleagues in the universities 'provided the necessary external challenge within the interpretative planning process to inform a more critical treatment of the subject matter' (Blair 2016: 193).

The policy frameworks which Blair alludes to are the good relations strategies developed by the Northern Ireland Executive, *A Shared Future* (2005) and *Together: Building a United Community* (2013), whose emphasis on sharing and uniting communities, whilst well meaning, holds particular problems for historians and curators. The historian Mary Daly warns that 'concepts such as "shared history" must be treated with caution. The shared history may be one of mutual antipathy; while nationalists and unionists fought in the Great War they may have done so for different reasons' (MacBride 2014: 38). Blair's use of an 'external challenge' was a clear example of the Ulster Museum embracing the CRC/HLF Principles and using them to good effect. The Ulster Museum's History Gallery provided an important resource for community groups to engage with when planning their own projects and looking at issues of the past in general. For instance, historian Philip Orr brought community groups, who were at the heart of a Unionist protest about flags, to the gallery, using it as a stimulus for debate and discussion about identity-related matters (Orr, personal communication).

A second context-setting piece was through 'On the Brink: The Politics of Conflict 1914–18', a collaboration between the local authority managed Mid-Antrim Museum Service and the Causeway Museum Services. 'On the Brink' was a three-year community heritage project to explore the impact and legacy of the First World War, Battle of the Somme and Easter Rising within a local, national and international context. As well as producing an exhibition, designed to travel beyond the Braid Museum in Ballymena, a key aspect of the project was for volunteers to be heavily engaged in the project's development. The 'On the Brink' Project highlighted another important aspect of the approach to the Decade, which was the involvement of Local Authorities. A number of Local Authorities had been engaging in the Decade roundtable, particularly those who recognised that the commemoration of 1916 events would prove a challenge to their Council. The CRC/HLF Principles were put at the heart of their proactive funding plans, as a tool to negotiate the various requests for funding support. The feedback to this author that Councils have given clearly suggests that without the underpinning principles and the informational resources that had been produced for the Decade, those Councils would not have been able to support the activities which they were ultimately able to fund.

Belfast City Council, the largest Council in Northern Ireland, had been involved in the Decade round table from the earliest meetings. An evaluation of their programme for commemorations in 2016 reflected on how the development of the CRC/HLF Principles empowered the council officials and enabled them to engage and get political support for commemorative activity. The CRC/HLF Principles were used as a foundation on which to stimulate discussion on the development of bespoke Belfast City Council principles. Encouraging the Councillors to reshape the principles in their own words secured their commitment to them. It was in Belfast, where many would have expected the greatest disruption from Decade-related activity, that such disruption was avoided. As well as the Council's well-received exhibitions on the Decade themes they have run many events and activities that have allowed for thoughtful engagement. The Council also agreed a sum of £250,000 to be split equally between the Nationalist and Unionist communities for community-directed projects that worked to the Council principles. Once again, the period passed off with a sense of genuine reflection and thoughtful engagement with the past without deepening sectarian tensions.

HLF supported a wide range of projects from both sides of the community throughout this period and continues to do so. One project saw a group of Republican ex-prisoners research the connections between Nationalist West Belfast and the First World War. This type of project could not have been imagined a decade ago and exemplifies just how taking a wider perspective allows for the recovery of repressed or forgotten memory. Not surprisingly, however, given the importance of the First World War to the Unionist community the vast majority of First World War projects were located in loyalist and Unionist areas, most exploring their local connections to 1914–1918.

One of the most interesting HLF projects was when a cross-community group, the Bellanaleck Local History Group from the border county of Fermanagh, decided to explore the forgotten story of resettled First World War soldiers on Cleenish Island. After the war had ended, the British Prime Minister, David Lloyd George, made a promise to create 'homes fit for heroes' for the returning survivors. Cleenish Island on Lough Erne was chosen as one of the Northern Ireland sites for this purpose. Through the help of the Irish Land Act 1919, twelve homes were built for soldiers with the hope of helping them to build new lives. This HLF-funded project explored what had happened to those soldiers. This was a story that had been largely forgotten, even within the area, because the resettlement had not been successful. What was uncovered was the tale of human struggle against nature and bureaucracy. At the time of resettlement, the Island did not even have a bridge, making sustainable life challenging if not impossible. The historical group's work on the project captured wide attention creating a great interest locally and nationally in what they were doing (BBC 2014; Bellanaleck Local History Group 2017). The richness of what they uncovered exemplified the value in bringing out the complexity of past events to uncover a deeper meaning that goes beyond simple commemoration: a meaning which in a divided society can uncover shared experiences and understanding.

Conclusions

A number of themes run through this chapter, but perhaps the most important is the ethical responsibility around engaging with the past. The CRC/HLF Principles have endeavoured to create a space within which the past can be engaged with in an ethical and thoughtful way. The approach is not dissimilar to that of Hannah Arendt who suggested 'the more people's standpoints I have present in my mind while I am pondering a given issue … the stronger will be my capacity for representative thinking' (Arendt 2006: 220–221). Looking back, many of the fears about the disruptive potential of the Decade of Centenaries have not been realised. The initial concern had been that groups within communities could have mobilised the Decade in ways that would have created significant community tensions. This did not happen. A harder question to answer at this point is whether this has been due to the efforts made to steer a thoughtful path through the Decade. The belief of the many stakeholders involved in the roundtable discussions is that their work has made a difference. HLF's ability to fund strategic and local projects has been important, as has that from other groups such as Northern Ireland Government departments and the Irish Government. But equally important has been the commitment of stakeholders and groups who were able to share and learn from what everyone else was doing. The resources that were developed have been widely used; in particular, engagement from museums, libraries and the Public Records Office has allowed expertise and knowledge-driven approaches to engage with local communities. The CRC website continues to host a vast array of relevant material to this discussion (CRC 2017). The approach taken by CRC, HLF and the Round table has at least ensured that in public space there has been an opportunity for thoughtful exploration of the period. By providing the opportunity and resources for communities to explore the Decade, many groups have been exposed to the multiple narratives at play in the past. One of the volunteers involved in the 'On the Brink' Project commented that 'for the first time I realised what was happening at the same time, a real parallel history' (McVey 2017).

When commemoration takes in a series of events as with the Decade of Centenaries period, 1912–1923, there is opportunity to widen the focus and not be trapped in one single uncontextualised event. This enables connecting of complex and interconnected stories, allowing the examination of historical events that go beyond the tribal and simplistic narratives that too often sit at the heart of Nationalist and Unionist memory. For example, when the Ulster Museum refreshed its modern history gallery it placed the 1912 Ulster Covenant, a significant document for Unionists, and the 1916 Easter Proclamation, significant for Nationalists, side by side. This provided an opportunity for thoughtful comparison and analysis. Also, the close proximity in time, April and June 1916, of the Easter Rising and Battle of the Somme enabled many rich and interconnected stories to be uncovered. It was significant that the commemorative narrative in the Republic of Ireland in 2016, which had in 1966 focussed solely on the Easter Rising, was developed to include the role of Irish Nationalists in the First World War as well as providing an inclusive Unionist dimension. The process of working with the 'principles' has reinforced the importance of an historically based approach that complicates tendentious one-sided narratives of commemoration. Todorov reminds us, 'While history makes the past more complicated, commemoration makes it simpler, since it seeks more often to supply us with heroes to worship or with enemies to detest' (Todorov 2003: 133). Equally how language is used will challenge Northern Ireland's political parties when they come to address the forthcoming centenaries of the establishment of Northern Ireland and the Irish Free State in 2021. In their 2016 election material the DUP made a commitment to 'celebrate' 2021 (Foster 2016); such a celebration, which may be welcomed by some Unionists, is unlikely to be seen in the same way by the Nationalist community for whom 2021 will be little more than a reminder of the island of Ireland's division, which has been marked by community tensions and violence throughout the twentieth and early twenty-first centuries. The CRC/HLF Principles discussed in this chapter provide a template as to how that exploration can happen. These provide hope for the period of 2018–2023 and the remainder of the Decade of Centenaries.

Another important theme is the importance of seeing events in their wider context. When we look ahead to the challenges of the next number of years this becomes particularly important. The ability to see beyond partition and division, recognising the global trends of history that were at work in the early twentieth century: in particular, the collisions and dismantling of the empires of the nineteenth century and the realisation of Woodrow Wilson's desire to see the post-First World War period as a place for smaller independent nations that could thrive within the context of a 'League of Nations' (McMaster 2016). As Reynolds in this volume discusses, 2018 sees the fiftieth anniversary of the Civil Rights movement, and 2019 will be fifty years on from the commencement of 'The Troubles'. This creates a new challenge, one of 'lived memory', a memory that will be experienced by people in many different and challenging ways. A broadening of the perspective in which this lived memory is placed has the potential to reconceptualise that experience and how it is deployed in the present. Contributing to one of the key themes of this book, the work that heritage can do for a society emerging from conflict, this chapter suggests there are approaches that can be taken to enable communities to explore their past in ways that alter the political and symbolic power of past events. By embracing the nuances and complexity of past events, a new understanding can emerge that may help mitigate the potential for further conflict.

Bibliography

Arendt, H. (2006). *Between Past and Future: Eight Exercised in Political Thought*. New York and London: Penguin Books.

Ashworth, G.J., Graham, B.J. and Tunbridge, J.E. (2007). *Pluralising Pasts: Heritage, Identity and Place in Multicultural Societies*. London: Pluto Press.

BBC (2014). *Cleenish, County Fermanagh: World War One soldiers' Home*, 11 June 2014 [online] Available at: www.bbc.co.uk/news/uk-northern-ireland-27785432 [Accessed 17 September 2017].

Bellanaleck Local History Group (2017). [social media post] www.facebook.com/bellanalecklocalhistorygroup [Accessed 5 September 2017].

Blair, W. (2016). Myth, Memory and Material Culture: Remembering 1916 at the Ulster Museum. In: Grayson, R.S. and McGarry, F., eds. *Remembering 1916: The Easter Rising, the Somme and the Politics of Memory in Ireland*. Cambridge: Cambridge University Press, pp. 181–203.

Butler, K. (1998). *Queen and President Open Anglo-Irish Peace Tower*. [online] *The Independent*. Available at: www.independent.co.uk/news/queen-and-president-open-anglo-irish-peace-tower-1184277.html;www.independent.co.uk/news/queen-and-president-open-anglo-irish-peace-tower-1184277.html [Accessed 17 September 2017].

Cohen, A.P. (1989). *The Symbolic Construction of Community*. London: Routledge.

Community Relations Unit (2005). *A Shared Future: Policy and Strategic Framework for Good Relations in Northern Ireland*. Belfast: Office the First and Deputy First Minister.

Cowen, B. (2011). A Decade of Centenaries: Commemorating Shared History. Dublin: Global Irish Institute, University College Dublin IBIS Working Papers, 108, 2011.

CRC (2010) *Decade Principles for Remembering in Public Space* [online] Available at: www.community-relations.org.uk/sites/crc/files/media-files/Decade%20 Principles.pdf [Accessed 30 January 2018].

CRC (2017). *Decade of Centenaries*. Belfast: Community Relations Council. [online] Available at: www.community-relations.org.uk/decade-centenaries [Accessed 30 January 2018].

Crooke, E. (2010). The Politics of Community Heritage: Motivations, Authority and Control. *International Journal of Heritage Studies*, 16(1–2), pp. 16–29.

de Souza Briggs, X. (1998). Doing Democracy Up Close: Culture, Power, and Communications in Community Building. *Journal of Planning Education and Research*, 18(1), pp. 1–13.

Foster, A. (2016). *Our Plan for Northern Ireland*. Belfast: Democratic Unionist Party.

Hall, S. (2008). Whose Heritage? Un-settling "The Heritage", Re-imaging the Post-nation. In: Fairclough, G.J. et al., eds. *The Heritage Reader*. London: Routledge. pp. 23–35.

Harrison, R. (2013). *Heritage: Critical Approaches*. London: Routledge.

Hewison, R. (1987). *The Heritage Industry: Britain in a Climate of Decline*. London: Methuen.

Hobsbawm, E.J. and Ranger, T. (1992). *The Invention of Tradition*. Cambridge: Cambridge University Press.

Hocking, B. (2014). Great Transformations: "Re-casting" Derry's Diamond War Memorial for the Demands of a "Shared" Future. *The Canadian Journal of Irish Studies*, 38(1), pp. 228–259.

Kearney, R. (1995). Narrative Imagination: Between Ethics and Poetics. *Philosophy and Social Criticism*, 21(5–6), pp. 173–190.

Kearney, R. (1996). *Paul Ricoeur: The Hermeneutics of Action*. London: Sage.

Lowenthal, D. (1998). *The Heritage Crusade and the Spoils of History*. Cambridge: Cambridge University Press.

Lowenthal, D. (2015). *The Past Is a Foreign Country - Revisited*. Cambridge: Cambridge University Press.

MacBride, D. (2012). Remembering the Future. In: MacBride, D., ed. *Remembering the Future: Understanding our Past, Shaping our Future*. Belfast: Community Relations Council.

MacBride, D., ed. (2014). *Remembering 1916: Challenges for Today*. Belfast: Community Relations Council.

Macdonald, S. (2009). *Difficult Heritage: Negotiating the Nazi Past in Nuremberg and Beyond*. Abingdon: Routledge.

McDonald, H. (2003). *A Brave and Generous Man*. [online] The Guardian. Available at: www.theguardian.com/politics/2003/may/25/northernireland.northernireland; www.theguardian.com/politics/2003/may/25/northernireland.northernireland [Accessed 4 June 2017].

McMaster, D.J. (2016). *Beyond 2016: Where Now for Commemorations?* Unpublished paper.

McVey, J. (2017). *On the Brink: The politics of Conflict 1914–16. Volunteer Strand Evaluation*. Causeway Museum Service.

Morrow, D. and Mullan, P. (2012). Remembering the Future. In: MacBride, D., ed. *Remembering the Future: Understanding our Past, Shaping our Future*. 2011, Belfast City Hall. Belfast: Community Relations Council. pp. 7–8.

Putnam, R.D. (2000). *Bowling Alone: The Collapse and Revival of American Community*. New York: Simon and Schuster.

Ricoeur, P. (1988). *Time and Narrative*. Chicago, London: University of Chicago Press.

Ricoeur, P. (1995). Reflections on a New Ethos for Europe. *Philosophy and Social Criticism*, 21(5–6), pp. 3–13.

Samuel, R. (2012). *Theatres of Memory: Past and Present in Contemporary Culture*. London: Verso.

Sennett, R. (1993). *The Fall of Public Man*. London: Faber and Faber Ltd.

Smith, L. (2006). *Uses of Heritage*. London: Routledge.

Smith, L. and Waterton, E. (2012). Constrained by Commonsense: The Authorized Heritage Discourse in Contemporary Debates. In: Skeates, R., McDavid, C., and Carman, J., eds. *The Oxford Handbook of Public Archaeology*. Oxford University Press, Oxford, pp. 153–171.

Todorov, T. (2003). Hope and Memory. *Lessons from the Twentieth Century*. Princeton, NJ: Princeton University Press.

Tunbridge, J.E. and Ashworth, G.J. (1996). *Dissonant Heritage: The Management of the Past as a Resource in Conflict*. Chichester: John Wiley and Sons.

4 Organised innocence in the paramilitary museum

Katie Markham

> The great maxim of all civilised legal systems, that the burden of proof must always rest with the accuser, sprang from the insight that only guilt can be irrefutably proved. Innocence, on the contrary, to the extent that it is more than "not guilty", cannot be proved but must be accepted on faith, whereby the trouble is that this faith cannot be supported by the given word, which can be a lie.
>
> (Arendt 1963: 87)

Questions of innocence and responsibility, whilst seemingly accounted for during peacetime by the court of law, are notoriously hard to mediate on a moral level in the aftermath of violent conflict. As Hannah Arendt (1945: 149) famously observed after the Second World War, innocence is particularly hard to establish in the wake of war, where

> the boundaries dividing criminals from normal persons, the guilty from the innocent, have been so completely effaced that nobody will be able to tell [...] whether in any case he is dealing with a secret hero or with a former mass murderer.

Of course, when it comes to those wars which are contained within the borders of a single nation, the boundaries distinguishing the so-called guilty from the 'innocent' are even more blurred and frequently become the source of considerable contestation in the transitional period towards stability.

For citizens of Britain and Northern Ireland, such debates occupy a particularly prominent position in relation to the Troubles, where responsibility for the conflict is incredibly diffuse, and the decision to prosecute specific people for their participation in acts of wartime violence are guided more by contemporary political agitations than any real desire to offer closure to victims of the Northern Irish conflict (Smyth 2000). Indeed, only in February 2017, Northern Ireland Secretary of State James Brokenshire invoked the so-called 'victims issue' in a speech to the House of Commons, where he lambasted the Police Service Northern Ireland (PSNI) Legacy

Investigation Team for their indictment of two ex-soldiers over the death of Irish Republican Army (IRA) commander John McCann. Declaring that government would 'never accept any kind of moral equivalence between those who sought to uphold the rule of law and terrorists who sought to destroy it' (Hansard 2017), Brokenshire's appeal to morality was no doubt a shrewd political move, designed both to pacify those Democratic Unionist Party (DUP) ministers present at the debate and to reposition the Conservative party as defenders of the British Armed Forces in the wake of other controversial prosecutions over the Iraq War (BBC 2017).

The issue of how best to deal with Troubles victims has long dominated Northern Irish society, where the very definition of victimhood has in itself become the source of an intractable conflict amongst its citizens. As the Troubles were dubbed a 'war by other means' by Marie Breen-Smyth (2009: 35), attempts to offer a universally acceptable definition of a 'Troubles victim' have been continually frustrated by a range of special interest and political groups, both in Ireland and Britain, with the result that twenty years after the signing of the Good Friday/Belfast Agreement, families of the deceased and those who were injured during the conflict have yet to receive appropriate financial or legal compensation for their losses. As a result, those living with the impact of the Troubles are more likely to be living in poverty, be in worse health, have lower life quality and suffer from depression and suicidal ideation than those without direct experience of the conflict, and Northern Ireland as a whole now has one of the highest rates of post traumatic stress disorder (PTSD) in the world (Ferry et al. 2008; Commission for Victims and Survivors 2011; Tomlinson 2013). Ongoing politicisation of the issue in Northern Ireland and mainland Britain means that the vast majority of perpetrators have yet to be brought to account for their role in another's victimisation, whilst broader definitions of victimhood, as advanced by the Eames-Bradley and Bloomfield reports, have also meant that on a policy level, distinctions between perpetrators and victims are becoming increasingly obscure, making the process of developing a universal framework for restitution increasingly difficult (Brewer 2006; Brewer et al. 2011).

In lieu of an established definition, a number of researchers have observed that the lexicon of victimhood in Northern Ireland is becoming increasingly implicit and reliant on a hierarchical approach to victimhood that often invokes the language of guilt, innocence and responsibility to discern between those 'deserving' and 'underserving' victims of the conflict (Rolston 2000; Morrissey et al. 2002; Brewer et al. 2011; Breen-Smyth et al. 2015). Such language is increasingly present in cultural responses to the Troubles, and in this regard the informal heritage sector in Northern Ireland is no exception, with many of those working in the so-called 'troubles tourism' (*Cultural Tourism Strategy* 2006) industry often utilising the language of innocent victimhood in particular to validate their own historical interpretations of the past. However, whilst academic literature has sometimes drawn attention to the way these discourses manifest in Belfast and Derry/Londonderry's oft-critiqued mural tours, or in broader landscapes of memorialisation (Graham et al. 2007; McDowell 2008; Goalwin 2013; Crooke 2016), the same discussions are often absent from the less-researched independent museum sector. Filling this gap, this chapter addresses cultures of victimhood in Belfast's paramilitary museums, drawing attention to the way that these sites draw on notions of innocence and responsibility to reinforce their own interpretations of the past. Paying particular attention to a recent orientation within museology towards the affective museum experience (Smith and Campbell 2015) this chapter touches on the intersections between the 'ideal victim' (Suski 2009) and the generation of empathy, arguing that both chosen museum sites (the Irish Republican History Museum (IRHM) and Andy Tyrie Interpretive Centre (ATIC)) appeal to this intersection as they develop their material for an increasingly incipient 'tourist gaze' (Urry et al. 2011) in Northern Ireland. Finally, arguing that both paramilitary museums are actively invested in the promotion of 'organisational innocence' (Jalusic 2007), this chapter will speculate on the centrality of the tourist figure to the post-Troubles imagination, arguing that we need to be more honest about the role contemporary tourism plays in memories of the conflict in recognition of the fact that what Debbie Lisle (2006: 27) calls the 'two communities thesis' is increasingly losing its relevance when it comes to scholarship on Northern Ireland (Conrad 2006; Nagle 2009; Crooke 2014).

The museums explored in this chapter come from opposite sides of the political spectrum in Northern Ireland and therefore offer some useful points of comparisons when thinking in more detail about the intersections between empathy, innocence and victimhood. Of the two sites, the IRHM is probably the most well known to tourists to Belfast, where, situated just off the Falls Road in the Conway Mill site, it encourages a reasonably steady flow of international visitors to its site, who come to the museum either as part of a black cab mural tour or after viewing the famous 'International Wall'. Established by ex-IRA Commanding Officer Eileen Hickey, the primary purpose of the museum (according to its volunteers) is to educate a new generation of visitors about the history of armed republicanism and to preserve artefacts connected to the long history of internment in Ireland, and the site itself is filled with a variety of objects donated from both local families in Belfast and supporters of republicanism from abroad. In contrast to this, the ATIC occupies a much less frequented space just off the Newtownards Road in East Belfast, and although it does receive international visitors (often through pre-organised tours), it is, as its volunteer confessed to me, much more oriented towards these visitors, and ex-members of the Ulster Defence Association (UDA), than the broader unionist or Protestant community. Set up by UDA commander Dee Stitt, the site opened in 2012 (five years after the Republican Museum) and was very much developed out of a growing awareness that the loyalist communities weren't as effective at selling their past to an international community as republicans have been (Interview with Anonymous, conducted by KM, ATIC 27 August 2015). Like the Republican Museum, ATIC receives the majority of its items from local donors, supplemented with purchases from eBay, and is operating on a shoestring budget. The financial independence of both these sites and their small-scale, 'do-it-yourself' (DIY) approach to museum curation make them perfect examples of what Fiona Candlin has described as the 'micro-museum'. However, whereas Candlin (2016: 11) tends to bracket these museums into amateur ventures, suggesting that they shouldn't be 'judged within dominant paradigms of good practice', I argue that these sites still curate a 'museum effect' (Kirshenblatt-Gimblett 1991: 410) for visitors, which combined with the reductive expectancy of the tourist gaze (Urry et al. 2011) means that however haphazard it might be, the 'curation' of objects at these sites still merits critical engagement.

Exhibiting victimhood

As indicated by the Arendt quote opening this chapter, one of innocence's more challenging features is that, whilst seemingly adjudicated by the justice system, on a social level it has inherited a kind of paradoxical un-utterability which enshrouds any outright declarations of innocence with immediate suspicion. As such, Arendt (1963: 87) writes, innocence 'cannot be proved but must be accepted on faith', the issue being, of course, that questions of faith, or the belief in someone's inviolability, are themselves highly socially controlled and subject to all the matrices of gendered, raced and classed logics. Nowhere has this been demonstrated more clearly than in relation to the Troubles, where, as Bill Rolston (2000: xi) has observed, the mainland media campaign against the North was so powerful that 'even the most obvious criterion of "innocence"', such as childhood, was dismissed in official accounts of state killings. In the years since the end of the conflict, these narratives have shifted considerably, and stakeholders at all levels have scrambled to enmesh themselves, and their organisations, within discourses of innocent victimhood on a cultural and a political level (Morrissey et al. 2002). However rather than overturning the balance of power with regard to victims of violence in the North, more often than not, the most successful cultural reimaginings emanate from those paramilitary organisations who were responsible for that violence in the first place, creating what Stephanie Lehner and Cillian McGrattan (2012: 39) have referred to as a 'foundational power gap' that separates those they consider to be 'true' victims of the conflict from those who represent victimhood in the cultural spheres.

As sites that are visited by tourists seeking a culturally authentic experience of Belfast (Jarman 1996; Murtagh et al. 2017), the IRHM and ATIC are deeply enmeshed in both the construction of innocent victimhood and the perpetuation of this foundational power gap. Both sites weave narratives of victimisation throughout their exhibitions, drawing attention to the fatalities and injuries inflicted upon members of the wider Protestant/Catholic community, often overstating the commonalities between republicanism/loyalism and these communities (McDowell 2007), and using these commonalities to justify their militarisation, thereby confirming Morrissey and Smyth's (2002: 5) observation that 'the violence of the victims is seen in the context of their victimisation'. At the IRHM, a memorial to female members of the IRA makes use of what Brian Graham and Yvonne Whelan (2007: 484) have described as the 'ritual rhetoric of volunteers' used elsewhere in the republican memoryscape, whereby the volunteer's cause of death is described in oblique terms as a 'premature explosion' or 'shot dead' by loyalist or state forces, without reference to any specific detail that might indicate the victim's responsibility for or collusion in the victimisation of others. At the ATIC, a similar pattern emerges, whereby the justification for taking up arms is framed through reference to the 'republican atrocities' inflicted upon Protestant communities, and very little detail is given of the revenge attacks carried out by various loyalist forces. Aside from the distinct differences that emerge in terms of how the sites situate their members within broader genealogical histories, at first glance, both museums appear to offer a similar expression of victimhood; one which for the most part focusses on the violence inflicted upon their communities by others that is unmatched by 'a corresponding willingness to own responsibility in relation to hurts and harms that have been done in their name' (Smyth 1998: 37).

However, such contextualisation, whilst mirroring broader practices of memorialisation in Northern Ireland (Graham et al. 2007; McDowell 2007; Goalwin 2013), is an anathema to many of the artefacts on display in these museums, which, contrary to attempts to subdue the inherent violence of paramilitary organisations, can evoke a vivid and deeply affective reminder of their complicity in some of the conflict's worst atrocities. Entering the IRHM for the first time, my initial apprehension and fear of being out of place in a republican enclave was initially confirmed when, trying to find some sense of continuity in my visit, and a clear narrative to latch onto, I was almost immediately confronted with the sight of a rocket launcher, which I noted seemed to be 'casually hanging from the ceiling, suspended above the heads of an unsuspecting couple'. At the time of witnessing such a blatant display of militarisation I found myself mostly registering shock and disorientation, which was intensified by the cheerful Irish music that was playing in the background at the time. A similar experience also presented itself at the ATIC, where, before moving premises in 2016, a loose display of rifles, baseball bats and flails (resting on metal hooks without protective screening) greeted the visitor as they walked through the door (Figure 4.1). On this occasion, even though my experiences at the Republican Museum prepared me for displays like this, an underlying sense of their viscerality persisted, aided no doubt by the sensation that they could all too easily be removed from their resting points and handled

Figure 4.1 Weapons on display in the Andy Tyrie Interpretative Centre (2016). Photograph by Katie Markham.

by members of the public (something which the volunteer later confessed happened with some frequency). Although these weapons have since been moved upstairs to another room where they no longer present themselves to the visitor in the same way, the sheer accessibility of these items (not to mention some of the ominous stains on the baseball bat) still makes sharing a space with these items an emotionally challenging experience at times, and they are a testament to the object 'liveness' that Fiona Candlin (2016) notes micro-museums often draw out of their artefacts.

Observing other visitors to these sites, it quickly became evident that the weapons on display were equally fascinating for tourists to the paramilitary museum. The average visitor to both the Republican and Andy Tyrie Museums arrives as part of a guided tour of the local murals, and whilst these tend to be more heavily concentrated around West Belfast (and hence closer to the Republican Museum) the mural tourist has a significant presence at both sites. When it comes to the IRHM, once let loose by their guide, the average visitor will tend to spend no more than thirty minutes wandering around its room, weaving their way through its exhibitions and stopping only briefly to examine its contents. In the absence of explanatory labels or detailed contextual information, visitors (who most often come in pairs or as part of groups) will stand in front of these cases, murmuring exchanges and occasionally pointing out items to each other. Without a doubt, the cases that always attract the most attention are those containing the hand-guns and petrol bombs, which people linger over for noticeably longer than the other cases (an observation also confirmed by multiple members of the curatorial staff). Occasionally I have overheard jokes being made about the weapons on display, but more often people's uneasiness is communicated through furtive silence as they look at these objects, sometimes glancing anxiously around, clearly uncomfortable to be seen staring for too long. When young children come to the museum as part of a family trip they are invariably drawn to these cases and will be unabashed about spending longer periods of time gazing at the weapons on display. However, what was striking about these interactions with the cases is that I rarely heard the children asking questions about the guns whilst in the museum, nor did parents particularly encourage them. The contrast between this and their interaction with other objects on display was particularly notable in one case, where a mother and son, after spending a period of time silently look-ing at one of the gun cases, moved on to a handcrafted crib which imme-diately prompted the child to exclaim, "Awh! That's amazing!" Listening to and observing visitors at the site it was clear that, like for me, handguns and rifles were the object of fascination, and yet these fascinations were never reflected in the comments in the visitor books, which instead refer-enced the photos of injured children or rubber bullets that surrounded these items. This discrepancy between people's engagements with the museum and what they chose to publicly record could suggest residual discomfit about expressing criticism in a space that doesn't invite it. Indeed, it was not unusual to see tour guides standing by the guidebooks, directing their clients to add a comment before they left the museum. Under such condi-tions, it would hardly be surprising for visitors to feel restricted in terms of providing an honest response to the museum. However contrary to this, and as this essay will later explore, the specific quality of the entries into these guestbooks also suggest a tacit endorsement of republican claims to innocence on behalf of the movement.

The decision to exhibit items which might cause visitors to question these museums' claims to victimisation might seem an odd curatorial decision; however, for the volunteers I spoke to at both sites, the inclusion of guns seemed unproblematic and was regarded as a matter of honesty. As the volun-teer at ATIC responded when I asked about the weapons on display, 'we tell the truth. We don't try to hide the gangster element that happened' (Interview with Anonymous, conducted by KM, ATIC 27 August 2015), suggesting a desire to be transparent about the organisation's past. Certainly, offering some degree of reflection on violent pasts is not unusual at sites such as the Andy Tyrie Museum and IRHM, where anything less would make them vulnerable to accusations of hypocrisy from their visitors and wider com-munity, and in this sense the display of weaponry fits neatly into the prac-tices of other memorial museums, which often exhibit objects that possess a certain 'sinister appeal' (Williams 2007: 31). However, such 'hot' objects, with all the emotional paunch they possess, are also hard for curators to control at an interpretive level 'due to their high capacity for personification' (Williams 2007: 34). In this sense, displaying guns and other items that have already been made iconic through their appearance in media coverage of both paramilitary groups (and which most visitors, myself included, would take as evidence of their responsibility for the horrors of the past) is a risqué move and one that suggests a particular level of confidence in the viability and power of their own narratives of victimisation.

Visitor books

Visitor books at both the ATIC and the IRHM, it is possible to see just how effective the narrative of victimhood is when it comes to reactions to the weapons and other items on display at these sites. Sharon Macdonald (2005) and Chaim Noy (2008b, 2008c) have already drawn attention to the role that the visitor book can play in our understanding of the museum experience, with Chaim Noy (2008b: 516) describing the visitor book's function as 'a *miniature stage*', on which visitors 'perform an act of documentation' (2008a: 513). At the IRHM, the performative aspect of signing visitor books was evident in the diligent queues of tourists who often lined up to sign their names and add a comment under the watchful eye of a tour guides. Although it wasn't always clear what the motivation was for getting clients to sign these books in this manner, the practice of the tour guide imploring their clients to sign the book before leaving was a frequently observable pattern, as visitors were requested to at least write a name and place of origin. From the volunteer's point of view, such a practice was useful in that it gave them a means of tracking visitor demographics, which could then be used as bragging rights in an ever-competitive troubles tourism sector. Staff frequently directed me to these books when I asked questions and would often highlight some of the more complimentary comments to me. In this sense, both the signing and reading of these books were deeply performative and controlled affairs, which seemed entirely appropriate given the space they were in.

Taking these coercions into account, it was hardly surprising to find across the ten years of visitor books at the Republican Museum, very little in the way of critique of the site, or suggestions for change (although to a certain extent this was still commensurate with the kind of reviews found on the museum's TripAdvisor site). The places where tacit disapproval was sometimes suggestive were the gaps left next to visitors who had signed their names (presumably under duress) without leaving a comment or a few cagier comments describing the site as 'ok', 'good' or the more neutral 'informative', although such omissions and comments may also have been the result of limited English or time restrictions. Of those who did leave comments in the books, most offered a variation on the usual banalities found in these mediums, with the site being alternately described as 'interesting', 'excellent', 'brilliant'. At the other end of the spectrum, and in notable contrast to the comments found at the Andy Tyrie Centre, signatories reported feeling 'moved' by the museum, describing the experience as 'emotional', 'heart breaking' and in some cases even 'life altering'. Strikingly, such comments were expressed by people from a range of backgrounds (from London to Honolulu). These comments were often written independently of the other comments in the book and were not part of the 'collective production' usually associated with visitor book entries (Noy 2008b: 517).

At the Andy Tyrie Centre, insights from visitor books were more limited given that the Centre only started keeping a record in the last eighteen months. However, in contrast to the Republican Museum, where comments were usually brief and general in tone, responses to the Andy Tyrie Centre were much more developed, usually covering a sentence or two, albeit without the expressions of emotionality found in the books at the Republican site. Like the Republican Museum visitor books, the one at the Andy Tyrie contains all the usual platitudes of 'brilliant', 'interesting' and 'very good'; however, they also offer additional notations, often from broader members of the UDA, expressing gratitude to the sites for 'preserving our history', in a nod to narrower audience for which the site was conceived. Also unlike the inscriptions at the Eileen Hickey, which tend to be more respectful and sombre in tone, there is an underlying jocularity and humour to some of the entries at the Andy Tyrie Centre, with one particularly notable commentator writing 'cheers for the lovely time UDA'.

These differences aside, what is striking across both visitor books is the way that visitors position themselves in relation to the material and narratives of the perceived community that they see at both sites. Returning to those displays in the Republican Museum that condoned the weapons on the premise that they were 'used to defend the nationalist people', visitor absorption of these slippages between the suffering of the Catholic community, the aims of nationalism and actions of Republicanism were evidenced through comments referencing the hurts issued against the 'community' or 'the Irish people', indicating a tacit acceptance (even if only performative) of the idea that republicanism in some way represents the general feelings and ideology of a broader (imagined) civilian community. Going further than this, a number of comments in both the Andy Tyrie Centre's and Republican Museum's books actually saw visitors using phrases associated with paramilitary forces, in an apparent gesture of solidarity with these ideologies. Whilst at the Andy Tyrie, slogans such as 'Quis Separabit' or 'QS' were most commonly used by those who indicated belonging to some kind of loyalist brigade, at the Republican Museum, notes that finished with "Up the Ra!", 'Viva la Republique' or "Go raibh maith agat" came from a range of actors from across the globe. Possibly this was the result of the museum's broader audience, which receives double the number of visitors on any given day than the Andy Tyrie Centre, and which is most heavily visited by those international tourists on a taxi tour of the city.

Possibly also, it reflects republicanism's wider success in importing its aims and ideologies to countries similarly engaged in conflict over their own colonial legacies (Lisle 2006; Rolston 2009). However, given that many of these comments also came from places without these legacies, such an explanation isn't entirely all-encompassing, and responses such as one from an Italian visitor who wrote, 'I feel more Irish now' suggest something else is also going on at the level of visitor experience. One the one hand, these declarative expressions of (mis)identification with paramilitary ideologies are certainly encouraged by what Chaim Noy (2008b: 523) sees as being the visitor book's performative element, through which the seasoned museum visitor uses the book's stage to demonstrate her understanding of 'both how she is expected to *react,* and how she is meant to *convey* her reaction'. However within this, the willingness to align themselves with a paramilitary ideology (however confusing the relationship between paramilitarism and wider communities in Belfast might be) in the face of such concrete evidence of their violent histories attests to another kind of performance, one that is deeply enmeshed in what Vlasta Jalusic has termed 'organisational innocence' (2007).

Organisational innocence

Writing on the questions of guilt and responsibility in relation to the Yugoslavian conflict, Vlasta Jalusic (2007: 1174) observes that understandings of how to talk about and understood 'the criminal past' were radically altered in the wake of Second World War. Noting that, following the Nuremberg Trials the possibility of denying collective responsibility for war crimes ceased, Jalusic suggests that those preparing for, or reflecting on criminal acts began to divert their attention away from the rhetoric of responsibility and towards that of innocence and guilt. Out of this shift, Jalusic (2007: 1174) writes about the concept of 'organised innocence', which she describes as 'an extended process of preparation' for 'a specific climate and mentality [...] created in order to prepare people to participate in, commit to, or tolerate' violence that is also a 'preparation process for an enterprise of organised guilt, producing a situation of inverted human values, where unimaginable things become conceivable and people can easily renounce their personal and collective responsibility' (2007: 1181). As a concept, organised innocence is heavily invested in an Arendtian interpretation of innocence and guilt that, stemming from the argument that only those excluded from the fullness of state participation are truly innocent, suggests by extension that all who benefit from the richness of national belonging (whether they are anarchists or not) must also admit complicity in that nation's wrongdoing. Organised innocence, Jalusic (2007: 1180) writes, works to invert this truth by first selling the lie that those belonging to a nation are, in fact, stateless and second encouraging citizens to renounce their 'basic political potential' by developing this lie through the construction of artificial victimhood.

Organised innocence can clearly be seen at work in the rhetoric of contemporary loyalism and republicanism in Northern Ireland, where the two traditions have essentially developed out of a reactionary fear about the disenfranchisement that the success of the other's campaign would bring. Within a museums context, such rhetoric becomes doubly potent, and alongside the visual evidence of the wounds that have been inflicted on both communities (captured in the array of deeply affecting photographs of the injured and dead) are references to militarised resistance to this, in a way that naturalises the association between the two. At the Andy Tyrie Centre, the most obvious manifestation of this militancy in the face of disenfranchisement is found in the arrangement of photos on the display, where amateur snapshots of various balaclava-covered UDA/UFF members, brandishing rifles in the disturbing familiarity of back gardens or countryside idylls, are situated alongside particularly graphic images documenting the stripping and beating of two young corporals, carried out by the IRA in 1988 in retaliation for the Michael Stone attacks three days before. The inclusion of this particular event, which actually occurred a decade after the formation of the UDA asks the visitor to make what was an implicit connection fully explicit; namely that loyalist violence emerged directly in response to this explicit assault on British soldiers and therefore unionists' British identity. Notably on the opposite side of this same display are images taken of a protest march conducted between Derry/Londonderry and Belfast, featuring banners emblazoned with the slogan "British citizens defend British rights!" that enable even the least discerning of visitors to pick up on this connection. Elsewhere, smaller, less obvious signs play into this ideology, with stickers subtly adhered to glass display cases with slogans such as "I am fully insured by AK 47" and calls to "Defend the Union". Such an interpretation is also cognisant with how ex-UDA members use the space: according to my interviewee, they will

> come in, take a look around, at some of the atrocities that the IRA committed, and they'll go, "you know what? Thank god that was on the wall because that's why I did this. To stop these men from doing this".
> (Interview with Anonymous, conducted
> by KM, ATIC 27 August 2015)

In this way Jalusic (2007: 1175) notes that organised innocence is also retroactive, used to reflect on crimes that were committed so that they are 'for the second time rendered into something righteous and are, accordingly, normalised'.

At the Republican Museum, this triangulation of militancy and innocence is in some ways subtler than at the Andy Tyrie, possibly in recognition of the fact that, thanks to the British media, the IRA's international reputation for violence has already been well established around the globe. Perhaps in response to this recognition, violence is abstracted rather than embodied at the Republican Museum, and it contains very few images of actual IRA men dressed in their military gear, in spite of the fact that the Roddy McCorley Museum down the road holds a significant collection in this regard. Instead, embodiment takes the form of abject photos of beaten hunger strikers and Catholic civilians or conversely a series of mannequins dressed in the uniforms of the RUC, British Army and Prison Guard, thus reconfirming the injured as solely victims and never perpetrators of violence. Subtle allusions to the necessity of republican militancy can be found, however, in labels that mark certain items down for their use 'in the cause of Irish Freedom', which avoids specifying against who and when they were used. In this way, the IRHM becomes not only the publicly acceptable face for republicanism, but also the visual front for its display of organised innocence, into which the tourist is guilelessly invited to take part.

Because, of course, as the distinction between the collections at the IRHM and its more militant cousin, the Roddy McCorley Museum, show, investments in the idea of organised innocence are not only deeply performative (a fact that Jalusic herself also picks up on), they are also performed for very specific audiences who, often in the case of the paramilitary museum, are for a far broader community than the one immediately imagined through paramilitary membership. As an imagined community, who over the years have been characterised by precisely the kind of statelessness needed for the abdication of responsibility, tourists are themselves often guilty of acts of violence that are concealed behind the 'veil of virtuous innocence' (Regina da Cal Seixas et al. 2016: 161). Hazel Andrews (2016: 5) has accused violence of being 'manifest in many aspects of touristic practices and encounters', whilst Julia Harrison (2003: 137) writes that 'the innocence with which the tourist imagine their travels blinds them' to the symbolic and real injustices that they may enact on the country and people that host them. Tourist declarations of allegiance with the IRA/UDA in the visitor books also need to be interpreted in this context, and in light of the debates around organised innocence, not least because as Jonathan Harden (2009) has identified, violent acts in Northern Ireland have always been framed around a certain performativity, in which witnesses play a crucial role as not just spectators but also performer and potential victim through the very diffuse nature of violence in the province. For most tourists, admitting responsibility for the perpetration or even condoning of violence is very discomforting. This is even more the case for the thanotourist who, Philip Stone (2009) observes, has already had to work to overcome significant media critique of the immorality of their venture and so is either completely oblivious to or completely convinced of their non-complicity in these practices. Nevertheless, it is through this understanding that comments expressing solidarity and emotiveness in these visitor books should be read, more so because it is these expressions that curators and organisers of the museum often use to justify their own existence and validate their particular interpretations of history.

Conclusions

As observed by Laurajane Smith and Campbell (2015) there has in recent years been an 'affective turn' in heritage studies, which often centred around example of difficult or 'dissonant' heritage (Tunbridge et al. 1996), has seen various scholars invest in the idea of empathy as a key driving force behind visitor understandings of the past (Landsberg 2004; Arnold-de Simine 2013; Witcomb 2015; Tolia-Kelly et al. 2016). Almost unilaterally, such studies tend to focus on the positive effects of empathy at these sites, the usual assumption being that their organisers are sincere in their attempts to address the past. However, as the case of the paramilitary museum demonstrates, expressions of sincerity can come at the expense of more nuanced and balanced approaches to the past, raising uncomfortable questions about what the political implications are of empathising with selective histories. Whilst neither the ATIC nor the IRHM explicitly states that they are trying to court visitor empathy, their self-positioning as victims and appeals to innocence are contiguous with popularised understandings of empathy, which usually position innocence as the baseline for emotional identification, and which Martin Hoffman and Martha Nussbaum say are key criteria for empathic engagement (Hoffman 1990; Nussbaum 1996, 2001). Certainly, the affective quality of the images of injured civilians at both sites compels an emotional reaction from the tourist that, if not entirely leading to complete empathetic identification, does gesture towards it and seems to override the equally affecting experience of being confronted with weapons used during the conflict. As one Australian visitor to the Republican Museum remarked whilst looking at a display case filled with rubber bullets and images of the children killed by them, 'if someone does something to you like that then you're going to retaliate', suggesting a similar level of identification with the republican cause to those expressed in the visitor books, which might be understood as both a cognitive and affectively driven demonstration of empathy (Coplan 2011). The museums explored in this chapter are not in themselves examples of 'bad' heritage (Lowenthal 1997) and particularly in a nation riven by traumatic experiences of the past, all forms of remembrance have a right to public expression. However, as Cillian McGrattan has argued, when such single identity work becomes enmeshed with discourses of empathy, these more selective interpretations of history become more problematic, particularly in relation to victims' issues, where the idea of indiscriminate empathy for all 'points to a generalised position where distinctions are no longer possible, and, since everyone is responsible for the 3,700 plus deaths, no one is individually culpable' (2013: 40).

As single-identity sites that are becoming increasingly popular amongst international audiences, both the ATIC and IRHM become complicit in this generalisation of justice, and in the absence of critically engaged visitors to these sites, discourses of innocence and empathy are not simply limited to their effects in the museum but become a route through which violence (symbolic and real) is condoned in the present. The effects of such empathetic victim narratives are not restricted to the tourist, but also have the potential to impact the broader heritage landscapes in Northern Ireland and understandings of the past. It seemed significant that, on one of the later visits to the Republican Museum, rifle pens and key rings with images of IRA militants were for sale, suggesting not just the commodification of violence, but also a guileless assumption that such items were 'innocent' and disconnected enough from contemporary issues to make their presence acceptable to the tourist visitor. Similarly, on one occasion at the ATIC, a museum volunteer gestured towards the posters and objects littered around the walls and chuckled that "this is basically like my bedroom", again suggesting a certain level of confidence about how I was perceiving the museum and its contents, and my inability to connect this to ongoing UDA gang violence in Belfast. As a place where such encounters take place, this chapter, as well as others in this volume, makes contributions to the areas of critical heritage studies working for closer scrutiny of 'the socio-political complexities that enmesh heritage' (Winter 2013: 533). The decision to exhibit, the choice of object, the interpretation, the method of display and the visitor encounter; each contributes to that complexity, demonstrating that the museum is a means for political agents to negotiate their place in the post-conflict narrative.

Bibliography

Andrews. H. (2016). ed. *Tourism and Violence*. Oxon: Routledge.

Arendt, H. (1945). Organised Guilt and Universal Responsibility. In: Bernauer, J. ed. *Essays in Understanding 1930–1954*. New York: Harcourt-Brace, pp. 146–156.

Arendt, H. (1963). *On Revolution*. London: Penguin Books.

Arnold-de Simine, S. (2013). *Mediating Memory in the Museum: Trauma, Empathy, Nostalgia*. Basingstoke: Palgrave Macmillan.

BBC (2017). Iraq War Allegations Probe to End. [online] 10 February 2017 Available at: www.bbc.co.uk/news/uk-38937053 [Accessed 7 July 2017].

Belfast City Council (2006). *Cultural Tourism Strategy*. Belfast: Belfast City Council.

Bigand, K. (2012). Peace in History and Heritage. Some thoughts on a Museum of Peace in Northern Ireland. [online] *E-rea*, 10(1). Available at: https://erea.revues.org/2825

Breen-Smyth, M. (2009). Hierarchies of Pain and Responsibility: Victims and War by Other Means in Northern Ireland. *Tropodos*, 25, pp. 27–40.

Breen-Smyth, M. and Cooke, S. (2015). A Critical Approach: Violence, 'Victims' and 'Innocents'. In: Kennedy-Pipe, C. Mabon, C. and Clubb, G. eds. *Terrorism and Political Violence*. London: Sage, pp. 69–85.

Brewer, J. (2006). Memory, Truth and Victimhood in Post-Trauma Societies. In: Delanty, G. and Kumar, K. eds. *The Sage Handbook of Nations and Nationalism*. London: Sage Publications, pp. 214–225.

Brewer, J. and Hayes, B. (2011). "Victims as Moral Beacons: Victims and Perpetrators in Northern Ireland. *Contemporary Social Science*, 6(1), pp. 73–88.

Candlin, F. (2016). *Micromuseology: An Analysis of Small Independent Museums*. London: Bloomsbury.

Conrad, K. (2006). Queering Community: Re-Imaging the Public Sphere in Northern Ireland. *Critical Review of International Social and Political Philosophy*, 9(4), pp. 589–602.

Coplan, A. (2011). Understanding Empathy: Its Features and Affects. In: Coplan, A. and Goldie, P. eds. *Empathy: Philosophical and Psychological Perspectives*. Oxford: Oxford University Press, pp. 3–18.

Crooke, E. (2014). The Migrant and the Museum: Place and Representation in Ireland. In: Gourievidis, L. ed. *Museums and Migration: History, Memory and Politics*. London: Routledge, pp. 189–202.

Crooke, E. (2016). Artefacts as Agents for Change: Commemoration and Exchange via Material Culture. *Irish Political Studies*, 31(1), pp. 86–100.

Commission for Victims and Survivors. (2011). *Troubled Consequences: A Report on the Mental Health Impact of the Civil Conflict in Northern Ireland*. Belfast: Commission for Victims and Survivors.

Ferry, F., Boulton, D., Bunting, B., McCann, S. and Murphy, S. (2008). *Trauma, Health and Conflict in Northern Ireland. A Study of the Epidemiology of Trauma Related Disorders and Qualitative Investigation of the Impact of Trauma on the Individual*. Londonderry: Northern Ireland Centre for Trauma and Transformation and University of Ulster Psychology Research Institute.

Goalwin, G. (2013). The Art of War: Instability, Insecurity, and Ideological Imagery in Northern Ireland's Political Murals, 1979–1998. *International Journal of Politics, Culture and Society*, 26(1), pp. 189–215.

Graham, B., and Whelan, Y. (2007). The Legacies of the Dead: Commemorating the Troubles in Northern Ireland. *Environment and Planning D: Society and Space*, 25(1), pp. 476–495.

Hansard HC Deb. (2017). vol. 621 col. 1194, 23 February 2017.

Harden, J. (2009). Performance and Potentiality: Violence, Procession and Space. In: Fitzpatrick, L. ed. *Performing Violence in Contemporary Ireland*. Dublin: Carysfort Press, Ltd., pp. 189–204.

Harrison, J.D. (2003). *Being a Tourist: Finding Meaning in Pleasure Travel*. Vancouver: UBC Press.

Hoffman, M. (1990). Empathy and Justice Motivation. *Motivation and Emotion*, 14(2), pp. 151–172.

McAtackney, L. (2013). *An Archaeology of the Troubles: the dark heritage of Long Kesh/Maze Prison*. Oxford: Oxford University Press.

Jalusic, V. (2007). Organised Innocence and Exclusion: "Nation-States" in the Aftermath of War and Collective Crime. *Social Research*, 74(4), pp. 1173–1200.

Jarman, N. (1996). Troubled Images. *Critique of Anthropology*, 12(2), pp. 145–165.

Kirshenblatt-Gimblett, B. (1991). Objects of Ethnography. In: Karp, I. and Lavine, S. eds. *Exhibiting Cultures: The Poetics and Politics of Museum Display*. London: Smithsonian Institution Press, pp. 386–444.

Landsberg, A. (2004). *Prosthetic Memory: The Transformation of American Remembrance in the Age of Mass Culture*. New York: Columbia University Press.

Lehner, S. and McGrattan, C. (2012). Re/Presenting Victimhood: Nationalism, Victims and Silences in Northern Ireland. *Nordic Irish Studies*, 11(2), pp. 39–53.

Lisle, D. (2006). Local Symbols, Global Networks: Re-reading the Murals of Belfast. *Alternatives*, 31(1), pp. 27–52.

Lowenthal, D. (1997). *The Heritage Crusade and the Spoils of History.* Cambridge: Cambridge University Press.

Macdonald, S. (2005). Accessing Audiences: Visiting Visitor Books. *Museum and Society*, 3(3), pp. 119–136.

McAtackney, L. (2013). *An Archaeology of the Troubles: The Dark Heritage of Long Kesh/Maze Prison.* Oxford: Oxford University Press.

McDowell, S. (2007). Armalite, the Ballot Box and Memorialisation: Sinn Fein and the State in Post-Conflict Northern Ireland. *The Round Table: The Commonwealth Journal of International Affairs*, 96(393), pp. 725–738.

McDowell, S. (2008). Selling Conflict Heritage through Tourism in Peacetime Northern Ireland: Transforming Conflict or Exacerbating Difference? *International Journal of Heritage Studies*, 14(5), pp. 405–421.

McGrattan, C. (2013). *Memory, Politics and Identity: Haunted by History.* Basingstoke: Palgrave MacMillan.

McLaughlin, C. (2016). Stories from the Inside: The Prisons Memory Archive. In: Andrews, C. and McGuire, M. eds. *Post-Conflict Literature: Human Rights, Peace, Justice.* New York: Routledge, pp. 69–80.

Morrissey, M. and Smyth, M. (2002). *Northern Ireland after the Good Friday Agreement: Victims, Grievance and Blame.* London: Pluto Press.

Murtagh, B., Boland, P. and Shirlow, P. (2017). Contested Heritages and Cultural Tourism. *International Journal Heritage Studies*, 23(6), pp. 506–520.

Nagle, J. (2009). The Right to Belfast City Centre: From Ethnocracy to Liberal Multiculturalism? *Political Geography*, 28(2), pp. 132–141.

Noy, C. (2008a). The Poetics of Tourist Experience: An Autoethnography of a Family Trip to Eliat. *Journal of Tourism and Cultural Change*, 5(3), pp. 141–157.

Noy, C. (2008b). Pages as Stages: A Performance Approach to Visitor Books. *Annals of Tourism Research*, 35(2), pp. 509–528.

Noy, C. (2008c). Mediation Materialised: The Semiotics of a Visitor Book at an Israeli Commemoration Site. *Critical Studies in Media Communication*, 25(2), pp. 175–195.

Nussbaum, M. (1996). Compassion: The Basic Social Emotion. *Social Philosophy and Policy Foundation*, 13(1) pp. 27–58.

Nussbaum, M. (2001). *Upheavals of Thought: The Intelligence of Emotions.* Cambridge: Cambridge University Press.

Purbrick, L. (2007). *Without Walls: Living Memorial Museum.* Belfast: Healing Through Remembering.

Regina da Cal Seixas, S., Luis de Morales Hoeffel, J., Botterill, D., Carnevale, P. and Rank, M. (2016). Violence, Tourism, Crime and the Subjective: Opening New lines of Research. In: Andrews. A. ed. *Tourism and Violence.* Oxon: Routledge, pp. 145–165.

Rolston, B. (2000). Introduction. In: Rolston, B. and Gilmartin, M. eds. *Unfinished Business: State Killings and the Quest for the Truth.* Belfast: Beyond the Pale Publications.

Rolston, B. (2009). "The Brothers on the Walls": International Solidarity and Irish Political Murals. *Journal of Black Studies*, 39(3), pp. 446–470.

Smith, L.J. and Campbell, G. (2015). The Elephant in the Room: Heritage, Affect, and Emotion. In: Logan, W., NicCraith, M. and Kockel, U. eds. *A Companion to Heritage Studies.* Oxford: Wiley-Blackwell, pp. 443–478.

Smyth, M. (1998). Remembering in Northern Ireland: Victims, Perpetrators and Hierarchies of Pain and Responsibility. In: Hamber, B. ed. *Past Imperfect, Dealing with the Past in Northern Ireland and South Africa*. Derry/Londonderry: INCORE/Ulster University, pp. 31–49.

Smyth, M. (2000). The Human Consequences of Armed Conflict: Constructing "Victimhood" in the Context of Northern Ireland's Troubles". In: Cox, M., Guelke, A. and Stephen, F. eds. *A Farewell to Arms? From "Long War" to Long Peace in Northern Ireland*. Manchester: Manchester University Press, pp. 118–135.

Smyth, M. and Moore, R. (1996). Researching Sectarianism. In: Smyth, M. ed. *Three Conference Papers on Aspects of Segregation and Sectarian Division*. Derry/Londonderry: Templegrove Action Research Limited.

Stone, P. (2009). Dark Tourism: Morality and New Moral Spaces. In: Stone, P. and Sharpley, R. eds. *The Dark Side of Travel: The Theory and Practice of Dark Tourism*. Bristol: Channel View Publications, pp. 56–75.

Suski, L. (2009). Children, Suffering and the Humanitarian Appeal. In: Wilson, R.A. and Brown, R.D. eds. *Humanitarianism and Suffering: the Mobilisation of Empathy*. Cambridge: Cambridge University Press, pp. 202–222.

Tolia-Kelly, D., Waterton, E. and Watson, S. (2016). *Heritage, Affect and Emotion: Politics, Practices and Infrastructures*. London: Routledge.

Tomlinson, M. (2013). *Legacies of Conflict: Evidence from the Poverty and Social Exclusion Survey 2012*. Belfast: Queen's University Belfast.

Tunbridge, J.E. and Ashworth, G. (1996). *Dissonant Heritage: The Management of the Past as a Resource in Conflict*. Chichester: John Wiley and Sons.

Urry, J. and Larsen, J. (2011). *The Tourist Gaze 3.0*. London: Sage.

Williams, P. (2007). *Memorial Museums: The Global Rush to Commemorate Atrocities*. London: Bloomsbury.

Winter, T. (2013) Clarifying the Critical in Critical Heritage Studies. *International Journal of Heritage Studies*, 19(6), pp. 532–545.

Witcomb, A. (2015). Toward a Pedagogy of Feeling: Understanding How Museums Create a Space for Cross-Cultural Encounters. In: Witcomb, A. and Message, K. eds. *The International Handbooks of Museum Studies: Museum Theory, First Edition*. Chichester: John Wiley and Sons, pp. 321–344.

5 Representing loyalist paramilitary heritage in non-museum exhibitions – aims, practices and challenges

Karine Bigand

The inherent dissonance of heritage, due to the multiplicity of ways of interpreting the past, is exacerbated when the past involves conflict (Tunbridge and Ashworth 1996). Amongst the vast terminology referring to heritage associated with war, violence and injustice (Samuels 2015: 111–114), the concept of "difficult heritage" is particularly operative for post-conflict societies. In a study of how the city of Nuremberg dealt with its Nazi heritage, Sharon Macdonald defines it as 'the past that is recognised as meaningful in the present but that is also contested and awkward for public reconciliation with a positive, self-affirming contemporary identity' (2009: 1). In a Northern Irish context, the recent conflict constitutes difficult heritage, as illustrated by the protracted debate on its legacy. Twenty years after the Good Friday Agreement, despite broad official aspirations to build a shared society, an agreed approach is yet to be found on issues relating to truth recovery, justice and how to remember or commemorate the past. Part of the challenge lies in the way different experiencing of the past leads to different perceptions of the present; as Paul Connerton reminds,

> Images of the past commonly legitimate a present social order. It is an implicit rule that participants in any social order must presuppose a shared memory. To the extent that their memories of a society's past diverge, to that extent its members can share neither experiences nor assumptions.
>
> (1989: 3)

Much of the ongoing effort to build a shared future for Northern Ireland is based on history and memory work. As Crooke (2007, 2010) has recounted, storytelling and heritage initiatives are legion, within community groups, as part of museum outreach activities or under the aegis of the Community Relations Council and various non-governmental organisations (NGOs). Memory work is instrumental in conflict transformation as it provides context and creates meaning, both for self and mutual understanding (Hamber 2015; Maddison 2016: 207–270). As other contributors to this volume have also noted, the difficulty is that memory work can reinforce or reshape identities and may therefore result in strengthening entrenched positions or bridging divides.

Amongst the various narratives of conflict, those of perpetrators of violence – loyalist paramilitaries in this chapter – are particularly contentious. There is no consensus about the promotion of peace and reconciliation through conflict heritage (Simone-Charteris and Boyd 2010: 180–184), which is seen either as a tool to reinforce existing divisions (Tunbridge and Ashworth 1996: 4) or as an opportunity to rethink the relationship between the past and collective identity (Macdonald 2015). Writing about "political tours" in conflict-afflicted areas in Northern Ireland, Sara McDowell warns against possible negative side effects:

> Support given by tourist visits, then, works to reinforce both the legitimacy of the landscape in question and the narratives being evoked. [...] In [the Northern Irish] context, selling conflict heritage must be seen as a spatial practice which, contrary to improving community relations and transforming the nature of the conflict, instead redefines and reinforces territorial politics and transforms the conflict into a war by other means.
>
> (McDowell 2008: 406)

Conversely, Simone-Charteris and Boyd suggest that

> Political tourism, despite being considered as controversial and even divisive by some public sector bodies and a few members of the tourism industry, is nevertheless contributing to reconcile the two communities, which for the first time ever, are being able to explain their different perspectives in a peaceful manner, thus discouraging the resurrection of violence and conflict.
>
> (2010: 195)

As places where the past is remembered and displayed through narratives and artefacts, museums and exhibitions take part in the conversation about the legacy of conflict. The contentiousness of their task is illustrated by the criticism the Ulster Museum faced in 2009 about its new artefact-free Troubles Gallery (Bigand 2016) or by the more recent controversy about an exhibit listing all those killed in the Free Derry area between 1969 and 1972 in the newly reopened Museum of Free Derry (Steel 2017; Derry Journal 2017). Permanent exhibitions about the conflict are few across the province. The Tower Museum in Derry/Londonderry and the Ulster Museum in Belfast present a multi-perspective narrative, whilst the Museum of Free Derry and the Irish Republican History Museum in Belfast look at the conflict from a republican point of view. The loyalist paramilitary viewpoint has been almost entirely absent.

This chapter looks at two exhibitions displaying loyalist paramilitary heritage. One is the Andy Tyrie Interpretive Centre (ATIC) on the Newtownards Road in East Belfast. It describes itself as a Loyalist Conflict Museum and tells the story of the Ulster Defence Association (UDA), from the early 1970s to the end of the 2000s. The other is called "Our Journey - Our Narrative" and is part of the Action for Community Transformation (ACT) Initiative, an organisation that helps former Ulster Volunteer Force (UVF) combatants go back to civilian life. The exhibition tells the story of the UVF from the 1910s to 1998 and in the transition period that followed. It was situated on the Shore Road in North Belfast until it relocated to the Shankill Road in West Belfast in April 2017. Each exhibition has been assembled and is run by former members of the paramilitary groups whose story they present. The exhibitions require a specific methodology to assess them, and I will explain this first. Based on on-site visits and interviews with staff, the analysis of the exhibitions will consider the aims of each in portraying former paramilitary organisations, the type of visitor experience they offer and the challenges they face as small-scale heritage initiatives.

Challenging research subjects – micromuseums, partisan museums and perpetrators' heritage

These exhibitions are not typical museum exhibitions, and as such they pose a challenge as objects of research. To start with, they operate outside the accredited museum sector in Northern Ireland, which includes local museums that are publicly or independently run. It means that they cannot avail of the support of the Northern Ireland Museums Council (NIMC), whose role is to assist museums in fields such as collections care, acquisition policies or education and learning. To become fully accredited museums, ATIC and ACT would have to meet a series of agreed standards relating to governance, collections care or public access that they are currently in no position to meet because of their funding, staffing capacity and/or facilities. Both are recently registered charities, operating from small premises. The exhibitions are displayed in two rooms in the case of ATIC and in one for ACT. Their visitor numbers are in the low hundreds. ACT's exhibition is a by-product of the social work the organisation carries out with former members of the UVF rather than its main purpose. In fact, both exhibitions can be described as micromuseums (Candlin 2015: 6–13), that is to say 'small, independent, single-subject museums' or, to be more specific,

> Collections that are variously run by trusts, businesses, special interests groups, and private individuals, and are open to the public; that concentrate on types of objects, themes, or individuals, that fall outside of the traditional academic compass, occupy a low level in the hierarchy of traditional classificatory tables, or that take a non-scholarly approach to subjects that could be encompassed by academe; and finally, they are

small insofar as they have relatively low visitor numbers and/or modest incomes and/or occupy a physically limited space.

(2015: 12)

Fiona Candlin's purpose in studying micromuseums throughout the UK was to challenge certainties about how museums operate and to open up new horizons in museology. She looked at how practices in micromuseums can question or affect the norms imposed by major institutions. She observed that, more often than not, micromuseums go against the grain of mainstream curatorial trends. In her view, they are generally not exemplars of good practice as 'the staff at micromuseums often lack the capacity, skills, money, or inclination to comply with health and safety legislation, to store and display the exhibits in a way that minimizes damage, or to develop interpretation strategies' (2015: 14). Criticisms are therefore counterproductive, she argues, as micromuseums have little power to improve their processes. Her observations provide useful methodology to study ATIC and ACT.

Another aspect that distinguishes the two exhibitions from mainstream museums is their open partisanship in support of a specific interest group. This is at odds with recent professional recommendations for museums to become social actors (Cameron 2005) that promote diversity and social inclusion (Sandell 2002), and adopt multi-perspective approaches in their displays (Witcomb 2003; Bradburne 2011). ATIC and ACT are charities classified as advancing, among other things, community development and conflict resolution, which defines them as social actors. It could be said that they promote diversity by giving a platform to groups whose voice is little, if at all, heard in exhibitions across the province. Yet they are, in Northern Ireland terminology, single-identity initiatives, and since they 'represent one communal, group or political voice', they fall in the category of 'sectional museums' (Brown 2008). Writing about the Northern Irish context, Kris Brown observed recurrent strong curatorial control in the sectional displays he visited. It took the form of a didactic or moralistic narrative that left little room for debate or alternative interpretation; of a central message articulated around ideas of victimhood, defensiveness or historical misrepresentation; of linear and ordered narratives which left aside difficult questions and highlighted the continuity between past and present; and of a lack of reflective criticism. Sectional, single-perspective or partisan museums are not exclusive to Northern Ireland. Examples abound, particularly in relation to difficult heritage. They reveal as much about the contemporary context as they do about the past events they represent. For instance, the Apartheid era in South Africa and racial violence and segregation in the US were memorialised differently in each country's historical narrative and museums (Autry 2017). Likewise, the controversy about the prospect of a Fascism museum in Mussolini's birthplace is forcing Italy to address its relation to its past (Loriga 2017).

At the core of these debates is the question of the curatorial control that museums or exhibitions wish to maintain or are willing to relinquish. The current trend is for museums to be less prescriptive, to shift from being 'sites of authority' to being 'sites of mutuality' (Hooper-Greenhill 2000: xi). Yet this seems contradictory with the idea of giving a voice to a group perceived to be, rightly or wrongly, voiceless. In her study about micromuseums, Candlin deals specifically with 'the problematic ethics of partisan museums' using a case study about Lurgan History Museum, a private collection of republican artefacts located in Northern Ireland. Her analysis of the visitor's experience serves to counter the assumption that good museum practice necessarily means a multi-perspective approach on a subject. Candlin argues that since partisan displays make no claim to neutrality, give a voice to marginalised groups and explain how their narrative results from a particular environment, their single-identity narrative should be valued. In such contexts, she argues, the requirement of a multi-perspective narrative may well be fairer, but it is not necessarily just and potentially oppressive (Candlin 2015: 75–92). Adrian Kerr, the director of the Museum of Free Derry, defends a similar viewpoint. He describes his museum as 'openly subjective' (2011: 348) and considers the sectional museum phase as a necessary step on the road to mutual understanding in Northern Ireland:

> Divided histories need to be addressed when the divisions are still causing conflict, and the only way to address them is accept they exist and tackle them head on. I would argue that the best way to do this here is to encourage smaller, subjective, community-based museums where different communities have the comfort and the freedom to tell their stories their way, and others have the same comfort and freedom to come and hear them and understand them.
>
> (2011: 367)

This vision of a mosaic of single-identity museums, into which ATIC and ACT might legitimately fit, begs a question: who will feel comfortable and free enough to visit the exhibitions? Despite continuous efforts at building a shared society, divisions remain, and post-conflict Northern Ireland has been described as a case of 'benign apartheid' (Nagle and Clancy 2010). Whilst it is accepted that dissonance in heritage is inherent and enhanced in conflict-related situations, an extra difficulty about ATIC and ACT lies in the fact that the groups they represent were active perpetrators of sectarian violence during the conflict. Loyalist paramilitaries caused just under 30% of the deaths during the conflict (McKittrick et al. 1999). Although officially defunct, the UDA (and associated group Ulster Freedom Fighters (UFF)) and the UVF (and associated group Red Hand Commando) are still proscribed and classified as terrorist organisations in the UK. Such elements may trigger different reactions among potential visitors: they may deter some people from visiting altogether, whilst others may object to what they perceive as a form of legitimation or glamourising of political violence. The debate about turning the Her Majesty's Prison (HMP) Maze/Long Kesh site into a heritage centre was replete with such arguments (McAtackney 2014, see also Purbrick this volume). The underlying question here is the place to be given to (former) paramilitary groups in the creation and promotion of heritage. Sociologist Lee A. Smithey views heritage and memory work in Protestant/Unionist/Loyalist (PUL) communities as part of conflict transformation (2011). He shows how community leaders have embraced heritage initiatives to make up for what they perceive as 'a deficit of historical knowledge among members of their organisations and communities that leaves them feeling insecure and unprepared to engage in cross-community dialogue and political debate' (Smithey 2011: 153). He identifies five functions of PUL heritage work: celebration, remembrance, education, unity and community relations (2011: 169–175). The weight given to each function is critical as too much stress placed on one may be detrimental to another. Smithey acknowledges the difficulty of dealing with paramilitary legacies, especially when sporadic unrest and criminality linked to paramilitary activity has continued since the organisations officially stopped operating. If heritage is to lead to better community relations, critical and historical reflection is key in order to avoid entrenched positions becoming fossilised (2011: 185–186). Smithey's analysis provides a useful toolkit to assess ATIC and ACT's exhibitions as snapshots of where the debate about dealing with the past stands.

ATIC and ACT's exhibitions sit awkwardly in the museum world, and traditional expectations and interpretative frameworks may not easily apply to them. Still, the exhibitions are valuable in the conversation about the legacy of conflict as they give opportunity to otherwise rather marginalised voices. Moreover, they fit the description Christopher Whitehead gives of museum displays as 'a political, public production of propositional knowledge intended to influence audiences and to create durable social effects' (2016: 2). It is precisely why, he argues, they must be studied.

Aims – empowering the voiceless

The ACT and ATIC exhibitions have been put together and are staffed by former members of the paramilitary groups they tell the story of: respectively, the UVF and the UDA. When I visited *Our Journey – Our Narrative* in North Belfast in November 2016, then in West Belfast in April 2017, I was shown around by ACT coordinator Dr William Mitchell. Billy Rowan, a volunteer in ATIC, guided me through the exhibition in East Belfast in November 2016. When asked how the idea of their respective exhibitions came about, each man insisted he wanted to have the story out there because the republican narrative dominated the environment. This is a commonly held view across loyalist communities that fuels a sense of social and political disenfranchisement, particularly in working-class areas (McAuley 2016: 142–147). Mitchell recalled how he once took an ACT group to Israel but realised, when the return visit happened, that he couldn't bring the young Israeli visitors to a specific place to tell them about the conflict from a loyalist point of view in the same way that they had been told about the republican point of view in the Irish Republican History Museum. He ended up giving them the loyalist vision of the conflict in an empty car park. The discrepancy between a highly visible republican narrative and a virtually invisible loyalist one prompted him to put the exhibition together to reach some sort of balance. It was not a question, in his words, of giving a 'comparative narrative', that is to say to counter each point of the republican narrative, but rather a feeling that the loyalist narrative needed to be heard too. Significantly, the exhibition opened on Ulster Day 2012 (29 September), exactly 100 years after the signing of the Ulster Covenant, one of the founding episodes of Unionism/Loyalism.[1] The same logic of giving a voice to the voiceless and reacting to a perceived dominant republican narrative applies for ATIC. Rowan reported how ATIC's founder David Stitt, whilst working as a community worker in East Belfast, would see Black Taxis from West Belfast (i.e. associated with the IRA) around the murals on the Newtownards Road, telling tourists about loyalist murals in a loyalist area: "David wanted the Loyalist people to be able to tell our story our way". ATIC opened at the end of August 2012, in the same commemorative context.

The desire to redress misrepresentation or, in this case, non-representation, prompted the putting together of the displays, to address both people from within and without the community. The exhibition leaflets articulate explicitly the intention behind them:

> The Andy Tyrie Interpretive Centre has been created to enable our community, as it emerges from forty years of violent conflict, to reflect on those years and hopefully that process of reflection may give us an understanding of what actually happened to us. There are reams and reams of press reports, pictures, books and TV programmes depicting many stories but all written by others. The Loyalist people have not told their story yet …
>
> (ATIC 2016)

> This [ACT] exhibition charts the major political developments which led to the creation of the Northern Ireland state, the social and political unrest that followed and the events which secured peace in the province. "Our Journey – Our Narrative" provides an insight into the journey of ACT members during this latter period of our recent history, as well as their efforts at securing peace and endeavours to transform themselves in the post ceasefire climate.
>
> (ACT 2016)

What is noticeable is the distinctive rhetorical positioning of each organisation. ATIC talks more to its own community than to outsiders, placing the focus of how the community needs to reclaim possession of its own story. In contrast, ACT primarily targets outsiders: the narrative is formally structured as a 'journey towards peace', the exhibition serving as an offshoot for the organisation's community work. As a result, the two groups are portrayed in different ways: one is still trying to make sense of its past and doesn't appear well grounded in the present, and the other is presented as being able to reflect critically on its own behaviour and having a sense of agency in the face of new circumstances. This expresses something of the history of the respective paramilitary groups after the Good Friday Agreement: the UVF was proactive in transitioning from political violence to the political arena, whilst the UDA was held back by internal divisions and localism (Spencer 2008: 227–245).

Practices: the visitor experience

Whilst their subject material and aims are largely similar, ATIC and ACT's 'productions of propositional knowledge' reveal differences between the organisations that make for distinctive visitor experiences. Visitors standing on the pavement outside ATIC in East Belfast are immediately faced with an ambiguous message: they are greeted with a welcome sign in five languages and a quote about peace-building by Albert Einstein, whilst the museum is described as a "Loyalist Conflict Museum". Its front displays the coat of arms of the UDA and the UFF, two officially defunct paramilitary organisations, and the centre is named after Andy Tyrie, a prominent figure of the UDA until the late 1980s. The combination of words and symbols may be confusing or overall contradictory for outsiders, who might be unfamiliar with the names, actors and history of the UDA/UFF.

Inside, the exhibition is organised over two floors. On the ground floor, newspapers clippings from the early 1970s to the late 2000s are displayed chronologically on the walls, charting the existence of the UDA from its emergence to its official disbanding. The collection of artefacts, donated or on loan from former members of the UDA, includes prison art, leaflets, caps, flags, scarves as well as a model replica of the H Blocks of HMP Maze/Long Kesh. A mannequin in full paramilitary regalia stands beside the portrait of the Queen and decommissioned guns hang on the wall. The exhibition continues on the first floor, with a focus on life in prison; larger exhibits, including a makeshift Lambeg drum made in the Maze out of a large plastic container; and more guns. The collection appears rather random, with no systematic labels. On a second floor, there's a space for group discussions.

Billy Rowan, who runs the exhibition single-handedly, guides visitors through the timeline of the organisation, using newspaper clippings as prompts to explain the creation of the UDA, first as a vigilante group, then as a paramilitary group; how it evolved through the conflict; and finally decommissioned its weapons in 2009. It is difficult to make sense of the display without his mediation as the clippings aren't all legible and there is very limited contextual interpretation. The same goes for the artefacts, especially the bigger objects like weapons and paramilitary regalia, some of which have no labels. The display is very raw, with context and interpretation mostly provided by the staff in charge. I have mentioned that lack of critical distance has been identified as one of the drawbacks of sectional displays and that a degree of it is deemed necessary to avoid entrenching existing positions. ATIC's narrative contains a few hints of reflective criticism: for instance, when Rowan explained how the UDA carried out most of its armed attacks under the name of the UFF, a strategy that allowed it to remain a legal organisation until 1992. When he mentioned that some members of the UFF began to engage in criminality in the 1980s, he was recognising that the UDA didn't always stay true to what the exhibition portrayed as its respectable *raison d'être* as a provider of safety for the community. But the nuances of the broader narrative may be lost on visitors, especially as some exhibits can be at best intimidating, at worst offensive. Apart from guns and masked men, a painted board panel adorned with the two coats of arms reads, 'Better to die on your feet than to live on your knees in an Irish Republic'. The lack of contextual panels may give visitors the impression that the narrative they're being given is binding, or that the story with which they are presented is incomplete. Some of them may find it daunting to enquire further. However, the contentious contents are almost secondary to the difficulty visitors may have in reading a micromuseum, especially if they expect to find familiar bearings, like interpretative panels. Candlin notes that micromuseums shouldn't be experienced the same way. In particular, she insists on looking for the museum's voice in the guidance of the staff since to 'concentrate on the more conventional forms of exhibition interpretation, such as wall-texts, could easily lead researchers to assume that very little information was disseminated and nothing could be learned from visits when the opposite situation may well be true' (2015: 17). The same could apply for visitors, but the experience may destabilise some because it requires unlearning usual museum habits.

ATIC also serves as a memorial of sorts, with one corner of the ground floor dedicated to deceased UDA members. Each day, a physical notice is posted that commemorates the dead; this is also posted on ATIC's Facebook page, often with less polished language. There is an undeniable element of nostalgia in the exhibition, of the sort Brandon Hamber observed in conflict museums in Chile, the Netherlands, China and South Africa, not so much for the conflict itself but for a time when the community was acting together, could defend itself, was organised and/or ingenuous (Hamber 2012). Such nostalgia is epitomised in ATIC by several exhibits, notably the makeshift Lambeg drum, prison art and various pictures of parades. But there is also a contrast between artefacts suggesting strength, stereotyped masculinity, possible threat – such as paintings of masked men kicking doors open or aiming at a target with a rifle – and the narrative of a victimised community. Rowan himself insists that the community feels cheated by the post-conflict arrangements and, if given the chance to vote again, would vote against the Belfast Agreement. His story is a sad one, but he tells it earnestly. The narrative of deprivation applies to the area where ATIC is located: where the community used to thrive in the nearby shipyard, poverty is now stark. The surrounding urbanscape, marked by the iconic defunct Harland and Wolff cranes and commemorative, paramilitary-related murals, conveys the same sense of loss, outward-facing aggression and defensiveness.

To Rowan, the exhibition is about the past, not the present, and yet ATIC's front door and leaflet talk about peace-building and conflict transformation. The ambivalence of the message is also to be found in the ways the 'Other' – republicans – are referred to. They are mostly demonised in ATIC's written material, but the conversation reveals them to be invisible contributors to the collection. Rowan explained how, after he saw a model of the H blocks in the Irish Republican History Museum, he had one made for the museum by the same man, a former IRA prisoner. All of this makes for an unsettling visitor experience, the educational value of which may be difficult to grasp and/or questionable to some, depending on their own experience or knowledge of the conflict. Some may feel confused by conflicting messages or even antagonised. If we consider Smithey's list of five identified functions of PUL heritage initiatives, celebration, commemoration and unity seem to weigh more than education or community relations. Overall, the message in ATIC is a rather fuzzy one, mixing tangible displays of strength, defensiveness and sacrifice with intangible touches of vulnerability, helplessness and reflexive criticism.

By comparison, the ACT exhibition offers a more focussed visitor experience. At the time of my first visit in October 2016, it was set up in the association's offices, on the first floor of a commercial block on the Shore Road, in a predominantly PUL area of North Belfast. What was advertised on the street was the ACT initiative, not the exhibition, which meant that visitors would hardly stumble upon it. In April 2017, ACT moved to a shop unit on the Shankill Road, a predominantly PUL area in West Belfast. Its front now bears a 'Shankill Road Museum' sign, giving the exhibition more visibility for passers-by, both locals and tourists. In both locations, the display is in one large single room, with panels organised chronologically from the signing of the Ulster Covenant to the post-Belfast Agreement years. The artefacts on display are linked either with the 1910s or with the prison experience of UVF members during the Troubles. The exhibition is text-rich and didactic. There is a small newspaper archive as well as TV footage shown on a screen. The only uniforms present date from the 1910s. Children can dress up in cap and sash and pose with a wooden replica of an early UVF rifle: no modern UVF uniform or weapons are displayed. A collection of academic books about the conflict is available for visitors to consult. Tables and chairs are at hand for group discussions and community activities.

The choice of the 1910s as a starting point for the narrative is significant for several reasons. The events of the decade, in particular the signing of the Ulster Covenant (1912) and the Battle of the Somme (1916), are essential parts of the PUL collective identity (Brown 2007; Viggiani 2014: 128–149). 1913 was the year when the first UVF was formed as part of the anti-Home Rule movement. In its transition to political activism, the modern UVF looked back to the period of the Home Rule Crisis and described its agents as "the founding fathers of unionism" (Mitchell 2002). Including the 1910s and the historic UVF in the exhibition serves to stress the continuity – and thereby legitimacy – of the loyal tradition through the years. The link with the past is made even more prominent in the Shankill Road premises, where panels on the decade are visible from the pavement and thus used as pull factors for visitors.

During my first visit, William Mitchell briefly explained how the exhibition was organised, detailed a few artefacts in the 1910s section and in the prison art section and left me to look at the displays on my own. The format of the exhibition, combining contextual panels and artefacts, is closer to that of a mainstream museum than ATIC's. A large place is given to context, with half the panels devoted to the period before the recent conflict began. Critical distance is also a major element, as the conclusion of the paragraph about the Civil War in 1922–1923 exemplifies, 'the events of extreme violence and upheaval of early 20th century Ireland – which included the creation of Northern Ireland and Eire – set the stage for future conflict and discord'. This is a broadly received historical interpretation of the twentieth-century origins of the conflict, which gives the visitor a sense of being given a dispassionate narrative of the past.

The emergence of the modern UVF is treated with similar distantiation. The panel entitled 'Early Campaign of the UVF, 1965–1969' includes the following extracts: 'Many current scholars posit that the UVF was reformed by right-wing Unionist opposition to liberal thinking of Prime Minister Terrence O'Neill'; and 'The UVF's aim was to mislead authorities. They believed blaming the IRA would erode confidence in O'Neill and his 'bridge building' policies' (ATIC 2016) and, a quote from UVF leader, Gusty Spence:

> The UVF was not reconstituted because of a threat from the IRA. There might have been – there probably always was an implied threat from the IRA – but I believe it was reconstituted in order to oppose or be used as a bargaining counter against some of the things which O'Neill[2] had brought out into debate.
>
> (ATIC 2016)

As many members of the modern UVF, including former prisoners, moved on to create the Progressive Unionist Party in the 1970s, a working-class-based party supporting a democratic socialist ideology, the continuity of the UVF from the 1910s to the 1960s and later is not straightforward, and it is worth noting that the display addresses the issue. The narrative is informative but not narrowly binding. For instance, two dates are mentioned as the starting date of the Troubles: 5 October 1968 as 'Often seen as the day the Troubles started. Confrontation between Police and Civil Rights protestors in Londonderry draws international attention' and 14 August 1969 as 'Officially recorded as the day the Troubles started. British Army is placed on active service in Londonderry and in Belfast the next days'.

Reflective criticism appears in several panels, which openly recognise the violence of conflict, the lethal actions of paramilitaries on both sides and the tragic loss of civilian lives. For instance, the date when Peter Ward, a Catholic man, was killed by the UVF in 1966 is included, which some would consider as the starting point of the Troubles. Likewise, on the one panel giving the timeline of the Troubles, the victims of bomb attacks perpetrated by loyalist and republican paramilitaries are acknowledged (Dublin and Monaghan in 1974, Enniskillen in 1987, Omagh in 1998). The narrative continues with a large section devoted to life in prison, mixing personal testimonies (including from former female prisoners) and artefacts. The final part of the narrative includes the transition to politics, the impact of conflict on former combatants, their wives and families, and the post-Agreement timeline. The focus is clearly on the experience of UVF members and their journey to the present day. The narrative is not a counter-narrative to the republican one: the 'Other' whose behaviour is critiqued is the Unionist middle-class establishment. One testimony from a former prisoner reads,

> There is so much hypocrisy around … There are these SuperProd figures who tell you how they nearly did what you did. But if you asked them for a job they wouldn't want to know you because you're a Loyalist prisoner. I've seen the same people sit in Church and say "Oh I don't condone what has been done but we didn't start it …" People who would never dream of being actively involved but who sit in front of their televisions, and when a certain person comes on, they have murder in their hearts.

The personal testimonies, most of which are from a male perspective, do not shy away from expressing emotions, relating the hardships of imprisonment and the devastating impact on paramilitary engagement on families and on the community at large. They offer models of masculinity that are less brash and stereotyped than in ATIC. This is where ACT's work in helping former combatants go back to civilian life, notably through self-reflection, is the most discernible. The exhibition is tailored both for outsiders and the members of the working-class loyalist community it represents, who have moved on from being agents of conflict to agents of conflict transformation. The dimension of empowerment, despite hardships, is essential, both in the exhibition and in the work of the organisation. The exhibition prioritises the functions of educating and remembering over celebrating and unifying. With its critical depiction of the past, it offers a more engaging starting point to further community relations than ATIC.

Challenges – funding, visitor numbers and best practices

As loyalist heritage initiatives, ACT and ATIC define themselves as agents of conflict transformation in post-conflict Northern Ireland. Yet their role as social agents has not reached its full potential because of several challenges. The first challenge has to do with funding, on which development, sustainability and staffing rely. Personal communication with Billy Rowan suggests a precarious future for ATIC: the centre has no stable source of funding and relies on donations from visitors and friends, charging £5 per person for groups. In 2015–2016, it had an income of just over £6,500 and spent a little over £5,000.[3] Rowan works there as a volunteer four or five days a week, more if there are group tours at weekends. In practice, he says ATIC runs "from month to month". Not only does this make it difficult to envisage significant changes to the display, but the uncertainty regarding the future of the exhibition echoes the sense of powerlessness that emerged from the story he tells. The ACT Initiative is in a slightly more stable position. The exhibition doesn't have a specific external funding source, but the Joseph Rowntree Foundation currently supports the organisation. This British charity sponsors initiatives promoting social change, including conflict transformation in Northern Ireland, one of its five priority areas (Joseph Rowntree Charitable Trust website). ACT is one of thirty-one projects that have received a Joseph Rowntree grant since 2014. Previous funding has come from the International Committee of the Red Cross. Securing funding from such well-regarded charities is a sign that ACT is a proactive member of the voluntary sector and that its work is valued and recognised. This helps to further empower the group it represents and can, in turn, serve as a stepping stone for future projects, even if future funding is never guaranteed.

Another challenge for both organisations is how to promote their exhibition, given they operate outside the official museum sector and deal with contentious heritage. Although neither keeps strict records of visitor numbers, both are looking to increase annual visitor numbers, currently in the low hundreds. Billy Rowan explained how the Twelfth of July and the weekend of Remembrance Sunday in November were the busiest periods in ATIC. Student and youth groups are common visitors, both locals and from further afield, including from the Republic of Ireland, Canada, Switzerland and the US. William Mitchell said ACT welcomed twenty-five groups in 2016, hailing from various parts of the globe, notably Ukraine,

Israel, Palestine and the US. Overall, about 300 people visited the exhibition in 2016, a third of which identified as being from a nationalist background. Both organisations use their own networks of community workers and conflict transformation initiatives as the main channel of promoting the exhibitions. A small number of visitors find out about the exhibitions through Facebook and word of mouth.

The two organisations have adopted different strategies to increase the visibility of each exhibition. ATIC has contacted Visit Belfast, the main tourist information centre in the city centre, to display its leaflets there. According to Rowan, Visit Belfast hasn't been very responsive, with the consequence that the centre isn't advertised to the flow of tourists going through Visit Belfast. The lack of response has generated disappointment in ATIC but no further action has been undertaken to press the matter. It is worth mentioning that the front page of the leaflet combines inspirational slogans ('Building the Peace', 'Conflict Resolution and Transformation', 'Making a positive difference') with pictures of masked men parading on the streets. The leaflet is representative of the ambivalent message conveyed by the exhibition, and a possible reason for Visit Belfast's reticence. ACT's move to new premises in West Belfast has enhanced the visibility of the exhibition, not only because of the new, more accessible location, but also because of the possibilities of partnerships with other conflict transformation initiatives. West Belfast has long attracted the bulk of political tourism in the city, with tours available on both sides of the interface between the predominantly Catholic/Nationalist/Republican Falls Road and the predominantly PUL Shankill Road. ACT's plan is to avail of this more context to design a joint political tour with EPIC (a conflict transformation association for UVF ex-prisoners), the Crumlin Road Gaol where many political prisoners were detained during the conflict, the Black Taxi Tours and the Irish Republican History Museum, all of which already have the endorsement of Visit Belfast. Such a project would attract new visitors and further empower the community it represents as Mitchell hopes to train ACT members to run the exhibition and employ them to do so.

The last challenge has to do with best curatorial practices. If Fiona Candlin's recommendations are to be followed, this point is hardly worth mentioning, since the current budget constraints of ATIC and ACT mean they have very limited leeway to improve their practices. Basic collections care, such as monitoring temperature, relative humidity, light levels and air quality, is non-existent through lack of knowledge, funding or time. There is no storage room in ATIC and only limited storage space in the new ACT location. Not all the artefacts are in display cases – some can be touched and passed around. In ATIC, the display of guns on walls can be deemed as ethically problematic and glamourising violence (Centre for Collaborative Heritage Research, 2008). Again, applying the analytical framework for mainstream museums to heritage initiatives like ATIC and ACT only results in pointing out their shortcomings (Candlin, 2015: 13–15), when this chapter has sought to show the valuable aspects of the two exhibitions. Neither Billy Rowan nor William Mitchell has had any training in collections care or interpretation. Rowan said he learnt as he went along, talking to groups of visitors using the paper clippings as prompts and his knowledge of the organisation, whilst Mitchell explained he designed the exhibition after visiting several museums, notably in Poland. If staff in ATIC and ACT were to be encouraged to get training and improve their curatorial practices, who could they turn to? As small-scale, independently run, non-accredited exhibition spaces, ATIC and ACT operate outwith the aegis of the Northern Ireland Museums Council, who would have the relevant expertise. Northern Ireland Museums Council is also part of the Museum Development Network (which provides support to accredited museums) and works in collaboration with the Association of Independent Museums. These bodies may sound too formal for grass-roots initiatives like ATIC and ACT. Indeed, even though the artefacts on display and the narratives told are uncomfortable and contentious, their priority is to empower the communities they represent. Any expertise on best curatorial practices, if required and provided, would have to be passed on in a manner that would comply with the same imperative, and not be perceived as constraining or binding. Ways and means need to be imagined that would take into account the built-in limitations of such small-scale heritage initiatives, the fragile post-conflict environment in which they operate and the enduring sense of disenfranchisement and related trust issues in the communities they represent.

Conclusions

For the last twenty years, Northern Ireland has been having a conversation on how to deal with the difficult heritage of the Troubles. Adjectives used to describe this conversation – challenging, uncomfortable, necessary – could also describe the two exhibitions discussed in this chapter. ATIC and ACT challenge the researcher in museum studies and the visitor by upsetting the rituals of museum analysis and experience. To many people, the very fact of engaging with their contentious subject matter requires leaving their comfort zone. The two exhibitions perform some of the functions of mainstream museums by creating meaning, for the communities they represent and for outsiders, thereby advancing self, mutual and general understanding. As such, they are necessary social agents. They also contribute to conflict transformation in Northern Ireland by empowering the groups they represent and giving them the voice they feel is missing from the conversation. Their very existence helps understanding the peace process: the distinctive characteristics of the narratives and displays they have produced are telling signs of where these communities stand at after twenty years of peace as is the fact that their success or shortcomings depend on their social, political and even geographical environments.

In her study on how past wrongdoings were memorialised in Nuremberg, Sharon Macdonald described how difficult heritage may disrupt the present (2009: 1). In an article on the now global turn to difficult heritage, she argues that

> The act of publicly addressing terrible historical acts undertaken by the collective is no longer necessarily a disruption to positive identity formation. On the contrary, increasingly it seems to be a sign of moral cleanliness and honesty, and, as such, a performance of trustworthiness.
>
> (2015: 19)

Even if difficult heritage poses 'moral and representational challenges', she considers the growing confidence in addressing difficult heritage may open up new representations of the past, transcending the polarisation between perpetrators and victims to include the role of the silent majority (2015: 19–20). Such representations of the conflict haven't yet entered Northern Ireland museums or exhibitions, but the degree of reflective criticism at play in the exhibitions mentioned, however limited, is a step in that direction. The imperative of social responsibility imposed on museums (Janes 2007) can hardly be expected from such small-scale initiatives as ACT or ATIC. Yet for their social role to expand as heritage initiatives, conversations with critical friends – visitors, academics, museum professionals – might prove fruitful.

Notes

1 In the context of the debate about the Third Home Rule Bill in 1912, supporters of the Union were encouraged to sign the Ulster Covenant, by which they pledged to defend their position in the Union. The text was signed by just under a quarter of a million men. A distinct text, the "Declaration", was signed by about the same number of women.
2 Captain Terence O'Neill was a moderate Unionist who became Prime Minister of Northern Ireland in1963. The conciliatory measures he sought to introduce to reduce sectarianism were perceived to be detrimental to Unionist interests. He faced increasing criticism from his own electors as well as escalating violence and resigned in 1969.
3 https://apps.charitycommission.gov.uk/ccni_ar_attachments/0000100616_20160401_CA.pdf

Bibliography

Action for Community Transformation Initiative. (2016). *Leaflet*. Belfast: ACT.
Andy Tyrie Interpretative Centre. (2016). *Leaflet*. Belfast: ATIC.
Autry, R. (2017). *Desegregating the Past. The Public Life of Memory in the United States and South Africa*. New York: Columbia University Press.
Bigand, K. (2016). The Role of Museums in Dealing with the Legacy of the Troubles in Northern Ireland. *RISE – Review of Irish Studies in Europe*, 1(2), pp. 40–53.

Bradburne, J.M. (2011). Visible Listening. Discussion, Debate and Governance in the Museum. In: Marstine, J. ed. *The Routledge Companion to Museum Ethics. Redefining Ethics for the Twenty-First-Century Museum*. Abington and New York: Routledge, pp. 275–297.

Brown, K. (2007). 'Our Father Organization': The Cult of the Somme and the Unionist 'Golden Age' in Modern Ulster Loyalist Commemoration. *The Round Table*, 96(393), pp. 707–723.

Brown, K. (2008). Living with History: Conflict, Commemoration and Exhibitions in Northern Ireland: The Case of Sectional Displays. *Social History in Museums*, 32, pp. 31–37.

Cameron, F. (2005). Contentiousness and Shifting Knowledge Paradigms: The Roles of History and Science Museums in Contemporary Societies. *Museum Management and Curatorship*, 20(3), pp. 213–233.

Candlin, F. (2015). *Micromuseology. An Analysis of Small Independent Museums*. London: Bloomsbury Academic.

Connerton, P. (1989). *How Societies Remember*. Cambridge: Cambridge University Press.

Crooke, E. (2007). Museums, Communities and the Politics of Heritage in Northern Ireland. In: Watson, S. ed. *Museums and Their Communities*. London and New-York: Routledge, pp. 300–312.

Crooke, E. (2010). The Politics of Community Heritage: Motivations, Authority and Control. *International Journal of Heritage Studies*, 16(1–2), pp. 16–29.

Derry Journal. (2017). Families Say 'Yes' to Free Derry Museum Exhibit. [online] 8 September 2017. Available at: www.derryjournal.com/news/families-say-yes-to-free-derry-museum-exhibit-1-8141525 [Accessed 7 October 2017].

Hamber, B. (2012). Conflict Museums, Nostalgia, and Dreaming of Never Again, *Peace and Conflict: Journal of Peace Psychology*, 8(3), pp. 268–281.

Hamber, B. (2015). Dealing with Painful Memories and Violent Pasts. Towards a Framework for Contextual Understanding. In: Beatrix, A. and Fischer, M. eds. *Transforming War-related Identities*. Berghof Handbook Dialogue Series No. 11. Berlin: Berghof Foundation.

Hooper-Greenhill, E. (2000). *Museums and the Interpretation of Visual Culture*. London and New York: Routledge.

Janes, R. (2007). Museums, Social Responsibility and the Future We Desire. In: Knell, S., McLeod, S. and Watson, S. eds. *Museum Revolutions. How Museums Change and Are Changed*. London and New York: Routledge, pp. 134–146.

Joseph Rowntree Charitable Trust. (2017). Northern Ireland. [online] Available at: www.jrct.org.uk/northern-ireland [Accessed 13 October 2017].

Kerr, A. (2011). Sitting on the Fence, What's the Point? In: *Museums of Ideas: Commitment and Conflict. A Collection of Essays*. Edinburgh: MuseumsEtc, pp. 428–450.

Loriga, S. (2017). Can Italy deal with its fascist past? *The Conversation France*. 28 July. Available at: https://theconversation.com/can-italy-deal-with-its-fascist-past-81077 [Accessed 7 October 2017].

Macdonald, S. (2009). *Difficult Heritage: Negotiating the Nazi Past in Nuremberg and Beyond*. Abingdon: Routledge.

Macdonald, S. (2015). Is 'Difficult Heritage' Still 'Difficult'? Why Public Acknowledgment of Past Perpetration May No Longer Be So Unsettling to Collective Identities. *Museum International*, 67, pp. 6–22.

Maddison, S. (2016). *Conflict Transformation and Reconciliation. Multi-level Challenges in Deeply Divided Societies.* London and New York: Routledge.

McAtackney, L. (2014). *An Archaeology of the Troubles: The Dark Heritage of Long Kesh/Maze Prison.* Oxford: Oxford University Press.

McAuley, J.W. (2016). *Very British Rebels. The Culture and Politics of Ulster Loyalism.* New York and London: Bloomsbury Academic.

McDowell, S. (2008). Selling Conflict Heritage through Tourism in Peacetime Northern Ireland: Transforming Conflict or Exacerbating Difference? *International Journal of Heritage Studies*, 14(5), pp. 405–421.

McKittrick, D., Kelters, S., Feeney, B. and Thornton, C. (1999). *Lost Lives, The Stories of the Men, Women and Children Who Died as a Result of the Northern Ireland Troubles.* Edinburgh: Mainstream Publishing.

Mitchell, B. (2002). Principles of Loyalism. In Internal Discussion Paper. [online]. Available at: www.pup-ni.org.uk/loyalism/principlesdocument.aspx [Accessed 13 October 2017].

Nagle, J. and Clancy, M. (2010). eds *Shared Society or Benign Apartheid?: Understanding Peace-Building in Divided Societies.* Basingstoke: Palgrave Macmillan.

Samuels, J. (2015). Difficult Heritage: Coming "To Terms" with Sicily's Fascist Past. In: Lafrenz Samuels, K. and Rico, T. eds. *Heritage Keywords: Rhetoric and Redescription in Cultural Heritage*, University Press of Colorado, pp. 111–128.

Sandell, R. (2002). ed. *Museums, Society, Inequality.* London and New York: Routledge.

Simone-Charteris, M.T. and Boyd, S.W. (2010). Northern Ireland Re-emerges from the Ashes: The Contribution of Political Tourism towards a More Visited and Peaceful Environment. In: Moufakkir, O. and Kelly, I. eds. *Tourism, Progress and Peace.* Wallingford: CABI. pp. 179–198.

Smithey, L. (2011). *Unionists, Loyalists, and Conflict Transformation in Northern Ireland.* Oxford: Oxford University Press.

Spencer, G. (2008). *The State of Loyalism in Northern Ireland.* Basingstoke: Palgrave Macmillan.

Steel, P. (2017). Museum of Free Derry Removes Exhibit Following Protests. *Museum Journal*, 5 (September) p. 6.

Tunbridge, J.E. and Ashworth G.J. (1996). *Dissonant Heritage: the Management of the Past as a Resource in Conflict.* Chichester: Wiley and Sons.

Viggiani, E. (2014). *Talking Stones: The Politics of Memorialization in Post-Conflict Northern Ireland.* New York and Oxford: Berghahn Books.

Whitehead, C. (2016). Critical Analysis Tool (CAT) 2: How to Analyse Museum Display: Script, Text, Narrative. *Critical Heritages (CoHERE): performing and representing identities in Europe* [online]. Available at: http://digitalcultures. ncl.ac.uk/cohere/wordpress/wp-content/uploads/2016/10/WP1-CAT-1.2.pdf. [Accessed 9 January 2017].

Witcomb, A. (2003). *Re-Imagining the Museum: Beyond the Mausoleum.* London and New York: Routledge.

6 Long Kesh/Maze

A case for participation in post-conflict heritage

Louise Purbrick

When I first visited the prison officially named Her Majesty's Prison (HMP) Maze, also known as Long Kesh, on a bright, cold day early in January 2002, it had been emptied of prisoners for a year. I vividly recall three aspects of the site. First was the scale of the prison. Enclosed within high, long walls was an expanse of flat land, with the same structures duplicated, over and over; there were walls everywhere. Second was the colour grey. Concrete, corrugated iron, mesh fencing and barbed wire were all grey. The brick facing on the eight H blocks, the cell units for which the jail is most famous, was pale yellow, but since all buildings from the Nissen huts, the oldest structures erected in 1971 to house internees on a disused Royal Air Force (RAF) base, to the additional visiting area that was constructed in 1990s were encased in their own wire cage, everything appeared grey. The bright light of the January day became opaque inside the jail. Third was the atmosphere of oppression; this sense of restriction was most acute inside the H blocks. They were cold, damp and discomforting. Only a little daylight filtered in, and a feeling of weighty nothingness pervaded the entire space of the empty prison. Of course, structures create sensations. Any official building, prisons especially but also courtrooms, hospitals and even some schools, can cultivate hesitancy, a fear of free movement. These forms have been studied as systems of control and discipline (Foucault 1979; Cohen 1985). The scale of Long Kesh/Maze and the similarity of its structures, its long views that always ended in walls, evoked the enormity of imprisonment and offered to a fleeting visitor, such as myself, a fraction of the sensation of prolonged isolation; it is not possible for a single body to fully register the affects felt by others, by the approximately 10,000 male prisoners (Ryder 2000) suspected of or sentenced for 'conflict-related' offences, many of whom spent much of their youth in Long Kesh/Maze.

The brutal sameness of the walls and blocks initially obscures the material complexity of the site (Figure 6.1). An architectural survey in 2004 identified over 300 building types that belonged to two prison systems, geographically adjacent and historically overlapping, within the same perimeter wall. Twenty-two compounds, containing the shared spaces of four Nissen huts, comprised Long Kesh internment centre, whilst the eight H blocks

Figure 6.1 View of H blocks, yards, internal fencing, walls and watchtowers (2004).
Photograph by Louise Purbrick.

contained ninety-six single cells. It is the H blocks, constructed between 1976 and 1978, that carry the most widely known history of the prison: the Republican prisoner protest over political status, which began with the refusal to wear prison clothing and ended with the hunger strikes of 1981. The older compounds reveal layers of prison history: the sectarian nature of internment in the very first years of the 1970s, then, by the middle of the decade, the establishment of both loyalist and republican self-organisation within the spaces they called the 'Cages'. Other prison structures, such as the visiting areas, of which there were two, are little remarked upon but once contained intersecting experiences of conflict: the separation of families, the love of friends, political solidarity. Whilst the H block narrative has coalesced around the figure of Bobby Sands, who died of starvation after his election as Minister for Parliament (MP) for Fermanagh and Tyrone, the 1981 hunger strikes are also a history of the political bonds between individuals and collectives. The nine men that followed Bobby Sands were drawn from two republican organisations: the Provisional Irish Republican Army (IRA), to which Sands belonged, and the Irish National Liberation Army (INLA). The prison was a site of everyday confrontation, including that between Loyalist prisoners and prison officers, which reveals one of the most contradictory relationships of the conflict. Cells represent most powerfully the containment of a prisoner's life, but there were journeys within each H block, repeatedly undertaken, such as the prison officers' walk along the wings. Also, in each wing were dining and association areas, which from the mid-1980s were forums for political discussion that led to the ceasefires of the mid-1990s, the Good Friday Agreement and, ultimately, to the period of post-conflict heritage examined within this book (Challis 1999; McKeown 2001).

The prison and post-conflict heritage

Long Kesh/Maze has been called both a microcosm and an icon of 'The Troubles' (Dorrell 2005; Keenan 2006), the conflict 'in and about' Northern Ireland (Healing Through Remembering 2017). It presents both a summary of the conflict and is its most recognisable image, a portrait. For this reason, it may seem the most obvious and appropriate place for post-conflict heritage. But, for the very same reason, it has also proven to be the most difficult. Most importantly, all the key protagonists to the conflict occupied some of the space of the prison; they had a place within it. It was built at the behest of the British government, and its perimeter was patrolled by the battalions of the British Army; prison officers, usually locally recruited, were aligned to Northern Ireland's security forces; republicans and loyalists were its prisoners. Who are soldiers or civilians, the perpetrators or the victims? Categories overlap. Relatives of those killed in the conflict may well regard prisoners sentenced for their involvement in the death of their family members as the perpetrators of violence. Those same prisoners detained under emergency powers, arrested under draconian terrorist legislation and sentenced by no jury courts, can also be considered as victims of the conflict. Under what conditions does a member of a republican or loyalist community, a British soldier or a prison officer carry weapons, then use them against another person? Long Kesh/Maze and its formerly occupied spaces raise the most fundamental issues relating to the causes of violence and conflict as well as the most pressing political concerns about the extent of victimhood.

The 1998 Good Friday Agreement provided for the early release of prisoners sentenced for conflict-related offences. As Long Kesh/Maze emptied, a debate, increasingly fierce, circled around the past and future of the site. The contested nature of the heritage of Long Kesh/Maze is well established (Graham and McDowell 2007; Flynn 2011; McAtackney 2014; Welch 2016). The possibility of the prison site as one of heritage became one of the causes of a series of stalemates within the power-sharing consociational arrangements devolved upon Northern Ireland since the Good Friday Agreement. It was, and still is, one of the sources of political disagreement: the resolution of the destiny of the former prison is bound up with the resolution of the conflict itself. But twenty years on, much has changed at the site itself.

As prisoners were released, entire wings, then blocks, were emptied; the interiors of the cells were dismantled; standard cell furniture of beds, shelves, curtains and even light fittings were removed and stored. Some blocks, kept in 'warm storage', were repainted and refitted. Others were simply cleared and cleaned: marks of political affiliation erased, for the most part. The removal of materials to be reused within the prison estate and of remaining documentation to the Public Record Office was more systematic once the prison was formally decommissioned in 2002. In April 2005, the Environment and Heritage Service gave the following listed building status, thus establishing them as being of historic interest: (yards, fences, vehicle entrance, airlock gates, Northern Ireland Prison Service watchtowers), one prison chapel, the prison hospital, two sections of the perimeter wall and two British Army watchtowers. One compound (number 19), comprising four Nissen huts and its high wire fence, were also listed with a view to relocation closer to the H block structures. Buildings relating to the earlier history of the site as the RAF base, the hangars and shelters have been scheduled as historic monuments. The rest were demolished between 2006 and 2008. When the remaining buildings of Long Kesh/Maze were flattened, gradually, the site altered. Its prison structures once overlaid the airbase, but now fencing, cultivated hedges and formal lawns demarcate Second World War heritage from that of 'The Troubles'. The geographical scale of the prison site, and with it some of its historical significance, has visibly shrunk.

Tracing the debate surrounding Long Kesh/Maze, the task to which this chapter is addressed, should offer some insights into the wider politics of post-conflict heritage as well as that of the former jail. I want to suggest that there are three phases in the politics of heritage in Northern Ireland since the signing of the Good Friday Agreement that have manifested around the former prison: a time of hope, a period of government management and another season of conflict. In the years since Long Kesh/Maze was emptied, its buildings became effaced and its space became reduced and overgrown. Since then the practice of heritage has also changed. Public engagement is valued more highly than pristine preservation, immaterial values matter more than material values and 'doing' heritage (Smith 2006) is more important than simply seeing it or just knowing it is there. All this could be summarised as heritage practice as participation, which, I argue in conclusion, could find a place at Long Kesh/Maze. Before I start sketching the phases of post-conflict heritage and then embark on a discussion of participation as a heritage practice, I want to note that in the two decades since the signing of the Good Friday Agreement and the whole period of post-conflict heritage to which this volume is addressed was, is, one of global political change summarised as neo-liberalism. Perpetual war has created a global crisis that has reshaped power relationships between the Middle East and the US and intensified the divisions and inequalities between Europe and North Africa, Europe and the Middle East, Europe and

Syria, Pakistan and Afghanistan, and West and East. Division and inequality is most forcefully evident in defended borders and displaced peoples. It is to this contemporary global context that practice of participation in the cultural domains of museums, art galleries, social centres and heritage is addressed. What I suggest in this chapter, then, is that a contemporary global practice developed as a critique of conflict and its consequences might find a place in Long Kesh/Maze or elsewhere in contested landscape of Northern Ireland.

A time of hope

The first phase of an emerging politics of heritage began when the last prisoners were released under the terms of the Good Friday Agreement from Long Kesh/Maze, eighty-four people being released on a single day (28 July 2000). In both local and national media, the dualism of the conflict was reinstated in heritage discourse: two traditions, two positions translated into Republican and Unionist, were played off against each other in a simplified opposition between preservation and demolition. Former Republican prisoners suggested that the prison could be turned into a museum; Unionists responded that it should be razed to the ground. The power of the two warring tribes' media narrative, established through years of reporting the conflict, should not be underestimated; it fed an entrenched political opposition that has subsequently settled upon the site, but it did not hold sway in this initial phase of post-conflict heritage.

The emptying of Long Kesh/Maze generated interest in the history of the jail for two reasons. First, former prisoners drew attention to their experience of imprisonment during the conflict. Prisoners' stories, especially but by no means only Republican prisoners' stories, had circulated throughout the conflict, but the mass releases under the Good Friday Agreement raised the political and cultural status of all prisoners and allowed for more sympathetic reception of their histories. Second, the condition of the prison building changed; into now empty spaces, another future was projected. Closed structures were a source of speculation; reoccupying a site of incarceration seemed possible. This early phase was one of open debate and some indeterminacy: not all positions on the future of Long Kesh/Maze were decided in advance. For example, Sir Reg Empey, then Enterprise Minister in the Northern Ireland Executive, stated that 'a museum could play a part' in a mixed development at the site (BBC 2002), whereas Antony McIntyre, 'dissident' Republican and Long Kesh/Maze prisoner between 1975 and 1993, stated, 'I don't care what they do with it as long as I don't get sent back there'.

McIntyre's contribution to the Long Kesh/Maze debate was made in a public discussion held in the photography gallery Belfast Exposed, during an exhibition of Donovan Wylie's work *The Maze* (2004). These images and this exhibition were just one of a much wider series of art productions and cultural events that responded to the end of imprisonment at Long Kesh/Maze, to Good Friday Agreement and to the beginning of the end of conflict. Photography, film, exhibitions of material culture and sculpture, and other artworks offered a series of perspectives upon the prison and its post-conflict heritage. Wylie, for example, sought an objective rendering of depopulated prison structures, whereas Cahal McLaughlin's *Inside Stories* (2005), a collaborative film project, enlivened the empty prison spaces with the return journeys of a Republican prisoner, a Loyalist prisoner and a prison officer. Their three narratives were shown simultaneously on three screens in one gallery space, a juxtaposition that convened past coexistence and present inclusivity. The material culture of Long Kesh/Maze, seized prohibited items, such as sills, radios, banners and weapons, was the subject of Amanda Dunsmore's film *Billy's Museum* (2005). Billy was a prison officer who held this collection of objects; his act of keeping was one of the recognition of the jail and its artefacts as historically significant. The film and the collection cannot be reduced to a single narrative: the objects reveal the struggle between prisoner and prison officer, strategies of resistance against the prison regime and the attempt to impose it. Two cinema releases, *H3* (2001) and Steve McQueen's *Hunger* (2008), drew upon only the Republican experience of prison protest, but neither can be reduced to a single community interest: both films privilege a human over a political story. However, a former Republican prisoner created artworks of universal meaning. Raymond Watson's *Hands of History* (2003) sculpture repeatedly casts the metonym of humanity in an overtly optimistic artwork that restages the politicised handshake of official agreement as an act of unity between communities. In this all too brief review of works made about Long Kesh/Maze in the years immediately following its closure more could be said, but these are offered as ways of thinking about the site: as objective records of conflict, as historically significant, as a site of human experiences, as a place of co-existence and a new unity. Importantly, it was cultural centres and art galleries in particular that were open forums for discussions of post-conflict heritage. Such discussions, initiated by former prisoners, especially those organised under the wing of Coiste na n-Iarchimí, and the sustained work of artists, photographers and film-makers intersected with an initiative from the political sphere: a public consultation.

On 14 January 2003, the then Secretary for Northern Ireland, Ian Pearson, announced a public consultation on *A New Future for Maze/Long Kesh*, to be conducted by a Maze Consultation Panel composed of four political parties: the Ulster Unionist Party, the Democratic Unionist Party, the Social Democratic Labour Party and Sinn Féin. Public and community meetings were held, and submissions were invited by post and email. The Maze Consultation Panel was a mechanism for channelling aspirations about the development of the prison site, creating a process through which individuals and organisations, people and communities, could present their views on what should happen. Anyone could submit proposals, and almost 60% of those who did were 'private individuals'. Openness, a defining feature of this moment of post-conflict heritage, characterised the consultation process. However, proposals were required to meet 'government objectives' that set high stakes for the site: submissions had to provide evidence of how the plans could transform the former prison site into 'an internationally recognised beacon for Northern Ireland'; they had to 'be new and innovative', bringing 'economic', 'social' and 'community' benefits, but also 'deliverable and sustainable', meeting 'Physical, Supply and Demand constraints'. Such ambitious criteria may have deterred smaller-scale projects and people without the skills of long-term financial planning, offsetting some openness, but the criteria certainly were optimistic. Hope resided in an important aspect of Maze Consultation Panel's purpose: it was a conflict resolution process. The Panel's work could be described as an attempt to manage the debate about the past of the prison and to direct the consideration of its future. It tried to balance the aspirations for and repugnance towards the site, the desire to preserve the prison and a demand that it be razed to the ground.

The Maze Consultation Panel published its *Final Report* in February 2005. Its role as mediating different aspirations that manifested around the site, thus its conflict resolution, was demonstrated by its selection of recommendations that could command 'the broadest possible support from all sections of society' (Maze/Long Kesh Consultation Panel, hereafter, MCP 2005: 10). A mixed, even eclectic, zoned development included a multi-sports stadium in a Sport Zone, a Rural Excellence and Equestrian Zone, a hotel and leisure village, an International Centre of Conflict Transformation and a Community Zone, light industrial development, a healthcare part and a regional arts centre. The Panel tried to fit all proposals into the space, but the two proposals prioritised were described as 'government-led' and set to 'proceed simultaneously and with all possible speed' (MCP 2005: 10).

In the weeks before the publication of the Maze Consultation Panel's report, the Environment and Heritage Services Northern Ireland, the state body for heritage matters, listed a 'representative' number of buildings: a compound, an H block, the administration buildings, the hospital. The preservation of particular prison buildings informed the Panel but it is their *Report* and not the official heritage management decisions that have affected the site itself and post-conflict heritage more generally. It is around the new buildings, the stadium and the International Centre for Conflict Transformation that a post-conflict heritage was articulated. At this point, the official process of listing was largely unnoticed.

The multi-sports stadium was largest single structure proposed for the site, requiring a disproportionate amount of any investment, justified because it would define the site as a visitor destination. The *Final Report* dwelt upon its social benefits at some length, making a case for its positive contribution to conflict resolution: 'the potential to play an important part in promoting a shared society' (MCP 2005: 11). Northern Ireland's 'three main sporting bodies', the Gaelic Athletic Association, the Irish Football Association and the Irish Rugby Football Union, were all offered a stake in the same place. Shared use was central to its role in reconciliation. As a new location, 'home ground', for the fixtures of these different sports (Gaelic football, football and rugby) and for their associated communities (nationalist and republican, unionist and loyalist), the stadium challenged the sectarian geography that characterises the cultural life in Northern Ireland; it provided space, and the same space, for different 'cultural traditions', with the hope the stadium itself would promote 'tolerance and respect for diversity' (MCP 2005: 11).

The role of the International Centre for Conflict Transformation was similar to that of the stadium, complimentary to a great extent. It, too, would contribute to 'promoting a shared society'. It would provide 'a facility that would support and facilitate the ongoing processes of dialogue and building trust and confidence within and between communities'. Conference, office and archive rooms were envisaged as a shared space in which conflict resolution of the conventional kind, that is, talks, would occur. But it was also conceived as 'a neutral, inclusive and constructive place apart' (MCP 2005: 14). Whilst the multi-sports stadium and the International Centre for Conflict Transformation were both new buildings, the former seemed to carry the future, whilst the latter looked, just a little, to the past. A small note to bear in mind '[s]ensitivity to built heritage did not detract from the contemporary design aspirations for the stadium: 'the best of its type in these islands' (MCP 2005: 11). Spatial and political connection between the International Centre for Conflict Transformation and the preserved buildings was closer; the Panel stated,

> Since part of the purpose of the Centre would be to acknowledge and learn from the past while looking to and building for the future, it would be fitting to do so in a setting which played a major role in the conflict.
>
> (MCP 2005: 11)

It is only in relation to the International Conflict Transformation Centre that the prison buildings feature in the report and they only do so as background. They are just there without interpretation: 'Straight forward information should be available on site for those wishing visit either the centre or the protected buildings' (MCP 2005: 17). Their heritage is not mentioned. Indeed, the *Final Report* could be read as one long announcement of how to supplant an old regime of meaning for a new one, a rebranding exercise. The whole site, stadium and International Conflict Transformation Centre would be covered with 'key brand or recognition symbol for the site'. An international art and design competition might supply 'iconic art elements in the specification sufficient to signify the major social investment in promoting peace and prosperity and the transformation of society' (MCP 2005: 16), from 'symbol of conflict' to 'symbol of on-going transformation from conflict to peace' (MCP 2005: 14). Thus a commercial language, often antithetical to heritage, contained both hope and optimism that the meaning of the prison could be changed. This was not without its problems, played out in later period, for it denied the specific historical significance of the site.

Government management

The second phase of post-conflict heritage began, I suggest, when the consultation process ended. This period is defined by government involvement. A cross-party group of Members of the Legislative Assembly, under the auspices of the Office of the First Minister and Deputy First Minister of the Northern Ireland Executive, was convened as the Maze/Long Kesh Monitoring Group to receive the *Final Report* of the Maze/Long Kesh Consultation Group. The purpose of the cross-party group was 'implementation strategy', to consider how practically and financially such the plans in their *Report* could be brought into being. The group generated planning scenarios based on where buildings, the stadium and the Centre for Conflict Transformation in particular, would be located in the site, and the transport networks required to make these, especially the former, viable. Whilst the Long Kesh/Maze Monitoring Group declaimed they were allocating without resources for government decisions, their work was grounded in the territory of economy, which appeared safer than that of history.

Post-conflict heritage was bound to economic development once government took up its control of heritage sites. Economic advantage began to be presented as the primary purpose of heritage; this economic heritage discourse, a version of an Authoritative Heritage Discourse (Smith 2006), was underpinned by an economic mechanism, the Regeneration and Reform Initiative, through which sites managed by the Northern Ireland Office or Home Office were transferred to Northern Ireland Executive, from British government to that of Northern Ireland. Long Kesh Maze was one of four, including Crumlin Road Gaol, the Magherafelt security base and Ebrington Barracks transferred without charge in 2002 for reinvestment. The Maze/Long Kesh Monitoring Group released a Masterplan in May 2006. Hope and optimism for shared spaces or place apart was dissembled into a notion of economic benefit. A rhetoric of conflict resolution remained in one statement released to the press. Monitoring Group Deputy Chair, Paul Butler, described The International Centre for Conflict Transformation as symbolising 'where we have come from in this society and points us in the direction of where we want to go, towards a society which looks outward in hope and not inward in fear' (Maze/Long Kesh Monitoring Group, hereafter, MMG 2006b). He repeated a well-known pacifist phrase that hints at productive gain. 'It is not a cliché to say this is really about turning swords into ploughshares' (MMG 2006b). Monitoring Group Chair, Edwin Poots, however, associated the International Centre for Conflict Transformation with the past of the site offset by the future promised by the stadium. He stated, 'we believe a balance has been struck between recognising heritage in the form of the International Centre for Conflict Transformation and embracing a dynamic future symbolised by the multi-purpose sports stadium and other developments' (MMG 2006b).

The multi-sports stadium was largest single structure proposed for the site, requiring a disproportionate amount of any investment, justified because it would define the site as a visitor destination. The economic benefit it would bring, including becoming a 2012 Olympic venue if built in time, seemed to convince the Maze/Long Kesh Monitoring Group that it was a structure around which agreement about the whole site could be secured. Its symbolic role was scaled down. Some detail was added: it was stated that the stadium would have a capacity for 'about 42,000 spectators' and not only used for Gaelic sports, rugby and football but for 'open air concerts and other large events'. It would also 'contain a hotel, conference facilities, and offices'. Rather vaguely, it was noted that the stadium could provide for 'a range of community uses', including helping to 'fulfil needs of young people' (Maze/Long Kesh Monitoring Group, hereafter, MMG 2006a), but the concept of shared space between different communities is absent, along with the rhetoric of conflict resolution that suffused the earlier *Final Report*. Only in the concluding comments about the social and economic potential of the whole site does the *Masterplan* revert to the Maze/Long Kesh Consultative Panel's vision of conflict resolution at the site:

> The overriding objective is to provide an internationally recognisable physical expression of the ongoing transformation from conflict to peace and to provide an inclusive, shared resource for the people of the region and beyond, reflecting the broad range of aspirations expressed during the work undertaken by the Maze Consultation Panel.
>
> (MMG 2006a: 121)

It was in this phase of post-conflict heritage, government-led heritage practice that the site itself was transformed. Demolition began. The partial listing, the Regeneration and Reform Initiative, the *Final* report of the Maze/Long Kesh Consultation Panel, the Masterplan of its Monitoring Group, all paved the way for demolition (Figure 6.2). The act of destruction appeared as one of developments, like the clearing of a pathway to the site, moving forward, to use a phrase of the peace process.

The financial offer of the future facing multi-sports stadium, intended to solicit agreement since it had none of the historical weight of the International Conflict Resolution Centre associated with the preserved parts of the prison

Figure 6.2 Demolition of H blocks (2006). Photograph by Louise Purbrick.

and the idea of a museum, was opposed, vehemently. Northern Ireland football supporters campaigned against the stadium at the former site. Their opposition was articulated in sporting terms: it was argued that the different size pitches required for Gaelic football and rugby would not allow growing numbers of Northern Ireland football fans to get close enough to the action. There were claims that stadiums never succeed outside major cities combined with criticism of the inadequacy of transport links to the Maze's Lisburn location. But the underlying issue was the past embodied in the preserved prison buildings. The past was not dispelled by its sporting future. Colin Dunn, in a letter to published in March 2006 issue of *When Saturday Comes*, wrote,

> The idea of a national stadium sharing a site with a terrorist museum is a complete anathema to me ... if there are to be museums/memorials then let them be built in the Republican and Loyalist hinterlands, not at a sporting venue.
>
> (Dunn 2006: 44)

Opposition to the stadium became a party position. On 23 June 2007, the *Newsletter* reported that 'Senior DUP figures yesterday queued up to say "no" to a national stadium at the Maze while it includes a "shrine to terrorism"' (Dempster 2007: 8–9). North Belfast DUP MP Nigel Dodds stated, 'However it is dressed up, whatever spin is deployed, the preservation of a section of the H-Blocks – including the hospital wing – would become a shrine to the terrorists who committed suicide in the Maze in the 1980s' (McGinn 2007: 8). The media narrative had been rumbling on. It was continuous noise against which the second phase in the politics of heritage of Long Kesh/Maze got underway and was now heard more loudly by the politicians than by the artists, activists and community groups that shaped the debate in the earlier phase. In 2009, the Sports Minister and DUP MLA Gregory Campbell announced that multi-sports stadium would not be built at the site.

All heritage policies are, to some extent, shaped by party politics at local, regional and national levels: in Charlottesville, US, the Republican Party defence of statues to Confederate generals is just one case in point. Party positions often polarise and especially so in consociational arrangements such as in Northern Ireland. That different communities are represented separately through the duplication of political office allows for the negotiation of differences at governmental level and its entrenchment. Opposing views are assumed and become unwavering positions that bar agreement. Long Kesh/Maze became caught up in consociationalist politics. The period of government involvement in post-conflict heritage is also characterised by the dualism of the conflict itself.

What government-led heritage politics had failed to address was the materiality and meanings of the site, how the buildings continued to contain the past, a Republican past, in particular. The Masterplan was an attempt to draw attention away from the past with the promise of financial gain in the future and thus did not acknowledge meanings. Such meanings could not be wished away. This denial, an attempt to get agreement to the implementation of development plans by avoiding the matter of history of imprisonment and the heritage of conflict, failed. The proximity of new buildings to old ones was a source of opposition: the distance between old and new was unacceptably close.

The loss of stadium meant the site, now razed bar the listed buildings, was in abeyance. Empty, unused and in stasis, it begins to function as a problem of the past and is no more a space of optimism. Driving heritage debates through an economic discourse also leaves hostages to fortune. Investment appears as a cost as well as a profit: the media narrative took detour to position Long Kesh/Maze as money pit. *The Belfast Telegraph* reported, on 14 August 2009, that a 'remediation strategy' preparing new plans for the site, including some decontamination of soil and water, would cost £5 million (Belfast Telegraph 2009). BBC Northern Ireland announced that £12.5 million had already been spent (BBC 2010a). The figures were accompanied by complaints about the waste of taxpayers' money. Without the stadium the International Centre for Conflict Transformation was the sole lead development. The economic promise of the former became attached to the latter, under an amended name, a Peace Building and Conflict Resolution

Facility. Deputy First Minister Martin McGuinness repeated some of the optimism of the Maze Consultative Panel when he announced on 29 July 2010 a European Union funding application for the Long Kesh/Maze site: '"It is anticipated that the centre will be a world-class facility of international importance designed to strengthen our peace-building expertise and to share our experiences with others throughout the world"' (BBC 2010b). First Minister Peter Robinson stuck resolutely to the economic argument for post-conflict heritage. 'The constitution of a development corporation for this strategically important Maze/Long Kesh site will enable us to realise the full economic potential of the site', he noted. 'The site represents a unique opportunity to help revive our economic output in these difficult times' (BBC 2010b). Their announcement was a cue to turn up the volume on the media narrative of inevitable division. 'Row continues over the Maze site plans' ran the headline of an article in the Unionist paper the *Newsletter*, published a few days later (Gray 2010). Fear of the heritage of the prison, or more precisely of the Republican history attached to buildings that prisoners occupied, was raised. A representative of Families Acting for Innocent Relatives, Willie Frazer, quoted at some length, stated, 'When people visit the Maze they will be very quickly steered away from any conflict resolution centre toward the H-block, which in reality will be little more than an obscene shrine to IRA terrorism' (Gray 2010: 7). Again, the concern and cause for disgust was the proximity of the original remaining structures to any additional architecture. The news in August 2012 that Daniel Libeskind would work with Belfast-based architects McAdam Design (Fulcher 2012) on the variously titled £18 million 'new peace building centre', 'conflict transformation centre' or 'Peace and Reconciliation Centre' or 'conflict resolution centre' was followed by another instalment of the same old story.

Daniel Libeskind, architect of post-conflict iconography in Berlin and New York, did fulfil, albeit briefly, the hopes of the Maze Consultation Panel for buildings 'specified to the highest architectural standards' that would carry a 'key brand or recognition symbol for the site'. It globalised the site; it was part of a trend of heritage management across the world that cultivated reconciliation through economic regeneration (de Jong and Rowlands 2008). However, as Patricia Lundy and Mark McGovern note, the global patterns of conflict resolution are not simply played out or straightforwardly reproduced in Northern Ireland. The question of '[h]ow should a society emerging from conflict remember and deal with the violence and injustice of the past' has been preceded by another: 'should we be remembering the past at all?' (Lundy and McGovern 2008: 29).

On 15 August 2013, Peter Robinson called a halt to the plans for a conflict resolution centre of any kind; he claimed there was no wider consensus for construction of new building and spoke of prohibiting public use of preserved buildings. The second phase of government management of post-conflict heritage ends without resolution, indeed, in conflict over the site of Long Kesh/Maze. Heritage had become a repository of unresolved differences about the past. Robinson's withdrawal of support for development at the Long Kesh/Maze site immediately preceded Peter Haass's involvement in brokering power-sharing (Moriarty 2013). Power-sharing in the Northern Ireland Executive had broken down, and the fate of Long Kesh/Maze prison was an integral difficulty in the peace process itself.

Another season of conflict

The third and current phase of post-conflict heritage began unfolding in 2013 and continues to the present day. The past itself is a source of conflict and site of the Long Kesh/Maze, that icon of the Troubles, remains the most contested manifestation. The past, alongside flags and parades, was one of three issues addressed by the 2014 Haass talks. In the early agenda setting stages, it was reported that Long Kesh/Maze itself was to be discussed (Rowan 2013a). It was not. It was ruled out to attempt agreement on other issues. A 'source' quoted in the *Belfast Telegraph* claimed that, initially, 'issues were included that, realistically, were undeliverable, put there to be taken out (such as the Maze peace centre)' (Rowan 2013b).

The whole period of post-conflict heritage, in whatever way that period is distinguished or understood, has been one of restricted access to the site. For the most part of twenty years since the signing of the Good Friday Agreement, the site is not visited or studied, recorded or interpreted in any sustained way. Whilst site is the subject of debate, the contest is over established political meanings rather than those that may be contained in its remaining material forms. Its meanings have tended to be fixed through media narratives and thus according to political perspectives rather than through practices of heritage. Indeed, divisions have thrived, and stalemates sustained by its closure. Lack of investigation of the complex materiality of the prison as a space and a system has permitted a political simplification of history in which a binary opposition is perpetuated: Republican commemoration against Unionist denial.

Although access to the site has always been limited, during the initial hopeful time of post-conflict heritage and conflict resolution, it was possible to apply to the Office of the First Minister and Deputy First Minister to join group tours. Guided by local civil servants working for the Northern Ireland Executive, the tours encompassed the listed buildings (the administration buildings, the hospital, H block 6, compound 19, a section of a wall and a watchtower). There was no wandering. The route was prescribed, and its script presented as intermediate account whilst site was prepared for both development and an agreed interpretation. On this limited tour, with its own prohibitions on entering buildings that were not listed, the whole site could still be seen, and it was possible to gather sense of the scale of the prison and feel its atmosphere. The demolition that came later abolished this view; collapsing buildings and removing the materials from which they were made is an absolute denial of access. What was left of the Long Kesh/Maze has also been open on one weekend of occasional years from 2011 as part of the European Heritage Open Days. Infrequent but less prescribed once at the site, these visits have been welcomed as far as it is possible to tell from visitor figures (200 on the first open day) and online postings.

But tours and open days are the exception. At Long Kesh/Maze there has never been the most basic requirement of access: widely published regular opening times allowing people to enter with anonymity and without announcement. For example, whilst no one was refused permission to join a Northern Ireland Executive guided tour, the act of requesting it cannot be described as publicly accessible: making these arrangements is not the same as just turning up. Public access to sites that are as open as possible, as free as possible to as many people as possible is an imperative of heritage practice: it has become priority above preservation. The purpose of heritage is participation.

Conclusions

I suggest that participation offers an alternative to the denial of access that has fostered the ossification of political positions about the past and future of the Long Kesh/Maze; a reopening rather than closing the site could do the same for its meanings. The political standoff over the conflict resolution centre at site of the H blocks and hospital, a polarisation over the proximity of peace building, was too fixed, too far apart. Consequently, its cause could not be discussed and was excluded from the Haass talks. It is now a political silence that prevented the practice of heritage. It is heritage practice that is required, a practical consideration of strategies through which contested heritage can be made accessible. Potential lies in heritage as participation. This is not a straightforward alternative to heritage as preservation, but it does not rely upon it. Preservation and its role within plans for economic regeneration are dependent upon high-level political decision-making, which is not necessary for participatory events. Participation, moreover, requires no permanent interventions at a site that might fix its meaning for the future. Participation is temporary, a performance, which, as all actions, will leave trace but one that intrudes a little less on the site and certainly does not seek to make structural changes associated with architecture.

Theories of participation have become most fully articulated within art theory that has explored of the relation between art and politics in period of disenfranchisement in the late twentieth and early twenty-first centuries: the reduced public space of neo-liberal regimes and the dominance of the global markets over local communities. Forms of participatory art are traced back to early twentieth century, but participatory art has accumulated a critical mass at since the 1990s. It is one of the 'hallmarks', to borrow a term from Claire Bishop, of 'artistic orientation towards the social in the 1990s'. She observes, 'the work of art as a finite, portable, commodifiable product is reconceived as an ongoing or long-term *project* with an unclear beginning and end; while the audience, previously conceived as 'viewer' or 'beholder', is now repositioned as a co-producer or *participant*' (Bishop 2012). In her introduction to the White Chapel Gallery publication *Participation* she summaries its imperatives. First, to 'create an active subject, one who will be empowered by the experience of physical or symbolic participation'. That experience of participating in art creates 'individual/ collective agency'. Such 'collaborative creativity', second, tends towards a 'non-hierarchical model' that allows for shared authorship; 'more egalitarian and democratic than the creation of a work by a single artist'. Inviting people to participate in space and a process in which they have an equal stake is, third and finally, addressed to a 'crisis in community and collective responsibility'. Whatever its specific project, participatory art attempts 'a restoration of the social bond through a collective elaboration of meaning' (Bishop 2006: 12). For Claire Bishop, the crisis of the late twentieth and early twenty-first centuries is global: capitalist alienation extending across all corners of the world. This scenario may not translate straightforwardly in Northern Ireland in and after conflict, but effects are similar: the dislocation of people from a political sphere, a lack of collective endeavour, an absence of society. Bishop's account of the potential of art participation to breathe renewed life into political subjectivity and to constitute a collective agent of change may seem out of place in the stillness of the closed site of Long Kesh/Maze. That is the point. Its space could be inhabited differently. Furthermore, the practice of participation as a form of shared authorship of art could contribute to a shift in the assumed relationships of opposing communities to the prison. A visitor who is a participant is not a recipient of an already determined meaning but a person who may add to its interpretation.

Current theories of heritage also favour forms of participation. Heritage studies has not simply borrowed from art theory or other philosophical enquires in humanities. Attention to the intangible rather than tangible heritage has led debates about the role of participation in the practice of heritage. Heritage is practiced by people rather than residing in things, located at a site or in specially object; heritage is not set in stone, so to speak. Thus, Rodney Harrison writes of how heritage practice relates to objects: 'We use objects of heritage (artefacts, buildings, sites, landscapes) alongside practices of heritage (languages, music, community commemorations, conservation and preservation of objects or memories from the past) to shape our ideas about our past, present and future' (Harrison 2009: 9). Practice and the object, Harrison suggests, are equally significant and are dependent upon each other. However, he does present practice 'in addition' to its certain 'physical' form (Harrison 2009: 9). The argument has been taken further. A radical rejection of heritage as an object is associated with the work of Laurajane Smith, she suggests: 'Heritage is not a thing, site or place, nor is it "found", rather heritage is the multiple processes of meaning making that occur as material heritage places or intangible heritage events are identified, defined, managed, exhibited and visited' (Smith 2012).

If Smith's argument is taken seriously, the heritage of Long Kesh/Maze has hardly happened yet. Lack of access has not allowed it. Its heritage could be permitted to unfold through forms of participation; its histories revealed by people who, for whatever reason, have a connection to the site. Participatory heritage practice, which intersects and overlaps with participatory art practice, has a track record elsewhere, at other contested sites of conflict. The development of the court and museum at Constitution Hill, Johannesburg, the site of an apartheid jail, began by repopulating the space with parties, raves to be most accurate and it remains a music venue. The global heritage project, Sites of Conscience, has initiated and supported many dialogues about the relationship between past and present oppression and exploitation at sites across the world. All are dependent upon participation: physical presence at the site. Examples abound and could be applied to Long Kesh/Maze.

Bibliography

BBC News. (2002). Empey Opposes Jail Museums. 4 May [online] Available at: http://news.bbc.co.uk/1/hi/northern_ireland/1967379.stm [Accessed 17 October 2017].

BBC. (2010a). Maze Prison "Indecision Bill" Cost 12.5 Million. 19 May [online] Available at: http://news.bbc.co.uk/1/hi/northern_ireland/8690992.stm [Accessed 17 October 2017].

BBC. (2010b). Maze Site Set to Be Redeveloped. 29 July [online] Available at: www.bbc.co.uk/news/uknorthern-ireland-10809186 [Accessed 7 November 2011].

Belfast Telegraph. (2009). Maze Site Cleaning Scheme Put Out to Tender. *Belfast Telegraph*, 10 November [online]. Available at: www.belfasttelegraph.co.uk/business/business-news/maze-site-cleaning-scheme-put-out-to-tender-14557375.html [Accessed 17 October 2017].

Bishop, C. (2012). *Artificial Hells: Participatory Art and the Politics of Spectatorship*. London: Verso.

Bishop, C. (2006). Viewers as Producers. In: Bishop, C. ed. *Participation*. London: Whitechapel Gallery and MIT Press, pp. 10–17.

Challis, J. (1999). *The Northern Ireland Prison Service 1920–1990. A History*. Belfast: Northern Ireland Prison Service.

Cohen, S. (1985). *Visions of Social Control: Crime, Punishment and Classification*. Cambridge: Polity.

de Jong, F. and Rowlands, M. (2008). Postconflict Heritage. *Journal of Material Culture*, 13(2), pp. 131–134.

Dorell, E. (2005). Problems and Opposition Dog Maze Stadium Plans. *The Architects' Journal*, 12 August [online]. Available at: www.architectsjournal.co.uk/news/problems-and-opposition-dog-maze-stadium-plans/583950.article [Accessed 14 January 2010].

Dempster, S. (2007). Not While It's Got a Shrine to Terrorists. *Newsletter*, 23 June, pp. 8–9.

Dunn, C. (2006). *When Saturday Comes*, 229, pp. 1–44.

Graham, B. and McDowell, S. (2007). Meaning in the Maze: the Heritage of Long Kesh. *Cultural Geographies*, 14(3) pp. 343–368.

Gray, B. (2010). Row Continues over Maze Site Plans. *Newsletter*, 2 August [online]. Available at: www.newsletter.co.uk/news/demolish-h-block-say-loyalists-1-1867287 [Accessed 15 October 2017].

Harrison, R. (2009). *Understanding the Politics of Heritage*. Manchester: Manchester University Press.

Flynn, M.K. (2011). Decision-making and Contested Heritage in Northern Ireland: The Former Maze Prison/Long Kesh. *Irish Political Studies*, 26(3), pp. 383–401.

Foucault, M. (1979). *Discipline and Punish: The Birth of the Prison*. Harmondswoth: Penguin.

Fulcher, M. (2012). Libeskind and McAdam Win Maze Prison Peace Centre Job. *The Architects Journal*, 31 August [online]. Available at: www.architectsjournal.co.uk/home/libeskind-and-mcadam-win-maze-prison-peace-centre-job/8635093.article [Accessed 17 October 2017].

Healing through Remembering. www.healingthroughremembering/org [Accessed 17 October 2017].

Keenan, D. (2006). History of Prison Stands as Microcosm of Northern Conflict. *Irish Times*, 30 October [online]. Available at: www.irishtimes.com/news/history-of-prison-stands-as-a-microcosm-of-northern-conflict-1.1022676 [Accessed 5 August 2015].

Lundy, P. and McGovern, M. (2008). Telling Stories, Facing Truths: Memory, Justice and Post-Conflict Transition. In: Coulter, C. and Murray, M. eds. *Northern Ireland After the Troubles: A Society in Transition*, Manchester: Manchester University Press, pp. 29–48.

Maze/Long Kesh Consultation Panel. (2005). *Final Report: New future for Maze/Long Kesh*. Maze/Long Kesh Consultation Panel.

Maze/Long Kesh Monitoring Group. (2006a). *Maze/Long Kesh Masterplan and Implementation Strategy*, Final Report.

Maze/Long Kesh Monitoring Group. (2006b). Maze/Long Kesh Monitoring Group Welcomes Masterplan, *Press Release*.

McAtackney, L. (2014). *An Archaeology of the Troubles: The Dark Heritage of Long Kesh/Maze Prison*. Oxford: Oxford University Press.

McGinn, D. (2007). No "Shrine to Terror" at Maze Demand. *Irish News*, 23 June, p. 8.

McKeown, L. (2001). *Out of Time. Irish Republican Prisoners Long Kesh, 1972–2000*. Belfast: Beyond the Pale Publications.

Moriarty, G. (2013). Richard Haass Faces Northern Political Process Going into Reverse. *The Irish Times*, 17 September [online]. Available at: www.irishtimes.com/news/politics/richard-haass-faces-northern-political-process-going-into-reverse-1.1529630 [Accessed 17 October 2017].

Rowan, B. (2013a). Maze Site to Feature in Critical Haass Discussions. *Belfast Telegraph*, 16 December [online]. Available at: www.belfasttelegraph.co.uk/news/northern-ireland/maze-site-to-feature-in-critical-haass-discussions-29841200.html [Accessed 17 October 2017].

Rowan, B. (2013b). Richard Haass Talks: Twists and Turns Stripped Away the Details of the Proposals. *Belfast Telegraph*, 31 December [online]. Available at: www.belfasttelegraph.co.uk/opinion/columnists/brian-rowan/richard-haass-talks-twists-

and-turns-stripped-away-the-details-of-the-proposals-29877997.html [Accessed 17 October 2017].

Ryder, C. (2000). *Inside the Maze. The Untold Story of the Northern Ireland Prison Service.* London: Metheun.

Smith, L. (2006). *The Uses of Heritage.* London: Routledge.

Smith, L. (2012). Discourses of Heritage: Implications for Archaeological Community Practice. *Neuvo Mundo, Mundos Neuvos,* [online] Available at: http://nuevomundo.revues.org/64148 [Accessed 17 October 2017].

Welch, M. (2016). Political Imprisonment and the Sanctity of Death: Performing Heritage in 'Troubled' Ireland. *International Journal of Heritage Studies,* 22(9), pp. 664–678.

Wylie, D. (2004). *The Maze.* London: Granta.

7 Discourses and practices of dealing with the spatial legacy of conflict in Belfast

The cases of Crumlin Road Gaol and Girdwood Park

Henriette Bertram

Protracted intrastate conflicts leave their mark on societies, on politics, on the way people organise their everyday lives and on the built environment. This is especially visible in cities, which can become intensive microcosms for tensions in society (Gaffikin and Morrissey 2011). After the conflict is settled officially, the political and societal contexts change dramatically. History and historical 'facts' are reconsidered and interpreted differently. Attitudes and beliefs that have been valid for decades or even centuries, however, do not change at the same pace and may leave society in a state of 'voluntary apartheid' (Baumann 2008: 6). Against this background, societies face the task of coming to terms with the conflictive past. Part of this task is to find a way of dealing with the spatial remnants of the conflict and to decide which strategies for redevelopment and what kinds of future use may be adequate and supportive for the creation of a peaceful society.

This chapter explores the discourse on and practice of dealing with the spatial remnants of conflict in Belfast after the Good Friday Agreement, the strategies applied to the sites and the aims and motives pursued by the various actors involved (see Coyles, this volume, for the hidden ways in which conflict continues to be articulated in the built environment). There is a broad consensus on the fact that the Northern Ireland conflict has impacted enormously on Belfast and vice versa. This consensus, however, seems not to facilitate a systematic policy approach towards the spatial heritage of conflict in the city. Agreement is not only problematic between members of the former conflict parties but also between those who see a need for commemoration and preservation and those who pursue policies of normalisation. It is therefore necessary to look at the strategies 'on the ground' that deal with the history and the stories of places that are connected to the conflict. By doing so, it is possible to find out which aims and motives are important to actors when dealing with the spatial heritage of conflict.

The second section of this chapter outlines the conceptual framework and discusses the role of cities and urban heritage during and after protracted intrastate conflict. In the third section I give a brief overview of post-conflict urban development in Belfast in general to explain the wider context in which the dealing with the spatial remnants in the city is happening. Two sites of spatial heritage of the Northern Ireland conflict in Belfast, Crumlin Road Gaol and Girdwood Park, are the topic of the fourth section. The two places lie adjacent to each other in North Belfast, and each is highly symbolic. Each has been redeveloped in recent years. Yet they are very different to each other, both in discourse and practice. Using the methodology of a discourse analysis, I analyse the strategies employed in the redevelopment of the sites and the aims and motives pursued by the various actors involved. The analysis is based on documents (newspaper and scientific articles, planning documents, minutes, websites, flyers and brochures) and interviews with representatives of organisations and bodies involved in the redevelopment processes. Some of the interviews are used in this chapter to highlight the points of views of the actors. I investigate which aims and motives dominate the redevelopment processes and discuss whether the strategies used in these two urban renewal projects can be regarded as responsible and sensitive ways of dealing with the spatial remnants of conflict.

The role of cities and urban heritage during and after protracted intrastate conflict

Post-conflict societies can be characterised by a variety of different and sometimes contradictory tendencies. Most peace processes do not proceed in a linear way once a peace agreement is signed. More often than not there are setbacks, sometimes violent. Furthermore, peace agreements on a national or elite level can provide a political framework for change, but the attitudes and behaviour of people only change over the course of a long period of time. The actual barriers and the physical danger are mostly gone, but the former conflict parties remain segregated and separated, not only in politics but in almost all aspects of daily life, from living to work to leisure activities (Baumann 2008). Due to the complexity of the new situation, peace processes invoke deep feelings of insecurity within post-conflict societies – even though peace itself is generally welcomed and regarded as positive (Lederach 2005; Mac Ginty 2010). A desire to retreat further into the safety of one's own community can emerge.

Even though protracted intrastate conflicts usually have their origins on the national or regional level, their effects are experienced locally and mostly in cities as the economic, political and cultural hubs of the region in conflict. Cities are shaped by conflict spatially and socially, and in a variety of other ways; in turn, their inhabitants, their political and societal actors, shape the conflict and its proceedings (Bollens 2000, 2013). The social repercussions and the spatial remnants of conflict are therefore closely intertwined and may take years or even decades to deal with. In cities, the spatial remnants or heritage of conflict are ubiquitous and manifold. They cannot be reduced to obvious places like memorial sites or physical barriers but can take the form of functional buildings, places of day-to-day activities or even spatial practices, like the flying of flags or the painting of curbstones (Kliot and Mansfeld 1999; Schofield et al. 2002; Calame and Charlesworth 2009; Bakshi 2012; Maddison 2016).

Heritage has been defined as the contemporary use of the past (Graham et al. 2000), as an element of history that, through its use and interpretation in the present, fulfils a need in the present and contributes to the creation of a collective identity (Dwyer and Alderman 2008). In any society heritage may invoke dissonance, though this need not be expressed in violent intrastate conflict. On the one hand, dissonance results from the double function of heritage as a cultural resource for the community and an economic resource staged for touristic use. On the other hand, interpretations of events and historic persons differ widely between the various societal groups and actors so that multiple perspectives feed into the use and display of heritage (Frank 2016). The interpretation of elements of heritage that are seen as dominant reveals the power structures of a society. Heritage can therefore take on a symbolic quality that links an element of history to the struggle for power and societal significance of a particular group (Assmann 2007; Meusburger 2011).

In post-conflict cities, views on the past, and of the related places of heritage, often seem to be particularly irreconcilable (Lederach 2005; Baumann 2008). Even after the conflict is officially settled, it is interpreted very differently between the former parties to the conflict, particularly where each group has fundamentally different commemoration needs and demands. The heritage of the conflict itself becomes contested, a 'dark heritage' that is particularly difficult to deal with (Lennon and Foley 2010). To find adequate means of dealing with it is one of the most challenging tasks for the newly emerging society. Prior to the Second World War in the West, most elements of dark heritage were ignored or deliberately destroyed because they did not fit in with the values and beliefs of the new societies emerging from empire. Recently, and especially after the regime change in the formerly communist countries of Eastern Europe, strategies to preserve and transform elements of heritage in a way that allows critical reflection have been applied successfully. Others have been turned into tourist attractions (Speitkamp 1997; Siebeck 2007; Czepczyński 2008; Sabrow 2015).

Finding an adequate way of dealing with dark heritage is made even more difficult by the fact that in addition to the different views of the former parties to the conflict, there are those actors and societal groups who would rather forget about the conflict as soon as possible, engaging in a process towards 'normalisation' (Nagle 2009). Normalisation can include a range of aspects that comprise a strong outside orientation: the promotion of tourism, investment in and revitalisation of the destroyed and decayed built environment, and the creation and communication of a new image (Bartetzky 2007; Bertram 2014). Conflict and the commemoration of the conflict are seen as an obstacle to normalisation and sometimes even to the development of the 'new' society (Charlesworth 2006; Till and Jonker 2009; Larkin 2010). One result of this strategy can be the emergence of 'pockets of affluence in capital cities and select tourist and recreational areas' that actually give the impression of a perfectly 'normal' society (Guttal 2005: 79). These newly emerging places and their attractions do not have the same significance for all members of the society. They may enhance and make visible the socio-economic inequalities of the society and thereby at the same transcend and overlap traditional conflict lines (Bittner 2010; O'Dowd and Komarova 2011; Muir 2014).

It is against this background that societies negotiate the potential redevelopment of spatial remnants of conflict. The chosen narrative of the past when dealing with symbolic and often contentious sites reveals which groups are most powerful in the post-conflict era and how past events are being interpreted by which actors. This means that when there is little public or documented discourse on a subject, one way of analysing it is to look at heritage and the discourse that emerges around certain elements of the urban environment. These sites can be regarded as proxies for the wider discourse which is being avoided. Bauriedl calls these elements of the built environment 'local stories' (Bauriedl 2007, 2009). They can be used to reconstruct the aims and motives attached to them, and thereby allow us to draw conclusions regarding the interests of the actors involved and the overall narrative of historic events or time periods. Thus, this built heritage reveals how post-conflict societies see themselves, how they want to see themselves in the future and how they want to be seen from outside.

Post-conflict urban development in Belfast

Although Northern Ireland officially became a post-conflict society after the signing of the Good Friday Agreement in 1998, the overall 'piecemeal approach' towards dealing with the past (Bell 2002) is visible too in the approach towards the spatial remnants of the conflict. It can be observed very well in Belfast as the capital city and the biggest conurbation in Northern Ireland. The city has been shaped spatially and socially by the conflict, with some of the deprived areas of North and West Belfast the most badly affected in terms of victims of violence and physical destruction. Some would even call the city itself a victim of the Troubles (Hepburn 2004: 182; Gaffikin and Morrissey 2006: 879–880).

Yet there seems to be little appetite and maybe even little imagination to deal with the places left by the conflict that can be found all over the city. Many of them have taken on a highly symbolic meaning due to their connection with the conflict. Strategic development plans and other planning documents, however, hardly mention those sites. One relatively recent policy approach is the government strategy Together: Building a United Community (TBUC), published in 2013. TBUC aims to dismantle all interface barriers – the so-called 'peace walls' – in Northern Ireland by 2023, which is seen as unrealistic, even though some barriers actually have been at least partly removed. Nevertheless, TBUC deals with one type of spatial remnant only, the interface barriers, and ultimately allows for only one way of dealing with them. Belfast remains deeply segregated and physically fragmented, whilst at the same time its physical appearance as well as its image has been changing rapidly during the last twenty years. Current urban development and planning in Belfast is mostly concerned with the transportation of a positive and renewed image to visitors, investors and inhabitants, an approach that has been labelled as 'lipstick on the gorilla' (Neill 2006). It focusses on the revitalisation of the city centre and waterfront area; quarterisation and theming of city space, and shows a general orientation towards culture, events and leisure (Bertram 2017).

These new developments are almost equally praised and criticised. On the one hand, tourist numbers have been on the rise in recent years, and many inhabitants enjoy using the new places. On the other hand, mostly critical scholars disagree with the 'twin-speed' in which the city is developing. They argue that the new attractions are first and foremost geared towards tourists and an affluent middle- or upper-class audience, and that all those new places do not change the realities for the working classes who are still living in deprived and segregated circumstances (Murtagh 2008; Nagle 2009; O'Dowd and Komarova 2011). The logic behind the new developments is criticised as neo-liberalised, superficial and inauthentic. These attempts to normalise the society by means of consumerism thereby avoid dealing with the legacy of the conflict through a meaningful and consistent approach towards the past.

Crumlin Road Gaol and Girdwood Park

Unsurprisingly, it is difficult to carve out a dominant narrative of the conflict in Belfast between the fundamentally different interpretations of history by the former parties to the conflict and under the pressure of the logic of moving on and normalisation. The diversity of interests and interpretations that flow from this are exemplified in two local stories, Crumlin Road Gaol and Girdwood Park, and the strategies applied in dealing with the symbolism of both places. They lie adjacent to each other in North Belfast, in an area that has been described as 'a site of much violence' (Fallon 2011: 15), as a 'microcosm for the conflict' (Interview with OFMDFM official, conducted by HB, 29 April 2014) and even as 'just the worst of everything' (Interview with Unionist community worker 1, conducted by HB, 7 May 2015). The strategies applied in both projects seem to have been able to establish a consensus that overcomes the dissonance regarding the interpretation of places closely associated with the conflict.

Crumlin Road Gaol, known formally as HMP Belfast, was designed by the renowned English architect Charles Lanyon. It was opened in 1845 and used as a prison until 1996. Especially from the 1960s onwards, many people who had been arrested for conflict-related crimes were imprisoned there and so became one of the key symbolic buildings during the conflict. It was officially given to the Office of the First Minister and Deputy First Minister (OFMDFM) in 2003 by the British Government and is now listed as a 'splendid example of Belfast's Victorian architecture' (Ulster Architectural Heritage Society 2016). The conflict-related symbolism of the site is complex and closely intertwined with the surrounding neighbourhoods in North Belfast. Many inhabitants felt and still feel a connection with the Gaol because they were either detained there themselves or went to visit friends or relatives who were. This closeness becomes evident in the following, rather personal statements of stakeholders involved in the redevelopment process:

> When we were in it, it was riddled with cockroaches and mice. A very aggressive place to be in at times. And it was jam-packed with people who were in. [...] And there's so many people who went through the jails from these areas, it sort of seems really surreal and weird sometimes going in to Crumlin Road Gaol for meetings.
>
> (Interview with Nationalist community worker 1,
> conducted by HB, 29 April 2014)

> Crumlin Road Gaol was viewed by everybody as a bad place...I had friends who were killed in it. There was an IRA bomb in the kitchen; two friends of mine blew up. 35 IRA men escaped from it. So each community will have their view.
>
> (Interview with Unionist community worker 2,
> conducted by HB, 6 May 2014)

Girdwood Park lies adjacent to the Gaol and was formerly known as Girdwood Barracks. The site was used by the British Army between 1970 and 2005, and was viewed very differently in nationalist and unionist communities. For people in the unionist community it was considered to be 'a natural part of the security arrangements that were required at that time' (Interview with Unionist community worker 2, conducted by HB, 6 May 2014). A nationalist community worker describes the connotation it had for his community very differently: 'Girdwood, that's what they came from to patrol our areas in their army vehicles and their blackened faces with their guns and their helicopters and land rovers' (Interview with Nationalist community worker 1, conducted by HB, 29 April 2014).

Other than that, there was no immediate interaction between the surrounding communities and Girdwood as the following statements show:

> It was a kind of dead space for local people because it wasn't anywhere you went. It was just a big corrugated ugly fence that you lived beside. And I'm not sure people had a lot of interaction with it.
>
> (Interview with former Police Officer,
> conducted by HB, 28 April 2014)

Girdwood Barsracks was an army barracks for all the time that I ever remember. And was not in the public realm, [...] it was not where you lived your life. It was not what you came up against. You know, it was there but it wasn't part of you.

(Interview with Unionist community worker 3, conducted by HB, 7 May 2014)

After the army vacated the site, it was bought by Department for Social Development (DSD), and the barracks were flattened without further public debate.

Redevelopment of the sites: discourse and practice

In 2006, the Northern Ireland Office set up an Advisory Panel with about twenty members – politicians, community representatives and urban planning experts – to oversee the development of a joint Masterplan for both sites. It was going to be the 'biggest regeneration project ever planned for north Belfast' (O'Dowd and Komarova 2011: 2016). The setting up of the Advisory Board marks the initiation of the public discourse around the two sites. The first action of the Advisory Panel was to agree on the following Mission Statement:

> To create a regeneration project of international significance which brings maximum economic, social and environmental benefits to the local and wider community and in doing so creates a vibrant, inclusive and diverse environment which attracts present and future generations to work, live and play.
>
> (Building Design Partnership 2007: 4)

This statement was later adopted by the planning firm commissioned to carry out the redevelopment of the site. Furthermore, the Masterplan adds another possible narrative to the redevelopment of the Gaol. To the authors of the plan, the Gaol is a 'high-quality, landmark building which has the potential to transform the appearance of the lower Crumlin Road and attract investment to the area' (Building Design Partnership 2007: 9), not primarily a site marked or even scarred by conflict. The wording used in both of these quotations shows that the Chair of the Advisory Board, as well as the planning professionals and consultants from outside, has high expectations for the redevelopment project.

Unfortunately, the Advisory Panel was unable to reach consensus on a number of issues, first and foremost on the question whether there should be housing on the former Girdwood Barracks site – and, if yes, what kind of housing. The site is situated on an interface between nationalist and unionist communities, and each has very different needs and wishes regarding the provision of housing. Whilst many in the growing and statistically younger nationalist communities would have liked to see mostly housing on the site; people in the unionist communities, however, feared for the site to lose its neutral character and become a site used by nationalists only (Building Design Partnership 2007: 6; Muir 2014: 59) (these same anxieties were manifest in the social housing debates in the 1970s, as identified by Coyles in this volume). The one thing on which there was some consensus between the communities was that whatever housing would be built on the site, it should be social housing to alleviate the need in the area and its deprived neighbourhoods (Interview with Nationalist community worker 2, conducted by HB, 30 April 2014).

The planning professionals had a different imperative. They advocated in favour of building apartments and different types of tenure. Their aim was to attract a wide mix of people to the new quarter:

> One of our ideas was to provide more student accommodation in Girdwood as an example of just one type of property tenure, to encourage students to come and live there. That's not gentrification, it's just a way of getting a broader mix of people into the area, of adding to its variety and bringing extra spending power to the benefit of local service providers. What is needed is a mixed community in all senses of the word.
> (Interview with Member of Advisory Panel and planning
> expert, conducted by HB, 18 June 2014)

Even though it is not completely agreed, the Chair of the Advisory Board presented the draft Masterplan to the then Minister for Social Development. Due to ongoing protest on the part of the local communities, the process came to a halt at that point, and the OFMDFM assumed responsibility for the immediate future of the project. Subsequently, an Equality Impact Assessment was carried out which recommended uncoupling the redevelopment of the two sites.

From that moment onwards, the development of the Gaol seems to be largely uncontentious and was taken forward relatively quickly, led by the North Belfast Community Action Unit as a subunit of OFMDFM. The building was refurbished in the following years. It was opened as a visitor attraction and cultural venue in December 2012 by two former inmates, the then First and Deputy First Ministers Peter Robinson and Martin McGuinness. Visitors can book guided tours through the building as well as attend concerts and art exhibitions. Some of the rooms can be booked for conferences or private functions. The history of the conflict told during the tours is incorporated into a wider historical context. Visitors will hear about the conflict and about the role of the Gaol and prisoners in it. They will also hear about Victorian times, about children being imprisoned, about the suffragettes and about executions that took place in the building. The building itself is restored to almost its original condition: it looks as it might have in 1845, with almost every trace of the heavy security equipment of the 1970s onwards has been removed. History, and especially the contentious parts, is presented in a way that is easily digestible.

The most prevalent aim of the redevelopment project is still to attract visitors from outside. At the same time, OFMDFM takes great care to bring in local people as well. They explicitly aim to establish the Gaol as a shared space, for example, by employing local people and by organising events for the surrounding communities:

> The local communities challenged me to say: 'We don't want you to develop this building where it's just for people from outside the area to come in, art exhibitions have nothing to do with us, they're for rich people'. So we had to maintain confidence there, and we also had to address the issue where those sorts of things are available to local people. [...] So we had to deal with that in two ways: Breaking down the perception of people outside the area so we can get them in; and also bringing in local people.
>
> (Interview with OFMDFM official,
> conducted by HB, 29 April 2014)

Within the communities, it is widely recognised that this double aim has been fulfiled:

> So the Gaol then adopted some of that ethos. And employed young apprentices and people from all the communities in the project. We could see from very early on that it was a genuine attempt to build shared space because the people who worked on it were from all over.
>
> (Interview with Unionist community worker 2,
> conducted by HB, 6 May 2014)

At the same time, there is a strong focus on social (as opposed to the contentious political) history to highlight the common experiences of many "ordinary people" in the surrounding communities as opposed to the still contentious political history:

> The Gaol is successful in two ways: It brings in tourists and foreigners, but it's also really successful in a way that – and this is heresy to say – in a way that Titanic isn't. [...] A lot of people go to Titanic Belfast when they have visitors in town. I know a lot of community groups who go to Crumlin Road Gaol because it's really interesting, it gives an opportunity to talk about politics and social history. It's of the people. [...] So the Crumlin Road Gaol has been hugely successful in attracting both audiences, that local community audience.
>
> (Interview with Project Manager Belfast City
> Council, conducted by HB, 1 May 2014)

There is a strong narrative that 'everyone was a victim of the Troubles', regardless of background or actual involvement in the conflict. The conflict appears as a largely abstract and depersonalised time period during which all people in all the communities suffered. Furthermore, new layers of historic significance are added to illustrate the progress of the peace process and to show that 1998 was not the 'end of history' for Northern Ireland. The redevelopment is perceived as the spatial manifestation of 'swords to ploughshares', as a 'reminder of just how far we have come' in the media and wider public (Clarke 2014). This became especially evident in 2014, when the Queen was guided through the building by Peter Robinson and Martin McGuinness, an image that combined well with the touristic appeal of the site.

Public debate on Girdwood, by contrast, quietened down for quite a while after the failure of the Advisory Panel. It seems that there was no strong idea for the use of the site that would have been able to convince a majority within all communities. In 2010 and 2011, two successive (nationalist) DSD ministers publicly announced that their department would start to build houses on the site, replacing 'watchtowers and sangers' with 'windows and washing lines' on the site, creating 'a much brighter future for everyone in the area' (Belfast Telegraph 2011). The announcements were followed by foreseeable protest by unionist politicians and communities. Girdwood is said to be a 'political football' during this period (Muir 2014), showing very well the struggle for interpretative dominance on behalf of all actors involved.

Only in 2012 was a compromise plan, facilitated by yet another – this time unionist – DSD minister presented to the public. The heart of that plan was a Community Hub building with the rest of the site providing for sports and leisure purposes. Two smallish plots are designated for residential development (Department for Social Development 2011; Devenport 2012). The new plan was 'explicitly a compromise plan' and as such criticised by a large number of people (DSD official, 6 May 2014), especially those who were hoping for a more ambitious scheme. They are disappointed and see it as a 'lost opportunity' (Interview with Member of Advisory Panel and planning expert, conducted by HB, 18 June 2014). At the same time, many residents and community representatives seem to be quite content about it, with agreement between politicians in the area – 'something that's never happened before in North Belfast' – being welcomed as a success in itself (Interview with Nationalist community worker 2, conducted by HB, 30 April 2014). The development of the Hub is then to be taken forward by Belfast City Council and funded by the Special European Union Programmes Body (SEUPB, 'PEACE Programme'). Belfast City Council establishes a Community Hub discussion forum in order to manage the process and to agree on details for the use of the building. Members are officials from DSD and OFMDFM, community representatives as well as politicians from North Belfast. The participation and active engagement of the communities has now become much more important than it was during the first process. This is seen as the key to its success by almost all of its members. The building of the hub started in April 2014, and it opened in January 2016.

It is used for a variety of purposes: there is a gym, multipurpose rooms, community and youth space as well as classrooms for courses with Belfast Metropolitan College.

It was stressed throughout the process that whatever was to go on the site would have to be 'safe and welcoming for all' and that it was important to create a shared space that people from all the communities and beyond would use (Interview with Project Manager Belfast City Council, conducted by HB, 1 May 2014). It was hoped that Girdwood would tackle 'some of the long term issues facing local communities, including poverty and health problems and provide more opportunities for young people' (Belfast City Council n.d.). The contentious past of the site was not mentioned throughout the whole process. It is still regarded as 'not agreed', as not what the communities want and certainly not what City Council wants and aspires for the site:

> Well, because it's not agreed, you know. And also, why would you freeze-frame it as an army barracks and not as a parkland? Just because it's kind of sexy from a conflict point of view, why would you do that? It may be interesting for tourists, but actually people have to live beside it.
> (Interview with Project Manager Belfast City
> Council, conducted by HB, 1 May 2014)

As a result, the redevelopment, the use of the site and the Hub building focus on meeting the present needs of the surrounding communities. Deprivation and division were interpreted as part of the legacy of the conflict and tackled explicitly during the redevelopment process. At the same time, the conflict itself or violent episodes during the conflict were not and are not part of the discourse even though they feature implicitly in every action and every discourse contribution of the actors involved.

Conclusions

This chapter has focussed on the strategies employed when dealing with the spatial remnants of protracted intrastate conflict and the aims and motives attached to the redevelopment of places shaped by conflict. Actors involved in the redevelopment process not only make decisions about the future use of a certain site, they also negotiate the dominant narrative of the conflict and the strategies applied to their redevelopment. They decide whether to ignore, demolish or transform the heritage of conflict and whether to use them as a tourist attraction for community purposes or critical reflection. Aims and motives for decisions range from normalisation on the one hand to retreat into the safety of one's own community on the other. In order to illustrate these tensions, two redevelopment projects, Crumlin Road Gaol and Girdwood Park, in the fragmented and deprived North of Belfast have been analysed as local stories (Bauriedl 200720092009). It is interesting to see that – even though the sites as well as the strategies and purposes are so different – the logic of 'normalisation' has prevailed in both cases.

In the case of Crumlin Road Gaol, somewhat ironically, it is the historical background of the site as a remand centre for political prisoners that attracts visitors and locals alike, and makes both roles, the tourism facility and the shared space for locals, possible. Precisely because many people in the area have some sort of relationship with and memories of the Gaol, there is also a certain amount of curiosity and interest in the site on the part of the local communities. The listed architecture and the interesting, easily digestible presentation of the historic background make it attractive for outside visitors, too. The strategy used is one of touristification and transformation of a former symbol of the conflict into a 'reminder of just how far we have come' (Clarke 2014). The focus on social history enables members of the surrounding communities to share their common experiences without the need to reconcile political points of view. In the case of Girdwood Park, reference to the 'unagreed past' of the site is made very differently. Or, more precisely, there is no reference to the past at all. The historic symbolism of the site is never explicitly mentioned throughout the process, it is ignored and thus fading away. This ignorance is in part ascribed to the fact that it was not a place that played an actual role in people's lives. The history of the site is seen to have been shaped by outsiders – members of the British Army who served in the barracks and have no connections to local people. The history and the stories of the soldiers are not a desirable narrative and do not fit in with the adopted focus on present needs. A third factor is the fact that it was perceived very differently between the former conflict groups. As a result of this, the site and its future use were a bone of contention for so long even after the official end of the conflict that its conflict-related symbolism has retreated into the background – even though the effects of the conflict on the communities, deprivation and division, have not. Girdwood therefore is an example of explicitly seeking compromise between the present wishes and needs of communities in conflict and of going one step at a time without even trying to negotiate a narrative of the past. It is an attempt to alleviate the effects of the conflict for communities without stressing their causes too much.

At both sites, the method of heritage interpretation, and its role in negotiating the peace process, is determined by multiple factors, ranging from the response of local communities and the commitment of urban planners – at one site this resulted in widening the historical context and focussing on social history and at the other the concentration on present needs whilst ignoring the contentious past of a site. Both strategies achieve to overcome or at least ameliorate dissonance between the interpretations of the different societal groups. In the case of the Gaol, the strategy even successfully incorporates an element of the difficult heritage of the conflict into the "normalisation" and touristification agenda of the city as a whole. As a result, both places are reconstructed as "shared space" that is intended to be safe and welcoming for all. Critical reflection, however, seems not to be an option for dealing with the spatial remnants of the conflict which means that one potential resource for shaping a peaceful society is not even considered in both redevelopment processes. This is not straightforward 'healing-heritage' (Giblin 2014); rather, it is a demonstration of the complexities of heritage in the post-conflict landscape that must be negotiated within and between communities.

Bibliography

Assmann, A. (2007). *Der lange Schatten der Vergangenheit: Erinnerungskultur und Geschichtspolitik, Schriftenreihe/Bundeszentrale für Politische Bildung.* Bonn: Bundeszentrale für Politische Bildung.

Bakshi, A. (2012). A Shell of Memory. The Cyprus Conflict and Nicosia's Walled City. *Memory Studies*, 5(4), pp. 479–496.

Bartetzky, A. (2007). Bauen für die Versöhnung'. *Frankfurter Allgemeine Zeitung*, 14 May.

Baumann, M. (2008). *Zwischenwelten: Weder Krieg noch Frieden*. Wiesbaden: VS Verlag für Sozialwissenschaften.

Bauriedl, S. (2007). *Spielräume nachhaltiger Entwicklung: Die Macht stadtentwicklungspolitischer Diskurse, Hochschulschriften zur Nachhaltigkeit* Vol. 27. München: Oekom-Verlag.

Bauriedl, S. (2009). Impulse der geographischen Raumtheorie für eine raum- und maßstabskritische Diskursforschung. In: Mattissek, A. and Glasze, G. eds. *Handbuch Diskurs und Raum: Theorien und Methoden für die Humangeographie sowie die sozial- und kulturwissenschaftliche Raumforschung* (2, unveränderte Auflage 2012), Sozialtheorie. Bielefeld: Transcript Verlag. pp. 219–230.

Belfast City Council (n.d.). The Girdwood Community Hub - A New Beginning, Belfast.

Belfast Telegraph (2011). 200 Homes to be Built on Former Belfast Army Base. [online] *Belfast Telegraph*, 14 March. Available at: www.belfasttelegraph.co.uk/news/northern-ireland/200-homes-to-be-built-on-former-belfast-army-base-28597185.html [Accessed 19 May 2017].

Bell, C. (2002). Dealing with the Past in Northern Ireland. *Fordham International Law Journal*, 26(4), pp. 1095–1147.

Bertram, H. (2014). A Long and Winding Road. Städtische Akteure in Belfast und die schwierige Anpassung an den Frieden. In: Altrock, U., Huning, S., Kuder, T. and Nuissl, H. eds. *Die Anpassungsfähigkeit von Städten: Zwischen Resilienz, Krisenreaktion und Zukunftsorientierung, Reihe Planungsrundschau*. Berlin: Planungsrundschau. pp. 59–84.

Bertram, H. (2017). Re-Imaging the Post-Conflict Quarter. Tourismus in Westbelfast zwischen Konflikt und kulturellem Erbe. Geographische Zeitschrift, 105(2). Themenheft zur Touristifizierung städtischer Quartiere.

Bittner, R. (2010). Baustelle Mostar. In: Bittner, R., Hackenbroich, W. and Vöckler, K. eds. *UN urbanism: Un-urbanismus*. Berlin: Jovis; Bauhaus Dessau Foundation, pp. 136–152.

Bollens, S.A. (2000). *On Narrow Ground: Urban Policy and Ethnic Conflict in Jerusalem and Belfast, SUNY Series in Urban Public Policy*. Albany: State University of New York Press.

Bollens, S.A. (2013). Urban Planning and Policy. In: Mac Ginty, R. ed. *Routledge Handbook of Peacebuilding*. London: Routledge, pp. 375–386.

Calame, J. and Charlesworth, E. (2009). *Divided Cities: Belfast, Beirut, Jerusalem, Mostar, and Nicosia, The City in the 21st Century*. Philadelphia: University of Pennsylvania Press.

Charlesworth, E.R. (2006). *Architects Without Frontiers: War, Reconstruction and Design Responsibility* Vol. 1. Amsterdam: Elsevier/Architectural Press.

Clarke, L. (2014). Royal Visit to Northern Ireland: Once Notorious, Now the Crumlin Road Prison is a Symbol of Our Journey to Peace. *Belfast Telegraph*, 22 June [online]. Available at: www.belfasttelegraph.co.uk/opinion/debateni/liam-clarke/royal-visit-to-northern-ireland-once-notorious-now-the-crumlin-road-prison-is-a-symbol-of-our-journey-to-peace-30381850.html. [Accessed 25 March 2017].

Czepczyński, M. (2008). *Cultural Landscapes of Post-socialist Cities: Representation of Powers and Needs, Re-materialising Cultural Geography*. Aldershot: Ashgate.

Department for Social Development (2011) Transformation Plan for Girdwood. [online]. Available at: www.northernireland.gov.uk/index/media-centre/news-departments/news-dsd/news-dsd-may-2012/news-dsd-210512-transformation-plan-for.htm. [Accessed 10 April 2017].

Devenport, M. (2012). Girdwood Barracks Development: Devil in the Detail? [online]. Available at: www.bbc.com/news/uk-northern-ireland-18162637. [Accessed 19 May 2017].

Dwyer, O.J. and Alderman, D.H. (2008). Memorial Landscapes: Analytic Questions and Metaphors. *GeoJournal*, 73(3), pp. 165–178.

Fallon, K. (2011). *"It's Just Not That Simple": Territory and Politics at Girdwood Park. Independent Study Project (ISP) Collection*. Washington, D.C: School of International Learning.

Frank, S. (2016) *Wall Memorials and Heritage: The Heritage Industry of Berlin's Checkpoint Charlie*, Routledge Studies in Heritage, Vol. 9. London: Routledge.

Gaffikin, F. and Morrissey, M. (2006). Planning for Peace in Contested Space. *International Journal of Urban and Regional Research*, 30(4), pp. 873–893.

Gaffikin, F. and Morrissey, M. (2011). *Planning in Divided Cities: Collaborative Shaping of Contested Space*. Hoboken, NJ: Wiley-Blackwell.

Giblin, J.D., (2014). Post-conflict Heritage: Symbolic Healing and Cultural Renewal. *International Journal of Heritage Studies*, 20(5), pp. 500–518.

Graham, B.J., Ashworth, G.J. and Tunbridge, J.E. (2000). *A Geography of Heritage: Power, Culture and Economy*. London: Arnold.

Guttal, S. (2005). The Politics of Post-war/Post-Conflict Reconstruction, *Development*, 48(3), pp. 73–81.

Hepburn, A.C. (2004). *Contested Cities in the Modern West*. Basingstoke: Palgrave Macmillan.

Kliot, N. and Mansfeld, Y. (1999) Divided Cities. *Progress in Planning*, 52 pp.167–225.

Larkin, C. (2010). Remaking Beirut. Contesting Memory, Space, and the Urban Imaginary of Lebanese Youth. *City & Community*, 9(4), pp. 414–442.

Lederach, J.P. (2005). *The Moral Imagination: The Art and Soul of Building Peace*. Oxford: Oxford University Press.

Lennon, J. and Foley, M. (2010). *Dark Tourism*. Andover, MA: Cengage Learning.

Mac Ginty, R. (2010). Hybrid Peace: The Interaction Between Top-Down and Bottom-Up Peace. *Security Dialogue*, 14(4), pp. 391–412.

Maddison, S. (2016). *Conflict Transformation and Reconciliation: Multi-level Challenges in Deeply Divided Societies*. London: Taylor & Francis.

Meusburger, P. (2011). Knowledge, Cultural Memory, and Politics. In: Meusburger, P., Heffernan, M. and Wunder, E. eds. *Cultural Memories: The Geographical Point of View, Knowledge and Space, Klaus Tschira Symposia*. Dordrecht: Springer Science+Business Media B.V. pp. 51–69.

Muir, J. (2014) Neoliberalising a Divided Society? The Regeneration of Crumlin Road Gaol and Girdwood Park, North Belfast. *Local Economy*, 29(1–2), pp. 52–64.

Murtagh, B. (2008) New Spaces and Old in 'Post-Conflict' Belfast, Divided Cities/Contested States Working Paper. [online]. Available at: www.conflictincities.org/PDFs/WorkingPaper5_10.9.08.pdf. [Accessed 11 January 2018].

Nagle, J. (2009). Potemkin Village. Neo-Liberalism and Peace-Building in Northern Ireland. *Ethnopolitics*, 8(2), pp. 173–190.

Neill, W.J.V. (2006). Return to Titanic and Lost in the Maze. The Search for Representation of "Post-conflict" Belfast. *Space and Polity*, 10(2), pp. 109–120.

O'Dowd, L. and Komarova, M. (2011). Contesting Territorial Fixity? A Case Study of Regeneration in Belfast. *Urban Studies*, 48(10), pp. 2013–2028.

Sabrow, M. (2015). Schattenorte. *Merkur*, 69(795), pp. 77–83.

Schofield, J., Johnson, W.G. and Beck, C.M. (2002). Introduction: Matériel Culture in the Modern World. In: Schofield, J., Johnson, W.G. and Beck, C.M. eds. *Matériel Culture: The Archaeology of 20th Century Conflict*. London: Routledge, pp. 1–8.

Siebeck, C. (2007). "Demontage statt Abriss" - oder: was ist ein Gedächtnisort? In: Schug, A. ed. *Palast der Republik: Politischer Diskurs und private Erinnerung*. Berlin: BWV Berliner Wiss.-Verl., pp. 84–108.

Speitkamp, W. (1997). Denkmalsturz und Symbolkonflikt in der modernen Geschichte. Eine Einleitung. In: Speitkamp, W. ed. *Denkmalsturz: Zur Konfliktgeschichte politischer Symbolik, Kleine Vandenhoeck-Reihe*. Göttingen: Vandenhoeck & Ruprecht, pp. 5–21.

Till, K.E. and Jonker, J. (2009). Spectral Ground in New Cities: Memorial Cartographies in Cape Town and Berlin. In: Staiger, U., Steiner, H. and Webber, A. eds. *Memory Culture and the Contemporary City: Building Sites*. New York: Palgrave Macmillan, pp. 85–105.

Ulster Architectural Heritage Society (2016). Crumlin Road Jail. [online]. Available at: www.uahs.org.uk/built-heritage-at-risk-register-northern-ireland/buildings-at-risk-success-stories/crumlin-road-gaol/. [Accessed 28 May 2016].

8 Legacies of conflict

Housing and the security-threat-community

David Coyles

Belfast is a 'contested' city where social and physical divisions remain most visible in its housing settlements. The so-called 'peace walls' separating its most contentious areas are perhaps the most recognisable form of post-conflict architectural heritage. This chapter moves beyond the penumbra cast by these interfaces to reveal a less discernible, yet equally important, aspect of conflict-era built heritage: a programme of social housing redevelopment between 1976 and 1980 that was initiated to reduce the threat of terrorism and inter-communal violence. Whilst government agencies at the time maintained that redevelopment processes did not possess any military agenda, suspicions have persisted that the security forces (the British Army and former Northern Ireland police force, the Royal Ulster Constabulary or RUC) were heavily involved in crucial decisions regarding the redevelopment processes (Alcorn 1982; Berseford 1982; Cowan 1982). This chapter reveals how the security forces intervened decisively in social housing redevelopment practice. Far removed from the blatancy of peace walls, these discussions illustrate instead the tactical use of 'everyday' residential architecture for the purposes of improving security and reducing terrorist threat in ways that contribute to the city's architectural heritage.

Whilst the extensive history of ethnic division, divisive population movement and residential segregation in Belfast is well understood (Jones 1960; Boal 1969; Hepburn 1996; Murtagh 2002; Shirlow and Murtagh 2006; Monaghan and Shirlow 2011), it was during the Troubles-era redevelopment of social housing stock that territorial divisions became formalised in the urban fabric of the city. The analysis here is of previously confidential government correspondence between the RUC, British Army, Northern Ireland Office (NIO) and Department of the Environment (DoE), the latter the government department responsible for planning and housing policy delivered through the Northern Ireland Housing Executive (NIHE). This chapter first establishes the novel and challenging asymmetries between social housing policy and security policy that emerged during this period. This analysis highlights the undervalued role of social housing in conflict operations between military and paramilitary forces, and exposes the central position played by pivotal social housing settlements in the development of the *Standing Committee on the Security Implications of Housing*, the undisclosed government body set up to reconcile a new and uncertain discursive territory where security and housing issues were inherently intermixed. In the political domain that emerges, the *assessment of the security threat* posed by the redevelopment of a particular social housing community replaces the *assessment of housing need* of that particular social housing community as the mitigating factor in the allocation of land and housing awarded to that community. This brings into being the *security-threat-community*, a discursive object targeted by government whereby all citizens are ostensibly designated by default as a potential security threat. This chapter then goes on to illustrate the first material visibilities of the decisions taken by the *Standing Committee on the Security Implications of Housing* under the auspices of reducing terrorist threat in a number of social housing developments. The architecture that was created through these processes demonstrates how the security-threat-community persists as a contemporary phenomenon that enables historic conflict-era forces to remain latently active within the present-day post-conflict city (Garland 1997, 2014).

Targeting the community

The architecture of the city has become recognised as a fundamental dimension in the complex operations of urban conflict (Savitch 2005). During the Troubles, 70% of terrorist bombings were aimed at housing in the Belfast Urban Area (Bollens 2000). Weizman (Weizman and Segal 2003, Weizman 2007, 2010), Graham (2009; 2011), Sassen (2002, 2006) and others have helped clarify the social, political and economic terrain subject to distortion and transformation through embedded connectivity between the processes of conflict and the urban material realm. This literature has helped establish a convincing critical narrative concerning the instrumental use of architecture by state authorities to target '(pre)insurgent citizens' (Anderson 2011) as a means of reducing potential terrorist threat. Anti-ram bollards (Coaffee and Murakami Wood 2006), closed-circuit television (CCTV) surveillance infrastructures (Graham and Wood 2003) and the pre-emptive 'kettling' of protestors and non-protestors (Cammaerts 2013) present a range of crude material practices addressing this domain of *potential* belligerents. The impact on community mobility is such that '[c]itizens and non-citizens alike are now treated as an always present threat… all are imagined as combatants and all terrain the site of battle' (Packer 2006). This parsing of civil liberty and social practice, through the design and implementation of architectural programmes, raises important questions about the long-term and mutually conditioning dynamics between people and their everyday architectural environment (Goffman 1961). In this sense, the security-threat-communities of Belfast present a prescient socio-material conciliation between the tensions of civil and security technologies that have come to typify post-9/11 discourses concerning societal liberty and the practice of individual social freedoms.

Transparency and opacity

The input by the security forces into social housing practices in Northern Ireland can be understood as a distinctly political operation. It was informed by the failure of both security policy and housing policy to respond to the proliferation of security issues arising within social housing estates in Belfast throughout the 1970s. Whilst in retrospect such a conundrum seems an inevitable consequence of the Troubles conflict, it is important to note that it was only in the mid-1970s that this confluence between security policy and housing policy became officially recognised. The state up to that time refused to publicly acknowledge the detrimental effects of sectarian conflict on housing development. The central role that social housing would play in a conflict with communities suffering through extensive bombing campaigns, sectarian intimidation and suburban flight was officially highlighted initially within a confidential 1976 DoE report. Commissioned by the Secretary of State, this dossier plainly acknowledged an imbalance in land distribution between Roman Catholic and Protestant communities that resided at the core of many of the related security issues:

> [T]here are fewer Catholic families (about 25%) to Protestant families in Belfast [and] the great majority (80% +) of the housing movements in the early years of the Troubles resulting from intimidation were Catholic families... Large numbers of refugee families have poured into the already over-crowded areas. It is absolutely inevitable therefore that the Catholic parts of the city will expand. But expansion is difficult in some areas as it would produce immediate confrontation with strong Protestant communities.
>
> (The National Archives of the UK [TNA] CJ 4/1559)

In November 1976, Minister for Housing Ray Carter made a presentation to a confidential gathering of the Secretary of State's Executive Committee which formally raised the issue of a 'housing crisis' for the first time. This presentation blamed 'past neglect' and 'sectarianism' as the primary causes of a dilapidated housing stock cited as being 'the worst in the UK and possibly in Western Europe', with 32,000 damaged dwellings and 10,000 unoccupied dwellings, which equated to what would then have been a two-year supply of new building (TNA CJ 4/1559). Kenneth Bloomfield, a leading civil servant within the DoE, was subsequently tasked with analysing this imbroglio and providing a strategy on which a policy response could be developed. Whilst his recommendations would lay the groundwork for the objectification of the security-threat-community that was to follow, his report was premised on the two specific problems that were particularly troubling to the Northern Ireland government: 'the impact of sectarian segregation on housing programmes' and 'whether it would not be beneficial to make a more open public acknowledgement of the situation'. Of note is how the report downplayed the historic divisions of Belfast's communities as a primary factor of concern:

> The frequent use of emotive terms such as "ghetto housing" should not, I think, lead to a sweeping generalisation that all forms of segregation are per se undesirable... In a great many instances, however, segregated communities have been created by a desire to live amongst congenial neighbours, and alongside one's own schools, churches and social recreational facilities. To characterise this trend as necessarily or in all circumstances bad in itself is to challenge the right of people to preserve that distinctive sense of community which is so strongly characteristic of life in Northern Ireland.
>
> (TNA CJ 4/1559)

Instead, the report placed the blame squarely on the malign influence' of sectarian violence and its impact on the 'vacancies, vandalism, squatting and territorial struggles at the sectarian interfaces: As mixed communities ...become solidly of one colour or the other, the inter-communal inter-face becomes a front line. Murders occur, people are intimidated, families move out, and houses are vandalised, squatted in or at best bricked up' (TNA CJ 4/1559).

When proposing how redevelopment planning might begin to address such problems, Bloomfield made two critical recommendations that would profoundly shape government formulation of subsequent social housing settlements. The proposal for a 'low-density' inner-city realm of 'smaller residential enclaves, surrounded by substantial areas of open space' contrasted sharply with the dense gridiron of interconnected Victorian terraces which characterised the industrial-era inner city. The interconnectivity and repetitiveness that epitomised the Victorian inner city are distinguished in Belfast by the fact that this highly permeable infrastructure afforded the terrorist (or would-be civilian rioter) easy access to opposing neighbourhoods as well as aiding in their escape from and evasion of the security forces. The overturning of this connectivity, alongside a 'steadily increasing pressure by the security forces', was put forward as a 'better and safer basis for the future'.

Equally significant was Bloomfield's second recommendation to acknowledge 'honestly and publicly' the impact that sectarianism strife was having on the progression of social housing programmes. However, of perhaps greater import was a policy briefing by the NIO which recommended to Minister for Housing Ray Carter that such thinking be cast aside:

> There would not seem to be a great deal of merit in provoking public debate on the evils of sectarianism... there is no great merit in

exhaustively discussing the symptoms without coming forward with some very positive proposals for tackling the source of the complaint... [We] feel that an inspired debate on the subject of sectarianism is likely to provoke the riposte that all would be well if only the security situation allowed people to live peaceably outside sectarian boundaries... Our general view is that for security and policing reasons the balance of advantage lies against provoking widespread discussion on sectarianism in housing...It would be unlikely to be actively supported by the army and the police who seem to find it easier to control violence in areas where community boundaries are clearly defined...better we feel to get on with the rebuilding of dilapidated areas...while trying to weaken sectarian boundary lines by stealth.

(TNA CJ 4/1559)

This lack of transparency is germane to the legacy of community suspicions that the disparate cul-de-sacs, courtyards and dead-end streets found throughout the contemporary city are the consequence of Troubles-era interference by the security forces in housing policy and not the experiments in place-making and defensive planning that they were purported to be (Dawson 1984, Coyles et al. 2013, Coyles 2017). In this sense, it becomes no longer appropriate to measure the presence and effectiveness of security or housing technologies as separate social or material entities. The security-threat-community is designated as a complicated socio-material problem to be explained through socio-material solutions.

Twinbrook and Suffolk: asymmetrical conflict

The events at the Twinbrook and Suffolk estates on the south-eastern fringe of Belfast would give further succour to the governmental bent towards non-disclosure. Crucially, these events would also make clear the increasing political dimensions of the social housing problem. Through tactics of manipulation undertaken by both paramilitary and military forces, Twinbrook and Suffolk highlight the strategic advantages of objectifying entire communities of social housing dwellings as a singular *potential threat*. In December 1976 a government press release detailed the establishment of a 'Ministerial Steering Group on Belfast Housing' that had been set up within the NIO and charged with 'masterminding' a full-scale response to the housing crisis: 'Belfast faces acute problems. In common with places like Liverpool and Glasgow the inner city has fallen into decay...In addition the Troubles have affected living conditions throughout the City' (TNA CJ 4/1559).

Whilst such public statements glossed over the true impact of conflict on housing issues, the dilemmas posed by the situations at Twinbrook and Suffolk demonstrated the complex role played by social housing in what was becoming a progressively asymmetrical conflict. Here, the instigation and facilitation of squatting by paramilitary forces helped place the individual social housing dwelling and social housing resident at the forefront of both territorial and political conflicts. A confidential report authored by the DoE in October 1977 for the NIO described how Twinbrook presented 'one particularly important lesson ... the dangerous consequences of allowing uncontrolled squatting in public housing estates'. Originally envisaged as a 'model mixed religion estate' of 3,000 families, the first arrivals to Twinbrook set up a 'Tenants Association' determined to keep the settlement mixed:

> the problem was that Twinbrook... was becoming increasingly regarded as a probable extension of Belfast's West Belfast Catholic areas. It became increasingly difficult to attract Protestant families... Many refugees, all Catholics [began] to squat in Twinbrook occupying homes that had been just built. The Twinbrook Tenants Association moved quickly and set up an anti-rumour service but the problem was clearly [the] desire of Protestants within the estate to leave it because of the influx of Catholic families.
>
> (TNA CJ 4/1985)

In 1977 around 156 persons displaced from other parts of the city conducted the non-violent political act of 'squatting' (Nathan and Spindler 2001; Sanyal 2010) in newly completed houses that had yet to be handed over by the contractor into the possession of the social housing authorities. Alongside this, a further 256 social housing tenants were illegally evicted by direct or indirect sectarian intimidation and replaced with 'tenants' selected by local paramilitary forces. The inability to enforce decrees for possession in the Twinbrook area would eventually force the social housing authorities to admit that they had 'lost management control of the estate' (TNA CJ 4/1985).

A similar story was also taking place at the equally contentious Lenadoon estate, a primarily Roman Catholic settlement adjacent to the predominantly Protestant settlement of Suffolk. Whilst a similar enmeshment of civilian-orientated and paramilitary-induced squatting was taking place, the scenario unfolding at Suffolk-Lenadoon made clear the explicit political connotations of the squatting issue:

> The [Suffolk] estate is becoming increasingly surrounded by Roman Catholic housing and [the] underlying threat is that what happened at Horn Drive will be repeated: i.e. that the IRA will mount intense pressure on the Protestant residents so as to accelerate their departure; that the UDA will counter by staging an organised withdrawal, while doing so much damage as they can to the houses; and that the new occupants will be chosen by the IRA rather than the Housing Executive.
>
> (TNA CJ 4/1559)

This helps to condition a scenario whereby the engagement of the security forces with the security-threat-community moves further from a normalised enterprise to protect the territorial rights of displaced tenants and the legal rights of landlords, to a latent operation of military conflict with increasingly intricate political dimensions:

> [T]he security forces consider that the situation could deteriorate at any time with the PIRA engineering a confrontation which would escalate as outside paramilitary assistance move in to support both sides... In the long term it is probable that Suffolk will become a Roman Catholic estate. However the pace at which this occurs and the way it happens should as far as possible be controlled by the Government and not a reflection of outside pressure orchestrated by the PIRA.
>
> (TNA CJ 4/1559)

As the conventional governance of housing allocation and management is broken it effectively splinters social and territorial rights (Sassen 2010) with the consequence that non-insurgent citizens become mobilised by the forces of military conflict into agents of paramilitary action. Just as the civilian squatter occupying the relinquished dwelling commensurately reinforces ethnic territoriality and security threat, the tenant illegally evicted by paramilitary forces is not afforded the tenancy protections of the law and in being dispossessed becomes a potential squatter and security threat. The controlled allocation of tenants by paramilitaries, and the 'control of this controlling' by the security forces, creates a situation where objects become military assets strategically positioned to address political objectives. As such, the ambit of conflict is extended, and the measures taken by both military and paramilitary forces identify the 'pre-insurgent' and the 'potential threat' as important objects in military and paramilitary strategy.

Squire's Hill-Ligoniel: community as security threat

The social housing proposals at Ligoniel on the northern boundary of Belfast's city limits would bring the nascent strategies of enclave-orientated housing settlements and clandestine security input together with the quandaries raised by the situations unfolding at Twinbrook and Suffolk. The complete absence of land in Belfast available to rehouse the Roman Catholic population dispersed from 'mixed' and predominantly Protestant parts of the city, and the extreme overcrowding in the Roman Catholic enclaves of West Belfast and Short Strand, situated the site at Ligoniel as the only land available within the city on which to build housing for the Roman Catholic population. The proposal consisted of two distinct phases totalling some 300 houses, with the phases being progressed consecutively. As such, a confidential report by the DoE on 'potential areas for Roman Catholic housing' emphasised the proposed development as having 'an extremely important part to play in easing the problems of re-housing people from Catholic re-development areas in Belfast' (TNA CJ 4/1985). However, both phases of the proposed development sat adjacent to long-established Protestant landmarks, most notably the largely owner-occupied settlement of Squire's Hill, which prompted the security forces to rally against the scheme:

> [Squire's Hill] residents were taking a firm line against the scheme... very strong objections would be made against the second phase which would bring Roman Catholic houses to the edge of the Squire's Hill estate. If [phase one] housing could be stopped some way of the [Primary School] playground then the... scheme would be acceptable on security grounds. The Squire's Hill residents would probably tolerate the situation.
>
> (TNA CJ 4/1985)

The fundamental nature of architecture as a socio-material practice becomes axiomatic to the modelling of a *better* or *worse* security practice by the security forces that, in turn, subordinates the encouragement of *better* or *worse* social practice. Humanitarian obligations to refugees from other parts of the city are reconceptualised as hazardous security choices. Quite distinct from the sectarian violence at interfaces between communities that had preoccupied Bloomfield's earlier report, no such pre-existing patterns of violence existed at the Ligoniel area. Rather, the security forces use the experience of Twinbrook and Suffolk to superficially target a community that is yet to find existence in bricks and mortar:

> If the Roman Catholic houses were built as far as the edge of Squire's Hill estate a point of conflict would be established. It was likely that the majority of the residents would move and would be replaced by hard-line Protestants (thus creating a confrontation zone) or the estate would become a 'no man's land' with perhaps some Roman Catholic squatters. In the latter circumstances a confrontation line may eventually develop across the Crumlin Road with the hard Protestant Ballysillan Estate. Furthermore the new Orange Hall (built to replace the one abandoned on the Ligoniel Road) on the Crumlin Road would be threatened and would be an additional emotional factor in Protestant reactions.
>
> (TNA CJ 4/1985)

Perhaps the most significant outcome of the Squire's Hill-Ligoniel discussions was that although construction on the Ligoniel site had not begun when the security forces gave their input in early 1977, the proposals had received full planning permission by the statutory authorities. Furthermore, whilst the announcement had not been made official word of the approval had been leaked to the public. This would inform the most decisive aspect of the policy mechanisms that were to emerge from these events, a more effective targeting of the security-threat-community through the capability to pre-empt potential behaviours rather than deal with the effects of exist-ing behaviours:

> [The] Squire's Hill case illustrates our current shortcomings and the prob-able limitations of any improved system. The security consultation was too late [and] the proposals [were] known in general far and wide; evi-dently security advice ought to be taken while the options are still open.
>
> (TNA CJ 4/1985)

The committee

A confidential memo by P.W.J. Buxton in June 1977 to NIO officials with overall responsibility for coordination with the security forces sought to clarify how this reoccurrence of competing-conflicting demands between housing policy and security policy could be most effectively resolved:

> [Squire's Hill-Ligoniel] raises in acute form the problems that are likely to recur frequently in the coming months. We have no objective grounds for contradicting security advice. On the other hand it plainly needs to be balanced against the over-riding need for more land for Catholic housing, and the predictable response of the Housing Executive and in particular its chairman to a 'political' request to amend its plans etc... whatever is decided is certain to cause offence somewhere and show that government decision-making has been less than perfectly co-ordinated... [T]roubles of the Horn Drive description [may] stem from previous vagaries, errors or inadequacies of housing policy. But in their current manifestations they are better treated as security matters, on the grounds that the security forces have to lead in dealing with them, not the housing authorities.
>
> (TNA CJ 4/1985)

Pre-emptive control of the social housing process is identified as a strate-gic operation to be enacted via the existing technologies of social housing policy. It is reasoned that the effective introduction of security advice as a pre-emptive insertion before the statutory process begins will avoid con-flict with other concerns. The planning process would provide the critical juncture (and subterfuge) where productive engagement is most beneficial:

> The problem lies in the planning area... what is needed is not inter-ference in the policy-making system...but practical working-level consultation between the housing planners and those with security concerns... the earlier they are given the opportunity to do so, in any planning process, the better.... the planners rightly feel that it can dis-tort their conclusions but they are well aware that they cannot ignore it.
>
> (TNA CJ 4/1985)

This logic details how housing policy becomes a tool not to assert *more control* over security-threat-communities but to establish *better control* through a mosaic of political and material practices. The memo would go on to affirm the need to form a 'committee' comprising of a 'fairly informal group [that] would regularly meet and would co-opt members of the security forces for particular matters as necessary' in order to 'regularise the rather loose practice' which had accompanied previous events:

> A sufficiently early consultation could provide many ameliorations and improvements of a scheme which the security forces intrinsically disliked. [The committee] could also contribute to the progressive tactical handling of an issue [from] a political and security point of view. It is in this context that I would see a useful political element in the arrangements. That is to say, housing policy itself is not political, but the prosecution and promulgation of it is... Security is merely a technical matter (although its requirements may of course have strongly political considerations). A given housing policy may have consequences for security, of a variety of kinds. Conversely, adjustments can be made to a given housing scheme, for the betterment of security... Their advice is technical, and following it or not is apolitical.
>
> (TNA CJ 4/1985)

The first meeting of the Standing Committee on the Security Implications of Housing *Problems* on 8 July 1977, under the chairmanship of A.W. Stephens of the NIO, would see Deputy Chief Constable John Hermon and Assistant Chief Constable David Chesney of the RUC join Brigadier John MacMillan and Lt. Colonel Malcolm McLarney of British Army to review 'the security aspects of housing in Belfast' alongside Messrs Semple and Steele of the DoE. This inaugural meeting focussed on three areas of major concern: how major housing policy decisions of the time were likely to involve in some instances 'the transfer of land from one community to the another which would have security implications'; trouble at 'sensitive interfaces'; and, crucially, 'the problems posed by trouble at individual houses' (TNA CJ 4/1985). The minutes of the meeting reveal the centrality of the social housing settlement to effective security strategy, in particular the 'the massive problem in the housing field because of the inequalities between the two communities' and the 'grave shortage' of Roman Catholic housing and the 'overall surplus' for Protestants. What emerges is a recognition of the 'absence of consultation and co-ordination between all the agencies involved' and the need for an ongoing mechanism to bring the planning and security side together to 'deal with crises and identify potential areas of conflict':

> It is the demolition of exiting buffers or 'the building of new houses in a previously neutral zone that develops flashpoints...Problems could be alleviated by the creation of a neutral zone. In positive terms industrial

development or the construction of amenity or welfare buildings would have the added advantage of providing an area for neutral contact. Failing that the creation of a wide open space, a dual carriageway or the erecting of fencing would at lease serve to separate hostile communities.

(TNA CJ 4/1985)

The committee represents a significant contingency where the government response to the security problems in housing areas moves away from being a reactive and ad hoc operation to one that was proactive in its amelioration of potential security threat. This gives birth to a formalised process whereby the potential threat posed by a potential social housing redevelopment could be pre-empted prior to redevelopment by altering the scale, scope and geography of a given proposal, outside of public scrutiny and irrespective of the social need that such a proposal might address.

Visibilities

An assessment of a number of the interventions made by the *Standing Committee on the Security Implications of Housing* helps explain the complexity and undervalued nature of much of the conflict-era heritage with which it is intricately connected. In this way, the Troubles-era social housing estate provides a 'grid of intelligibility' (Garland 2014: 375) for understanding how the historic decisions taken by the committee objectify the security-threat-community and continue to do so in the contemporary post-conflict city. Whilst the interventions range in scale, typology and application, they are consistent in their lack of visibility, residing largely unseen and embedded as parts of the functioning city structure. This condition can be exemplified by differing interventions made at Twinbrook and Ligoniel. With the squatting issue at Twinbrook spiralling out of hand in 1977, concerns were raised that the 'squatting problem' would spread across to the adjacent and largely Protestant Areema estate, separated from the eastern edge of Twinbrook by a 100-metre-wide green amenity space.

In September 1977, a DoE report described how this space had become a 'no man's land [which] serves as a battle-ground' between the Twinbrook and Areema estates (TNA CJ 4/1985). To eliminate the violence between the two communities and to thwart any spread of squatting to Areema the committee was able to co-opt the planning of a seemingly unrelated link-road aid security concerns:

It is understood that if the nearby Poleglass Estate goes ahead that a new road or motorway will be built on this ground. It is believed that a motorway would provide a fairly effective buffer zone between these two communities.

(TNA CJ 4/1985)

Figure 8.1 Dual carriageway between the Twinbrook and Areema housing estates. Photograph by David Coyles.

The resultant dual carriageway installed over the former 'no man's land' productively obliterates the former divide (and with it the security threat) and concretises this perpetual division by making it fundamentally resistant to any future social or material reintegration (Figure 8.1).

The interventions made at Squire's Hill-Ligoniel provide further visibility of such opaque use of statutory procedures, this time through passive interference with the planning process. Despite the Ligoniel proposal having received full planning permission, a briefing note issued by the NIO in September 1977 noted a 'continued pressure' from the security forces for modification of the Squire's Hill-Ligoniel scheme. This was premised on the continued objections of the residents of Squire's Hill who had met with Minister for Housing Ray Carter. A report prepared by the 'Squire's Hill Residents Association' and subsequently forwarded to Minister for Housing Ray Carter detailed the fears the local community had for an 'overspill from Roman Catholic parts of North Belfast' causing a deterioration in conditions in the area:

> If an excess of houses were built they would be allocated to people from Ardoyne and New Lodge. To bring families from these areas into one which is at present living in harmony would be inviting trouble...we feel

> that sectarian strife may develop between the residents of this new estate and those from Silverstream… the mixed community of Squire's Hill would be in the middle and our quiet streets would become an interface.
>
> (TNA CJ 4/1564)

Whilst the report recommended a considerably reduced Ligoniel scheme, based on 'taking these very real fears into consideration together with strong advice from sources within the military and RUC against the planned siting of the estate' (TNA CJ 4/1564), such drastic actions were not possible due to public awareness of the successful planning application. This greatly limited the options that were available for security remediation. However, in response to the concerns of the residents and the security forces, Minister for Housing Ray Carter directed the DoE to intervene in the planning process and incorporate compensatory 'conditions' into the granted planning permission for the scheme before the permission was publicly issued. These conditions, although quite inconsequential in appearance, profoundly impacted the relationship between the Ligoniel and Squire's Hill settlements:

1   that there should be particularly heavy planting, to a minimum depth of 12 metres, in the proposed landscape strip between the two developments;
2   that a physical barrier should be erected before any of the Executive houses immediately adjacent to the private development were occupied;
3   that the relevant Executive houses should not face towards the private development; and
4   that there should be no access whatever, vehicular or pedestrian, between the two developments.

> (TNA CJ 4/1985)

What appear as benign stipulations in fact propagate a productive disciplining of the security-threat-community of Ligoniel that passes undetected through the statutory processes of measurement and culpability. It would not be possible to reverse the arrangement of pre-approved housing layouts, therefore the quality of 'not facing' the 'relevant Executive houses' has been achieved through a reversal of the social programme of the dwelling rather than a reversal of its physical programme, thus avoiding any conflict with the permitted design of housing and roads. Front gardens have been reverse-engineered as backyards, large living room windows as disproportionately sized kitchen windows. Only the adjacent doorway cannot be disguised and remains 'front-facing'. The privileging of the social programme of Squire's Hill is bound to the disciplining of the social programme at Ligoniel. This is the most astutely precise and perverse targeting of citizens within the security-threat-community (Figure 8.2).

Moreover, whilst the divisive 12-metre-wide 'heavy planting' installed in 1980 is not on the list of interfaces recognised by the Northern Ireland

Figure 8.2 Back-to-front houses at Ligoniel repurposed to 'not face' Squire's Hill. Photograph by Donovan Wylie and David Coyles.

government (Department of Justice 2012: 25), it comprehensively separates the Ligoniel and Squire's Hill estates. Despite the continued absence of interface violence over the decades this division has been extended in more complex and problematic forms. Most discernible is the extension of the heavy planting barrier that has accompanied the extension of the Squire's Hill in 2013. Less noticeable are the fallow playing fields that have been wilfully abandoned by the primary school authorities to create a conclusive physical dislocation from the adjacent Ligoniel housing, effectively completing the continuous buffer first sought by the security forces in 1978.

Conclusions

The Together: Building a United Community Strategy (OFMDFM 2013) is the chief policy framework for post-conflict Northern Ireland. Under its auspices a range of initiatives are testing integrated education, integrated housing and shared community spaces. Given the principle of a peace process built on 'equality' it is understandable too that in matters of space, place and architecture, political attention is dominated by examples where outcomes common to both communities can be easily demonstrated.

Whether it be the shared and neutral tourist-orientated neo-liberalism of the Crumlin Road Gaol and Titanic Belfast visitor centre (Coyles 2013), the 'shared space' of the Girdwood Community Hub (Gaffikin et al. 2016), the Northern Ireland Executive 'Shared Future Housing' programmes or measures addressing the peace walls 'shared' between communities, these initiatives have been made possible by a common political will where the benefits are, at least in theory, equal to both communities. The elemental value this places upon architecture can be seen in the Together: Building a United Community Strategy:

> Some of our areas continue to be overshadowed by the physical reminders of the past, with residents living segregated lives as a result of dividing structures. These structures can come in a number of forms but their impact is exactly the same.
>
> (OFMDFM 2013: 20)

The 'peace walls' are recognised at international level and the political thinking underpinning them is well understood (Byrne et al. 2012). This has enabled incremental progress to be made towards ameliorating their divisive effects (International Fund for Ireland 2012). The lack of similar recognition of the security-threat-community means that implications of the legacy of Troubles-era social housing settlement become lost. The socio-material problems presented by the security-threat-community become recognised instead as distinct social problems and distinct material problems. However, the machinations of the Standing Committee on the Security Implications of Housing demonstrate the complex socio-material nature at the heart of its constitution. The processes which inform the assessment of threat posed by the full range of social housing communities redeveloped during the 1976–1980 period, and their consequences in socio-material forms, remain a fundamental historical praxis that requires comprehensive deconstruction and evaluation in the post-conflict era. Whilst others have theorised how the planning process might address post-conflict conditions, to class the security-threat-community as a planning issue is to miss the larger point. In the context of a post-conflict Northern Ireland, the historic and undisclosed involvement of the military in matters of social housing is foremost a political issue and a discrete legacy of conflict that requires a multifaceted approach that recognises the social, economic and environmental dimensions enmeshed in Troubles-era social housing development and management. This cross-cutting approach to policy is not unknown in Northern Ireland and explicitly underpins the 'four priority areas' of the Together: Building a United Community Strategy: 'Our children and young people; Our shared community; Our safe community; Our cultural expression' (OFMDFM 2013). The commitment of the strategy is to remove all 'peace walls' by

2023 (OFMDFM 2013:6). This is not planning policy but an interdepart-mental peace and reconciliation matter led by the Department of Justice (Department of Justice 2012). The examples of visibilities presented within this chapter are a small part of a wider programme of interventions across Belfast made by the Standing Committee on the Security Implications of Housing. As normalised and largely single-identity parts of the city many of these security-threat-communities lack the political currency of 'inter-face' and 'shared-space' endeavours. Yet the security-threat-community is an equally important legacy of conflict that demonstrates the need for a cross-cutting post-conflict policy to address its perpetual designation of citizens as potential security threats. If post-conflict policy seeks to enable social and material integration, can this be achieved when the his-toric forces that produced secure social housing settlements continue to reproduce the very security-threat-objects that they have been employed to resist?

Bibliography

Alcorn, D. (1982). Who Plans Belfast? *Scope,* 52, pp. 4–6.

Anderson, B. (2011). Facing the Future Enemy US Counterinsurgency Doctrine and the Pre-Insurgent. *Theory, Culture & Society,* 28(7–8), pp. 216–240.

Berseford, D. (1982). Security Forces Build on Belfast's Sectarian Divide. *The Guardian,* 13, p. 13.

Boal, F.W. (1969). Territoriality on the Shankill-Falls Divide, Belfast. *Irish Geog-raphy,* 6(1), pp. 30–50.

Bollens, S.A. (2000). *On Narrow Ground: Urban Policy and Ethnic Conflict in Jerusalem and Belfast.* Albany: SUNY.

Byrne, J., Gormley-Heenan, C. and Robinson, G. (2012). *Attitudes to Peace Walls.* Belfast: Northern Ireland Executive.

Cammaerts, B. (2013). The Mediation of Insurrectionary Symbolic Damage: The 2010 UK Student Protests. *The International Journal of Press/Politics,* 18(4), pp. 525–548.

Coaffee, J. and Murakami Wood, D. (2006). Security Is Coming Home: Rethinking Scale and Constructing Resilience in the Global Urban Response to Terrorist Risk. *International Relations,* 20(4), pp. 503–517.

Cowan, R. (1982). Belfast's Hidden Planners. *Town and Country Planning,* 6(56), pp. 163–167.

Coyles, D. (2013). Reflections on Titanic Quarter: The Cultural and Material Leg-acy of an Historic Belfast Brand. *The Journal of Architecture,* 18(3), pp. 331–363.

Coyles, D. (2017). Journeys through the Hidden City: Giving Visibility to the Material Events of Conflict. *Environment and Planning D: Society & Space,* 35(6), pp. 1053–1075.

Coyles, D., Wylie, D. and Spier, S. (2013). *Connected Communities: Communities as Constructs of People and Architecture.* Arts and Humanities Research Council [Online].

Dawson, G.M. (1984). Defensive Planning in Belfast. *Irish Geography,* 1(17), pp. 27–41.

Department of Justice. (2012). *Building Safer, Shared and Confident Communities: A Community Safety Strategy for Northern Ireland 2012–2017*. Belfast: Northern Ireland Executive.

Gaffikin, F., Karelse, C., Morrissey, M., Mulholland, C. and Sterrett, K. (2016). *Making Space for Each Other: Civic Place-Making in a Divided Society*. Belfast: Queen's University Belfast.

Garland, D. (1997). 'Governmentality' and the Problem of Crime: Foucault, Criminology, Sociology. *Theoretical Criminology*, 1(2), pp. 173–214.

Garland, D. (2014). What Is a "History of the Present"? On Foucault's Genealogies and Their Critical Preconditions. *Punishment & Society*, 16(4), pp. 365–384.

Goffman, E. (1961). *Asylums: Essays on the Social Situation of Mental Patients and Other Inmates*. Harmondsworth: Penguin.

Graham, S. (2009). Cities as Battlespace: The New Military Urbanism. *City*, 13(4), pp. 383–402.

Graham, S. (2011). *Cities under Siege: The New Military Urbanism*. London: Verso.

Graham, S. and Wood, D. (2003). Digitizing Surveillance: Categorization, Space, Inequality. *Critical Social Policy*, 23(2), pp. 227–248.

Hepburn, A.C. (1996). *A Past Apart: Studies in the History of Catholic Belfast, 1850–1950*. Belfast: Ulster Historical Foundation.

International Fund for Ireland. (2012). *Peace Walls Programme*. [online] Available at: www.internationalfundforireland.com/peace-walls-programmme [Accessed 29 January 2018].

Jones, E. (1960). *A Social Geography of Belfast*. Oxford: Oxford University Press.

Monaghan, R. and Shirlow, P. (2011). Forward to the Past? Loyalist Paramilitarism in Northern Ireland since 1994. *Studies in Conflict & Terrorism*, 34(8), pp. 649–665.

Murtagh, B. (2002). *The Politics of Territory: Policy and Segregation in Northern Ireland*. New York: Palgrave.

Nathan, C.D. and Spindler, Z.A. (2001). Squatting as a Transition Problem in South Africa. *Economics of Transition*, 9(3), pp. 657–673.

Office of First Minister and deputy First Minister of the Northern Ireland Executive. (2013). *Together: Building a United Community Strategy*. Belfast: OFMDFM.

Packer, J. (2006). Becoming Bombs: Mobilizing Mobility in the War of Terror. *Cultural Studies*, 20(4–5), pp. 378–399.

Sanyal, R. (2010). Squatting in Camps: Building and Insurgency in Spaces of Refuge. *Urban Studies*, 48(5), 877–890.

Sassen, S. (2002). Governance Hotspots Challenges We Must Confront in the Post-September 11 World. *Theory, Culture & Society*, 19(4), pp. 233–244.

Sassen, S. (2006). *Territory, Authority, Rights: From Medieval to Global Assemblages*. Princeton, NJ: Princeton University Press.

Sassen, S. 2010. A Savage Sorting of Winners and Losers: Contemporary Versions of Primitive Accumulation. *Globalizations* 7(1–2), 23–50.

Savitch, H.V. (2005). An Anatomy of Urban Terror: Lessons from Jerusalem and Elsewhere. *Urban Studies*, 42(3), pp. 361–395.

Shirlow, P. and Murtagh, B. (2006). *Belfast: Segregation, Violence and the City*. London: Pluto Press.

The National Archives DoE(NI), CJ 4/1559 Confidential report on 'Segregation in Housing in Northern Ireland', 29 October 1976.

The National Archives of the United Kingdom, CJ 4/1559/Housing Matters.

The National Archives of the United Kingdom, CJ 4/1985/Housing Problems in Belfast.

The National Archives of the United Kingdom, CJ 4/1564/Housing Policy in Belfast.

Weizman, E. (2007). *Hollow Land: Israel's Architecture of Occupation*. London: Verso.

Weizman, E. (2010). Legislative Attack. *Theory, Culture & Society*, 27(6), pp. 11–22.

Weizman, E. and Segal, R. (2003). *A Civilian Occupation: The Politics of Israeli Architecture*. London: Verso.

9 Migrants and the heritage sector
Issues of recognition, access and representation[1]

Philip McDermott

The chapters in this volume primarily focus on the tensions that exist between the unionist and nationalist communities in Northern Ireland. This, of course, reflects the dominant political blocks in the region and is testament to the durability of narratives of difference that have developed over centuries. However, the two decades after the Good Friday Agreement have also borne witness to shifts in demographics that have raised further nuances around the complexities of cultural difference. Immigration has become a more prominent aspect of Northern Ireland society in this period, bolstered by the success of the peace process, an economic boom in the early 2000s and European Union (EU) expansion in 2004. In 2011, despite four years of previous recession, the national census revealed that more than 4% of inhabitants were born outside Britain and Ireland, up from only 1% ten years previously (McDermott 2013: 1). Of the immigrant population, half were born in another EU country (other than the UK and Ireland), while the other half were born outside Europe. It is also important to note the presence of longer-established immigrant communities, such as the Chinese or Indian populations, resident in the region since before the onset of 'The Troubles' in the late 1960s. Up until the start of the peace process in the late 1990s, the presence of these groups was largely ignored by government and policymakers. Now in second, third or even fourth generations the Chinese and Indian communities have successfully maintained aspects of their cultural identities through grass-roots mobilisation and organisation.

The increased inward movement of people in the past two decades, coupled with the peace process objective of 'parity of esteem' and 'equality', has, therefore, ostensibly increased the position of migrant and ethnic minority communities in public policy. Nevertheless, civil servants and policymakers are often frustrated that their work on diversity issues has been hindered by the ongoing ethnonational competition between the largest political parties, which sometimes 'trumps' the pragmatic implementation of social policy over the concerns about the constitutional position of the region (see McMonagle and McDermott 2014). Moreover, there have been well-publicised concerns about a rise in racist incidents – especially in urban areas. All of this poses a series of questions about the changing nature of identity and particularly for public locations and cultural institutions where identities are represented and/or performed. For example, museums and galleries, given the ethos of the 1998 Agreement and wider international norms in minority participation, are now more than ever attempting to engage with ethnic minority and migrant audiences, while local authorities are now more proactive in promoting multicultural displays of identity in spaces such as regenerated places in city centres.

This chapter, therefore, assesses key considerations arising since the Agreement regarding the heritage sector's engagement with migrant and ethnic minority communities. While it is focussed on Northern Ireland, the rapid rise of migration internationally under pressures of globalisation means that the experiences here can provide insights to many other settings, both in societies emerging from conflict and societies dealing with diversity in ways that challenge existing cultural norms and heritage practices (Innocenti 2016). First, I deal with the practical question of how access to heritage services has been shaped by the wider objectives of the peace process. Second, I consider the impact that increasing levels of diversity have had on the representation of identities in the wider public space. These discussions have clear connections with the wider themes of a Peace Process which has touted equality, access to public spaces and the right to self-identity and representation as key focal points (McDermott 2012). The discussion in this regard also mirrors the situation internationally in which the arts and cultural sectors have become part of wider societal dialogue on multiculturalism.

Throughout the chapter I draw on fieldwork conducted as part of a project on migrant diversity in the cultural sector of Northern Ireland's post-conflict environment, funded by the British Academy. In particular I draw on a series of interviews conducted with heritage practitioners, migrant community representatives and individual migrants. These interviews were conducted between 2015 and 2017, and included ten interviews with individuals working in the heritage sector, six with representatives of community organisations and eight with individual migrants. As noted earlier, special consideration is given in the analysis to the ways in which relationships between heritage organisations/institutions and communities are critical in overcoming many of these challenges. However, first of all I provide a conceptual discussion on the recognition of minorities in multicultural societies and consider how this might be applicable to the circumstances of a diversifying Northern Ireland since the 1998 Agreement.

The 'politics of recognition' and the post-conflict environment: bicultural interpretations of a multicultural society

Conceptual discussions on the ways in which societies deal with their diversity have often been framed within the idea of a 'politics of recognition' (see Taylor 1994). Centring on the need for a segmental understanding of societies, the concept recognises that the majority of nation states are not homogenous and that in order to maintain cohesion different ethnic minority groups should have their cultural background represented at some level in the wider public space. The 'ethnic' culture of a minority group is, therefore, legitimately encouraged but importantly this is also balanced with a promotion of wider 'civic' values, such as citizenship rights, which act as point of commonality between all groups. This description, of course, appears utopian and does not adequately reflect the tensions caused in attempting to balance such distinctions between individual and group identities. Nonetheless, the ideas around the 'politics of recognition' illuminate the dilemmas faced by governments that are trying to deal with ethnic diversity within their borders. These debates can perhaps be understood as a quest to find a middle ground between the more ardent versions of ethnic and civic nationalisms which emerged in the nineteenth century.

The word 'recognition' can mean many different things depending on the 'type' of ethnic group under consideration. For example, communities which have a long-standing and historically embedded connection to a territory have been referred to by Kymlicka (1995) as 'national minorities'. These might include the Quebecois in Canada, the Catalans or Basque in Spain, or even the unionist and nationalist communities in Northern Ireland (or more precisely the UK). 'Recognition' for these groups, therefore, might involve demands for forms of regional governance which recognise the specific needs of a given territory. Equally, 'recognition' might involve the desire of these groups to obtain cultural and/or linguistic rights or special privileges for their cultural traditions and symbols. In a particularly divided place like Northern Ireland, although these are clearly matters of cultural diversity, they are rarely framed as 'multicultural' in wider policy or media discourse – a label maintained more for diversity caused by more recent immigration.

Kymlicka argues that immigrants have different and, on balance, softer demands when compared to national minorities, which he terms as 'polyethnic rights' (1995: 10). Whilst demands for recognition by national minorities are often justified in terms of history, and frequently relate to redressing past wrongs by a more powerful majority, polyethnic rights have tended to relate to pragmatic notions of recognition and representation in public places and spaces as well as certain levels of access to public services. The rights associated with immigrants, therefore, whilst overlapping with those of national minorities, do not necessarily come with the same burden of history. As a result of the entrenched nature of issues affecting national minorities, Kymlicka argues, somewhat controversially, that national minorities might legitimately claim a differentiated and perhaps a more robust set of rights than immigrants whose arrivals are more recent and, in many cases, voluntary (although the plight of refugees might refute this aspect of his argument). Also, importantly, this argument does not imply that the rights of immigrants should be ignored, just that their claims are often less vociferous and less imbued with the burden of the 'past' than the demands of national minorities – a point illustrated by many of the other chapters in this volume.

Examples of these softer polyethnic rights for immigrants might include state support for grass-roots organisations, financial assistance in running Saturday/community language schools, publication of government websites into other languages or assisting immigrant communities, through public programmes or initiatives, to participate more fully in the public space (Kymlicka 1995: 7). Significantly, in the context of this chapter, such policies might also advocate that locations like museums, galleries or other performance spaces for heritage be more open and welcoming to ethnic minorities. Indeed, as noted in the introduction, debates on how the heritage sector can engage with immigrant populations have been developing in countries with longer experiences of immigration. More recently, the refugee crisis in Europe has also instigated discussion on how migrant populations might gain access to institutions such as museums and how the narratives of migrants can be exhibited (see Levin 2017).

Given the demographic changes in Northern Ireland since the Agreement, the region provides a good case study of Kymlicka's distinctions between national minorities and immigrants. The establishment of power-sharing mechanisms in the political governance of the region has undeniably been driven by the long-standing historical perspectives of two national minorities, each with their own embedded narratives and identities. The justification of this prioritisation is, if I put it somewhat crudely, the criterion of indigeneity. This political system, some scholars contend, serves to cement ethno-national boundaries and thus acts as a barrier in the true recognition of diversity within social policies (see Horowitz 2001; Wilford and Wilson 2006). Others, however, note that the Agreement, and the subsequent power-sharing system, was the starting point in the introduction of a series of legal and equality mechanisms and policies which have ensured that groups, such as immigrants, who do not subscribe to either unionist or national identities have a societal voice (McGarry and O'Leary 2009: 37). The development of bodies such as an Equality Commission, established under the 1998 Agreement to protect minority rights, and the drafting of race relations legislation in the same period might therefore be viewed as moves that champion polyethnic rights. It is, however, clear that there are still challenges in pursuing a full ethos of cultural diversity across all policy areas – including the heritage sector. In order to contextualise the changes that have occurred since the agreement in arts and culture, the following section provides an overview of policy change in this time frame.

Policy change, the Northern Ireland peace process and cultural diversity

Prior to the late 1990s, Northern Ireland's policymakers placed little attention on racial diversity matters, although some minority ethnic communities had been resident in the region for many years – notably the Chinese and Indian populations (Kapur 1997; Irwin and Dunn 1997). During this period, the overwhelming focus of social policy initiatives on attempting to tackle questions relating to the 'traditional' divided between the unionist and nationalist communities.

However, the Northern Ireland peace process placed a greater focus on the notion of equality between communities. Subsequent policies and infrastructure to promote parity between the unionist and nationalist communities were introduced. However, the demography of the region has changed in the past twenty years due to processes of in-migration – particularly during the period of EU expansion from 2004 to 2008. As a result, the already existing equality focus on policy provided an emerging platform for multicultural debates, such as Section 75 of the 1998 Northern Ireland Act. This legislation provided a blueprint for devolved governance and contains stipulations to ensure equality of access to all public services, regardless of cultural or ethnic background. For example, schools and educational authorities, which previously had little in the way of policy and procedure to support pupils from migrant backgrounds, under Section 75 were obliged to provide strategies that would help newcomer pupils to integrate and generate an awareness of cultural difference in the classroom (McDermott 2008). In the past decade, equal opportunity laws also acted as the major impetus for the development of better translation and interpreting in areas like the health service and criminal justice system (McMonagle and McDermott 2014; González Núñez 2013). Both the Arts Council and Northern Ireland Museums Council also have equality schemes, driven by Section 75. These policies place emphasis on better connections with community organisations but also on monitoring the numbers of those from minority backgrounds engaging with these sectors. Therefore, at the very least, the twenty years since the peace process have created a policy infrastructure which is more aware of diversity issues and this question of access to those spaces and services.

Since the mid-2000s, a number of controversial attempts have been made by authorities to introduce specific regional frameworks to encourage a more unified society under the wider themes of a 'shared future' and a 'shared space' (OFMDFM 2006). Essentially these policy frameworks aimed to advance relationships between communities but have proven challenging to implement, given the contentions between the unionist and nationalist populations. The most recent manifestation, *Together: Building a United Community* (TBUC) (OFMDFM 2013), places great emphasis on the contestations between the two majority communities of Irish nationalists and British unionists. For example, questions around segregated housing, dealing with the past, the need to promote shared schooling and tackling sectarianism are all given prominence. Nonetheless, the document also refers to the emerging multicultural society due to more recent immigration, and it makes separate reference to the incorporation of minority ethnic communities into civic society and the right immigrants have to express group identity in the public space. The strategy encapsulates Kymlicka's arguments that rights for national minorities (in this case the nationalist and unionist communities) centre on issues which are more historically embedded, whilst ethnic minorities strive largely for a recognition which assists their wider integration. TBUC notes that Northern Ireland is a society which must 'identify and celebrate our differences' yet at the same time strive towards a 'shared and cohesive community' (OFMDFM 2013: 86). This is similar to assertions by some commentators that multicultural policies should bridge the need to recognise society as a 'community of communities' whilst promoting a strong sense of individual citizenship and commonality (Parekh 2000: xv; Young 1990).

The legislative changes during the peace process, therefore, have provided impetus for emerging multicultural awareness across a whole range of public services – including the arts and heritage sector. As noted earlier, the Arts Council and the National Museums Northern Ireland (NMNI) introduced policies to align with the obligations of Section 75. However, the wider ethos of equality and 'shared space' has also influenced other policies, which are equally reflective of widening diversity. NMNI, for instance, has furthered such objectives through its 2015 collection policy, which noted that museums would extend their collections in relation to the theme of migration and especially in relation to the experiences of ethnic minority and migrant populations in Northern Ireland (NMNI 2015: 15). Likewise, as part of the implementation of the TBUC strategy, the Arts Council has been involved in furthering a 'new annual shared community relations/Cultural Awareness week, to encourage cultural celebration and exploration for cultures and identities' (OFMDFM 2013: 7). For example, in 2015 a suite of events was organised under the multicultural theme 'One place, many people'.

In order to ascertain the practical issues involved in implementing these policies, in the next section I begin to draw upon fieldwork which has investigated the connected issues of access to heritage spaces for migrants. This is followed by a discussion on the nature of representation of migrant heritages within the cultural sector. Throughout the discussion the nature of power between communities and institutions is a key point of analysis in considering the success of such relations.

Exploring perspectives on access and representation

Accessing public spaces for heritage

Perhaps the most prominent example of migrant heritages in public places since the Agreement is reflected in the increase in the growth in community festivals which celebrate aspects of culture such as dance, music, film, poetry and crafts. Chinese New Year celebrations, the Polish Cultural Week in Belfast, the Ubuntu diversity festival in Derry and Omagh's half-term multicultural festival are now established events. Significantly, these frequently take place in what are perceived as shared spaces, such as the regenerated Craft Village in Derry, the Botanic Gardens in Belfast or the Sperrin Visitor's Centre in rural County Tyrone. In many cases, events which appear to focus on one community celebration, such as Chinese New Year or Diwali, will regularly feature heritage performances from other migrant communities or even from within the nationalist and unionist communities as a means of championing a sense of 'togetherness'. These events have constituted a reframing of spaces which, government argue, is more welcoming and accessible for newcomer communities to both celebrate their own cultural heritage whilst also engaging with the cultural heritage of other communities and members of the host population.

Many festivals started as community-based ventures which were sponsored through private funding, but as equality and diversity agendas have taken hold they have been more readily funded by public sources. The facilitation of performances and representations of different cultural expressions in prominent spaces is, therefore, part of the wider attempts by government to reframe the use of public space for reconciliatory purposes whilst concurrently opening up public space for previously marginalised communities (McDermott 2011: 196). For example, applications to DCAL's Community Festivals Fund, which awards significant resources for community events, must emphasise 'their commitment to promoting social cohesion, social inclusion, equality of opportunity and good community relations' (DCAL 2015: 2). This funding approach could be criticised as negating levels of community autonomy in determining the shape and outcomes of their own events. Moreover, the framing of events like Diwali and Chinese New Year as festivals which involve input from a variety of cultures (such as Irish, Ulster-Scots or Polish dancers) might dilute the effectiveness of such ventures as community celebrations, creating some kind of inauthentic hybrid.

However, others noted that festival initiatives had at the very least altered engagement with the heritage of their home country by bringing it into the public space. Mary, a member of the Chinese community who has been living in Northern Ireland since the 1970s, noted in interview that "back to the olden days, in the Chinese New Year, there were family get together, we always have it in the house. However, nowadays it is so convenient to just go and celebrate it outside. It is so much easier now than it was" (Interview with Mary, Chinese Community, conducted by PMcD 10 November 2015). Mary's experiences correlate with the international development of multiculturalism as both a political philosophy and government policy objective. For example, early discussions on dealing with new migration and subsequent diversity tended to take a 'two domains' response. Policies in countries like Britain, Sweden and the Netherlands tended to view the private home environment as the location where migrants would maintain and celebrate aspects of their ethnic identity (e.g. their language or cultural events).

By contrast, the public space was viewed as the location for migrants to integrate into civic life (e.g. acquiring the majority language, attending state education or celebrating state events). 'Private' and 'public' spheres were, therefore, viewed as operating separately yet combined to create a balance between a migrant's ethnic and civic identities (see Rex 2004: 10). This delineation between the public and private was also reflected in Mary's experience.

Modood, however, notes that such a 'strict division between the public and private spheres does not stand up to scrutiny' because the two domains of private and public are interdependent in the lived experiences of minorities (1998: 83). Moreover, it is not practicable to expect all aspects of a minority group to utilise only their private spaces as locations for the expression of their identity. If prominent public locations like city centres do not reflect the identities of minorities it is regularly the case that communities will utilise their immediate community environments to create their own counter-publics (McDermott et al. 2016: 621). Therefore, the manner in which communities in Northern Ireland draw upon flags, emblems and murals to define territory is in some ways a similar process to the redefinition of community spaces by ethnic minorities in urban spatial clusters via the use of multilingual signage or even community food stores with signage or facades painted in national colours. If these are the only types of representation of such groups' identities in spaces beyond the home this has been perceived as a form of ghettoisation and a barrier to integration/intercultural dialogue. Consequently, government policies internationally have now frequently broken down the 'two domains' approach to open civic spaces, such as city centre locations, to wider representations of identity (see Kymlicka 2007). Despite the challenges and potential posed by public performances of identity in a divided society this accommodative approach has been a feature of policy in Northern Ireland since 1998. Nonetheless, this policy approach has resulted in wider representations of the multicultural experience in the public space such as those noted by Mary.

Accessing heritage in institutional spaces

Perhaps for spaces like museums and galleries which are considered as 'institutional' there has been more difficulty in attracting members of minority ethnic groups. Unlike public festivals which are often in the open air there are a number of physical and psychological barriers to cross when entering the more enclosed space like the museum. In an interview conducted for the project with a representative of the Filipino community it was noted that lack of confidence for many individuals from ethnic minorities was a key challenge because this acted as a barrier in the initial decision to enter a museum or gallery space. It was commented that many individuals would have a perception that the museum is a culturally elite place which they perceived was not for them. This was further affirmed by a museum outreach worker who when interviewed noted that the staff at her museum were very aware of this as a critical challenge. She said,

> A lot of people don't like the word museum....I like the word museum, but I understand that it has connotations and people don't feel it is for them or they feel a bit – well like it's for people who are educated or people who, you know, are not the same as me.
>
> (Interview with Museum Officer 1, conducted by PMcD, 3 February 2016)

Both examples mirror the situation in other international settings, such as in Canada, the US and other parts of the UK, where the heritage sector has been perceived as the milieu of the middle classes. In other words, social divisions relating to race and class at a societal level are reflected in heritage institutions. This is despite an awareness and attempts by such institutions to open up to 'nontraditional' audiences or 'hard to reach communities'. In Northern Ireland, the museum and heritage services are undoubtedly influenced by the international debates on engaging marginalised communities with the heritage sector. Also the museum sector is acutely aware of the expectations of government in the promotion of equality and diversity as noted in the TBUC strategy and wider government policies relating to the peace process. Despite this, in my discussions with policymakers, heritage practitioners and representatives of ethnic minority communities there are still gaps which this study identified and which could potentially inform future policy and practice in this area. These relate specifically to two questions. The first is the means through which communities can be welcomed to heritage spaces through community partnership projects which aim to break down the elitist perceptions held by some towards the sector. The second relates to one of the most complex barriers of all: that of language.

A prerequisite in opening up any public space, therefore, is the creation of 'welcoming' spaces which attempt to overcome issues relating to confidence. For museums and galleries, a key issue is to consider the actual ways in which spaces are laid out. The physical geography can be extremely important as it is read by those who attend spaces like museums and galleries in a complex way. When a project that a museum/library has in conjunction with an ethnic minority group is in a 'hard to find' or peripheral location within a museum building this can generate bad feeling. As part of the observations of this project I noted on a number of occasions where an exhibition, usually a temporary exhibition whose general purpose is to provide a dialogue about diversity, was placed in a small exhibition room, normally displaced from the wider collection galleries. This use of space is potentially problematic as it can be read as denoting a continued marginalisation and subliminally transmits the message that a particular group or community are only there to meet an institution's equality objective. This was a point articulated by a representative from a Chinese community group who had worked on a partnership project with a local gallery. She relayed the following:

> We were offered a space in a gallery for our own exhibition. We got it all prepared but when I saw the space I was so disappointed. We were in a little room which was away at the back and upstairs. I noticed a space at the front of the building that would have been more appropriate, but how do you say this when you are being invited in?
>
> (Interview with Representative of a Chinese Community Group, conducted by PMcD, 9 February 2016)

An awareness of the basic geography of a museum or gallery space is an important consideration for practitioners when working with minority ethnic communities in creating the welcoming space. Another of the major difficulties in creating the 'welcoming space' relates to language barriers faced by ethnic minorities which continues to be a key reason in deterring groups and individuals from engaging with the heritage sector more broadly. Dawson (2014) notes that museums or galleries which facilitate visits by non-English speakers to a museum but which fail to address the language barrier in some way once visitors are there run the risk of deterring future visits rather than encouraging them and thus generating more harm than good.

As part of this research a research visit and workshop was coordinated at a local authority museum with a group from the Chinese Community, a group which has been in the region for many years, and also with a more recently arrived group of Syrian refugees who had been in Northern Ireland for a few months. The majority of people in both groups had no English language skills and their visit was coordinated with the help of an interpreter provided as part of the research project. There were a number of observations from these visits which indicated that this museum was ill-equipped to deal with individuals for whom English was not a first language. For example, it became apparent from a very early stage that the guides who were working with the interpreters did not alter their practice and were not prepared or trained to deal with this kind of scenario. For example, there were very long sections of information presented by the guide. This was most likely the same material that would be presented to a fluent English speaker, and it proved immensely difficult for both interpreters to transmit the guide's information to the group. During the visits, both interpreters requested that the guide provide shorter overviews of each display case so as to make the translation more manageable. The problems that both groups faced would suggest that it is imperative that guides are well prepared to deal with audiences who may not necessarily have English as a first language.

Improving accessibility to exhibitions for non-English speakers has been noted as good practice by bodies such as the British Council, given both an expanding global tourist industry and diversifying audiences (2015: 11). However, even for smaller museums there are other ways in which non-English speakers may become more engaged with the exhibits. For instance, during the fieldwork visit to the local authority museum there was no other written material available in languages other than English. However, many visitors from the Syrian group used their own technology to shape their own visitor experience. Many individuals used the camera on their mobile telephones to capture images of exhibits and the associated text panel. When asked why they were doing this they relayed via the interpreter that it was noted that the photographs were a means of capturing the experience, and the photos of the text panels could be used as practice for their recently started English classes. This example illustrates that museums should be aware of, and encourage, such practices, which might help non-English speakers engage more fully and which also assist in more formal English language learning (see Clarke 2013). Even in the museum in question, there were signs discouraging photography which may indicate that such restrictions are outdated for the diverse audiences which museums are aiming to attract. Overall, such examples illustrate that locations like museums and galleries can be appropriate locations for language learning which could be one way of attracting migrant groups to utilise museum spaces.

Questions of participation and representation

Another consideration in this chapter relates to the means through which the experiences of minority ethnic groups are represented in spaces such as museums. Crooke (2008: 15) notes that for communities, museums can be important locations 'in constructing a sense of place, belonging and self'. Likewise, the recent TBUC strategy also identifies the wider heritage sector in this regard noting that cultural institutions, such as museums, libraries, arts venues and organisations, 'can help to discover and share the stories of the people and places across the region and examine historical events from the distant and more recent past' (OFMDFM 2013: 95). The recognition of the heritage sector as a place for social dialogue has certainly resulted in an awareness amongst heritage practitioners of the need to forge relationships with communities. For example, the question of migration and diversity might now be explored by museums in projects which claim some element of participatory working between institution and migrant communities themselves. After all, 'cultural activity, whether through participation in the arts or through the formation of collections and display, must be read in the context of these forms of identity formation'; furthermore, 'museums and heritage can impact on the formation and representation of identity and we can construct and explore our identity through cultural participation'

(Crooke 2008: 15). The nature of the relationships forged between institution and community in this process are central points of critical reflection if such participatory engagement is to have successful outcomes.

When community partnerships are proposed between a heritage institution and a community organisation it might be argued that this is driven by emerging ideas around 'moral activism' and the need to empower communities (see Quinn 2017: 21). However, the challenge in this type of activity is that long-standing disassociation felt by communities has often hinged on perceptions that heritage and associated institutions as 'powerful' or 'elitist' (Davis 2007: 67). Therefore, any representative of a heritage institution may themselves be viewed in such terms by those communities that they aim to work with. If those working in community outreach in museums and galleries fail to address such concerns by the community from the outset, this can damage the overall success of grass-roots initiatives.

During fieldwork, the researcher spoke to various representatives from migrant organisations which had worked on arts projects with museums and galleries. There was a recognition that much progress has been made in this area and that the Northern Ireland heritage sector is now more adept at collaborating with communities both within and beyond places such as museums and galleries to co-produce exhibitions especially since the 1998 Agreement (Quinn 2017). However, there was frustration from some of those interviewed who felt that projects were driven too often by institutional or governmental expectation as opposed to the need for genuine partnership. For example, one representative stated that the apparent good will of official bodies and organisations in the heritage sector were often a pretence through which equality-based targets, introduced as a result of the peace process, could be met. She stated that regularly local councils, museums and galleries would contact her to attain 'ethnic' artefacts or performers for multicultural events. These requests also often came with the promise of payment which the participant interpreted as reducing her community development and the people she worked with as commodities to be bought and sold in a corporatised neo-liberal environment. Indeed, this has been an issue debated globally in relation to the arts and community engagement (Khan 2010). The example discussed earlier relating to the marginal locations often provided for partnership projects in galleries is also relevant here. The inability of a particular group to express its dissatisfaction to those with whom it is supposedly collaborating suggests unequal power relationships (see Korom 1999).

These anecdotes from Northern Ireland also concur with Lynch (2014) and Dodd and Sandell's (1998) findings which identify the nature of the relationships between heritage institutions and communities as requiring careful negotiation in the quest for success. Honest discussions at the beginning of partnerships about sectoral expectations and constraints of all the partners are fundamentally important in reducing the potential for conflict when developing collaborations – an issue arguably made more difficult by the lack of workforce diversity in the heritage sector (Sandell 2000). The participant mentioned earlier who was offered financial incentive for the provision of dancers and artefacts commented that she now refuses to collaborate. She said, 'now I just say no when they [official bodies] ask. It's all just to keep their targets' (Interview with Representative of Migrant Support Organisation, conducted by PMcD, 12 February 2016). Therefore, in a policy context an awareness of these power relationships is an important theme for staff training in many heritage organisations.

Enhancing the representations of minority ethnic communities in museum and gallery exhibits is often, although not always, a key objective of participatory work. In cases where there is no participation with communities or where there are poor collaborative practices participants might feel that their efforts in these contexts are overly objectified or commodified. The perception among ethnic minorities might be portrayals of their lives in such contexts are for the benefit of the wider host population to understand or 'look at' them with limited focus on representing the more complex and changing representations of their contemporary or historical experience in ways which are more multidimensional. The very utilisation of intercultural perspectives on identity has been noted as an objective of the wider Northern Ireland peace process because such narratives arguably break down boundaries between communities and find points of commonality. As such, intercultural perspectives on identity are viewed as appropriate in tackling both racism and sectarianism. Moreover such practices potentially bridge the gap between civic integration and the maintenance of cultural identity for migrants. This is a point raised by Tariq Modood who notes that multicultural democracies engaging with narratives of identity should find and cultivate 'points of common ground between dominant and subordinate cultures, as well as new syntheses and hybridities' (Modood 1998: 83).

In Northern Ireland, there are emerging opportunities for projects which connect the historical and contemporary experiences of ethnic minorities with those of the host population. In an interview with a representative from a local council museums' service in this area it was noted that such approaches were driven by a realisation that targeted projects with minority ethnic communities should be balanced with those which take a thematic approach across different cultural groups. She explained,

> Instead of saying, 'this is a minority community and we do targeted projects with them, for them, in their corner'. What we aim to do, is where we would have an opportunity within a more mainstream exhibition, was to explore a broader theme to include different perspectives. So, it kind of presupposes the idea that people from a range of cultural backgrounds can have a subject in common.
>
> (Interview with museum representative 2,
> conducted by PMcD, 16 May 2016)

Quinn (2017) identifies, the *Belonging Project* as one such success. This photographic exhibition which has toured various libraries and gallery spaces since 2013 involved a portrait of individual migrants holding a personal object alongside an associated participant narrative. Therefore, the use of a personal theme, objects and a personalised account has allowed for 'similarities and points of mutual identification to shine through' (Quinn 2017: 25). Indeed, the theme of migration is one deeply embedded in the psyche of the region given the historical and contemporary contexts of human movement to and from Northern Ireland which has impacted on many families (Devlin Trew 2016). For this reason, this focus was rightly regarded as a useful theme by which to encourage engagement and dialogue from a range of individuals and communities. One criticism of the approach, however, is the fact that the photographic output included only people who had come to Northern Ireland from another country. Whilst this is an important element of the migration story it somewhat omits the experiences of local people who may have experienced migration themselves. For example, return migration is a key issue for those who left the region (for example, during 'The Troubles') and returned later to a changed Northern Ireland where their own sense of belonging was challenged (Devlin Trew 2016). Arguably, even more complex interpretations/understandings of migration may very well have encouraged if those born in Northern Ireland had been represented in this exhibition itself.

Another example of emerging attempts at generating intercultural explorations of identity was the *Cultural Fusions* programme initiated by the museum services of the Causeway Coast and Mid-Antrim Council areas in 2011–2013. This project, funded under EU's peace initiatives, aimed to create a number of heritage activities which utilised museum collections to encourage those living in an increasingly diverse post-conflict society to engage 'in dialogue and interaction' which would 'lead to improved Good Relations and a more peaceful and stable society' (North East Peace III Partnership 2014: 7). One of the strands was the *My Treasure* workshop programme and community exhibition. The approach was similar to the *Belonging Project* in that it blended both the idea of narrative and artefact. However, in this case the project worked with a range of individuals, including migrant and non-migrants, 'to share treasured objects revealing their cultural background identity and beliefs' (North East Peace III Partnership). Whilst the project evaluations noted, again, the difficulties in breaching the language barrier when working with ethnic minority communities, there was an overall sense that the project had been 'a very useful approach, appealing to new audiences' and had 'supported new interest in participation' (North East Peace III Partnership 2014: 41).

In all of these cases though, there are difficulties in balancing group identity with the individual identity of self. If, for instance, discussions on identity are constantly framed within the context of one's perceived 'ethnic background' this may prove problematic and ignore the real complexities of an individual migrant's social experiences. While many people in Northern Ireland, migrant or otherwise, do inevitably place importance on ethnic identity as part of their sense of self, others may not. One musician, originally from the US, noted how she had established a Jazz music initiative in order to utilise public spaces for performance for everyone. She was acutely aware of the increasing diversity in Northern Ireland at the time she established her group and was keen to involve people from all backgrounds. However, she commented on the need for some projects to negotiate diversity with no presuppositions about participants as a means of enhancing access for the individual as opposed to for representatives of groups. For her whilst she was aware of the diversity, everyone's main point of connection was as a musician, as opposed to anything else. She noted,

> The one thing that I wanted to make sure that didn't happen though, was putting pressure on an individual so that they suddenly have to represent their country, their culture, their language so much so that they become this statue, or this spokesperson. I want to make sure that that never happens. So, with the musicians they are adding to a conversation as a musician first and foremost, everything else is secondary to that and that creates a great connection between the musicians because they are doing the same thing.
>
> (Interview with Musician Practitioner/facilitator, conducted by PMcD, 16 May 2016)

This final example from the fieldwork again shows that these questions of access and representation for individual migrants may not involve an engagement with ethnicity at all but may engage with other aspects of identity. Examples such as these may also be applicable to other aspects of the heritage sector and indicate that the questions of identity, representation and access are complex issues which heritage services need to consider when attracting members from migrant populations. The need to negotiate individual and groups senses of identity is a feature of the debate for consideration in the development of programmes, exhibitions and events. Whilst there is no one size fits all model, an awareness of these differing demands and a reflexivity generates opportunities for improvement and dialogue.

Conclusions

In the two decades since the 1998 Agreement society in Northern Ireland has diversified and this has had an impact in the heritage sector. Wider debates on equality were initiated by the peace process agenda, and this has seeped down to the workings of cultural institutions. Of course, while this has created an awareness of greater diversity, there is still much to do. Access issues are still clearly impacted on by the wider social factors that act as barriers for someone visiting a 'heritage place' like a museum.

Whilst resources are clearly a major issue, sometimes a greater awareness and discussion of such issues with communities are key to generating improvement. Also, the movement away from simple representations is a key task and there are certainly emerging examples of more complex considerations of identity – often starting at grass roots. Such complex fluid and intercultural representations of minority ethnic and migrant experiences alongside the host population are fitting given the wider equality and cohesion objectives of the peace process itself. In many other contexts where mass migration is occurring, there are similar challenges to social cohesion and equality. These examples from Northern Ireland demonstrate the opportunities available to heritage professionals to meet such challenges by engaging with migrant communities as co-producers of heritage and the dangers of increasing alienation when they do not.

Note

1 The author would like to acknowledge the support of the British Academy in funding this research. Grant number SG131810.

Bibliography

British Council. (2015). *International Tourism Toolkit* [online]. Available at: http://uk.icom.museum/wp-content/uploads/2015/08/Museums_International_Tourism_Toolkit_BC_FINAL.pdf [Accessed 7 July 2017].

Clarke, S.N. (2013). Adult Migrants and English Language Learning in Museums: Understanding the Impact on Social Inclusion. Unpublished PhD Thesis, University of Edinburgh.

Crooke, E. (2008). *Museums and Community: Ideas, Issues and Challenges*. London: Routledge.

Davis, P. (2007). Place Exploration: Museums, Identity, Community. In: Watson, S. ed. *Museums and Their Communities*. London: Routledge. pp. 53–75.

Dawson, E. (2014). "Not Designed for Us": How Science Museums and Science Centers Socially Exclude Low-Income, Minority Ethnic Groups. *Science Education*, 98(6), pp. 981–1008.

DCAL. (2015). Community Festivals Fund: Revised Policy and Guidance Framework. Belfast, Department of Culture, Arts and Leisure.

Devlin Trew, J. (2016). *Leaving the North: Migration and Memory, Northern Ireland 1921–2011*. Liverpool: Liverpool University Press.

Dodd, J. and Sandell, R. (1998). *Building Bridges: Guidance for Museums and Galleries on Developing New Audiences*. London: Museums and Galleries Commission.

González Núñez, G. (2013). Translating for Linguistic Minorities in Northern Ireland: A Look at Translation Policy in the Judiciary, Healthcare, and Local Government. *Current Issues in Language Planning*, 14(3–4), pp. 474–489.

Horowitz, D.L. (2001). The Northern Ireland Agreement: Clear, Consociational and Risky. In: McGarry, J. ed. *Northern Ireland and the Divided World: The Northern Ireland Conflict and the Good Friday Agreement in Comparative Perspective*. Oxford: Oxford University Press, pp. 89–108.

Innocenti, P., ed. (2016). *Migrating Heritage. Experiences of Cultural Networks and Cultural Dialogue in Europe*. London: Routledge.

Irwin, G. and Dunn, S. (1997). *Ethnic Minorities in Northern Ireland*. Coleraine: Centre for the Study of Conflict.

Kapur, N. (1997). *The Irish Raj*. Antrim: Greystone Press.

Khan, R. (2010). Going 'Mainstream': Evaluating the Instrumentalisation of Multicultural Arts. *International Journal of Cultural Policy*, 16(2), pp. 184–199.

Korom, F. (1999). Empowerment Through Representation and Collaboration in Museum Exhibitions. *Journal of Folklore Research*, 36(2/3), pp. 259–265.

Kymlicka, W. (1995). *Multicultural Citizenship: A Liberal Theory of Minority Rights*. Oxford: Clarendon Press.

Kymlicka, W. (2007). *Multicultural Odysseys: Navigating the New International Politics of Diversity*. Oxford: Oxford University.

Levin, A. (2017). *Global Mobilities: Refugees, Exiles and Immigrants in Museums and Archives*. London: Routledge.

Lynch, B. (2014). Whose Cake is it Anyway? Museums, Civil Society and the Changing Reality of Public Engagement. In: Gourievidis, L. ed. *Museums and Migration: History, Memory and Politics*. London: Routledge, pp. 67–80.

McDermott, P. (2008). Acquisition, Loss or Multilingualism? Educational Planning for Speakers of Migrant Community Languages in Northern Ireland. *Current Issues in Language Planning*, 9(4), pp. 483–500.

McDermott, P. (2011). *Migrant Languages in the Public Space: A Case Study from Northern Ireland*. Berlin: Lit.

McDermott, P. (2012). Cohesion, Sharing and Integration? Migrant Languages and Cultural Spaces in Northern Ireland's Urban Environment. *Current Issues in Language Planning*, 13(3), pp. 187–205.

McDermott, P. (2013). A 'Shared Society?' Attitudes on Immigration and Diversity. *ARK Research Update* [online]. Available at http://www.ark.ac.uk/publications/updates/update86.pdf [Accessed 7 July 2017].

McDermott, P., Nic Craith, M. and Strani, K. (2016). Public Space, Collective Memory and Intercultural Dialogue in a (UK) City of Culture. *Identities: Global Studies in Culture and Power*, 23(5), pp. 610–627.

McGarry, J. and O'Leary, B. (2009). Under Friendly and Less-Friendly Fire. In: Taylor, R. ed. *Consociational Theory: McGarry and O'Leary and the Northern Ireland Conflict*. London: Routledge, pp. 15–84.

McMonagle, S., and McDermott, P. (2014). Transitional Politics and Language Rights in a Multi-ethnic Northern Ireland: Towards a True Linguistic Pluralism? *Ethnopolitics*, 13(3), pp. 245–266.

Modood, T. (1998). Multiculturalism, Secularism and the State. *Critical Review of International Social and Political Philosophy*, 1(3), pp. 79–97.

NMNI. (2015). *Collections Development Policy National Museums Northern Ireland*. Belfast: NMNI.

OFMDFM. (2006). *A Shared Future-Policy and Strategic Framework for Good Relations in Northern Ireland*. Belfast: OFMDFM.

OFMDFM (2013). *Together: Building a United Community Strategy*. Belfast: OFMDFM.

Parekh, B. (2000). *The Future of Multi-ethnic Britain: Report of the Commission on the Future of Multi-ethnic Britain*. London: Profile Books.

Quinn, M. (2017). Intercultural Museum Practice: An Analysis of the Belonging Project in Northern Ireland. In: Antos, Z., Fromm, A. and Golding, V. eds *Museums and Innovations*. Cambridge: Cambridge Scholars Publishing, pp. 18–29.

Rex, J. (2004). *Multiculturalism and Political Integration in the Modern Nation State* [online]. Available at http://hanskoechler.com/John_Rex-Multiculturalism-Nation_State-2004.pdf [Accessed July 2017].

Sandell, R. (2000). The Strategic Significance of Workforce Diversity in Museums. *International Journal of Heritage Studies*, 6(3), pp. 213–230.

Taylor, C. (1994). *Multiculturalism: Examining the Politics of Recognition*. Princeton: Princeton University Press.

Wilford, R. and Wilson, R. (2006). *The Trouble with Northern Ireland*. Belfast: Democratic Dialogue.

Young, I. (1990). *Justice and the Politics of Difference*. Princeton: Princeton University Press.

10 Where are all the women? public memory, gender and memorialisation in contemporary Belfast

Laura McAtackney

Perhaps unsurprisingly the Good Friday Agreement (1998) (hereafter 'the Agreement') does not place a strong emphasis on the concept of 'heritage'. There is only one distinct use of the term, and this is in relation to the changes to the wording of the Irish constitution (in Annex B); likewise backward-looking themes of history, memory and 'the past' are largely absent. Undoubtedly the Agreement was conceived as a future-orientated mechanism that claimed the best way to honour the dead and injured of the past conflict was through a 'fresh start' (1998: 2). However, at an implicit level the past and heritage concerns were always central to the Agreement as ultimately it aimed to end a long-standing conflict by acknowledging difference whilst trying to strive for 'reconciliation and rapprochement' (1998: 2–3) as a starting point. Heritage is increasingly conceived as a means of engaging with the past, locating what people find meaningful in order to be reconfigured in the present as a means of future-making (see Holtorf and Høgberg 2015), and as such it would appear to theoretically have all the qualities needed to transform old identities to new through a changing contemporary. However, in practice, whilst the lack of explicitly 'dealing with the past' in the Agreement has been noted in commentaries on its efficacy (including McGrattan 2009) this does not mean that engagement with what the past was, and what it continues to mean in the present, has not been central to post-conflict Northern Ireland. In the period since the signing of the Agreement there have been significant heritage implications in its practical working out, implementation and funding. This has particularly been notable in the creation and relatively long-term (if sporadic) funding for community and heritage bodies, initiatives and projects that seek to work on intra- and cross-community identity issues through grants such as the European Union (EU) Peace Fund (see Byrne et al. 2008). Since the Agreement, heritage institutions have been perceived as a relatively problem-free and useable means to facilitate a wide range of both single identity and cross-community projects on potentially difficult and contested issues of identity, contested history and sectional memory despite the lack of specific training and skills at both the level of the institutions and practitioners to take on these roles (including Crooke 2010). In the twenty years since the Agreement there has developed a disjuncture between the future-orientated wording of the Agreement and the practical implications of moving forward in a society saturated and directed by the past. This disjuncture prompts further investigation in a number of ways, and this chapter will focus on memory-making practices that have emerged during the post-conflict context from both bottom-up and top-down initiatives, and some of their (often unforeseen) consequences in terms of gender.

Given the wide array of potential heritage issues that have continued, developed and escalated in post-conflict Northern Ireland – including the politicisation of language (Concubhar 2017); what to do with difficult (proto)heritage of the Troubles, such as Long Kesh/Maze prison (McAtackney 2014); and the continuing influence of paramilitaries in curating urban landscapes of memory (Bryan et al. 2010) – this chapter will focus on the role of gender and public memory. In some respects this chapter follows on from a publication by Sara McDowell – on the gendered implications of commemorating in post-conflict Northern Ireland, which was published on the tenth anniversary of the Agreement (2008) – as it will update a number of the themes that McDowell highlighted. Broadly speaking this chapter follows McDowell in dissecting the role of murals, memorials and active commemorations in Northern Ireland, and how they link to silencing women's experiences and narratives of the conflict in favour of implicitly androcentric perspectives. However, as we reach the twentieth anniversary of the Agreement the political and social context has changed somewhat since 2008. This includes an even more unstable political environment that is much more polarised and unsettled than it was in 2008. Internally, a number of controversies and shifts in voting patterns have resulted in the Democratic Unionist Party (DUP) and Sinn Féin increasingly dominating the sectarian vote of the respective 'unionist' and 'nationalist' electorates. This polarisation of the vote, controversies regarding financial mismanagement at Stormont and an open power struggle between the two parties have resulted in no effective government at Stormont since January 2017 (Hain 2017). Adding to, and exacerbating, this internal low in relationships within Northern Ireland one cannot ignore the instability caused by external pressures, especially the moves towards Brexit and its previously underconsidered impact on Northern Ireland (see Hayward 2017; Parr and Burke 2017). Lastly, and explicitly connected to issues of heritage in Northern Ireland, the inhabitants of the island of Ireland are currently transitioning through what has been called a 'decade of commemorations' (including DCHG 2017), a period of heightened public, political and academic interest in the creation of the states of Ireland and Northern Ireland dating from c.1913 to c.1923 that is currently progressing through a number of politically sensitive centenaries.

The first 'highpoint' of this so-called decade of commemoration was in 2016 when the centenary of the Easter Rising and the Battle of the Somme, foundational events for the Republic of Ireland and Northern Ireland, took place. This dual focus has been notable for providing comparisons and contrasts of how official and grass roots attempts have decided to remember, and especially reconfigure, particular personalities, events and outcomes from these periods. There has been a lot written in the Irish media about the importance placed on women's roles during the Easter Rising in 1916 during the centenary commemorations (although this has not all been positive), including work by Una Mullally, who has argued that the emphasis on women was not only needed but also reflected current realities relating to the high-profile involvement of women in the creative and governmental spheres that oversaw the commemorations (2016). It is also evident, especially in the Republic of Ireland, that the interest in women and their roles 100 years ago has become entwined with the activism and advocacy of the contemporary women's rights movement. As they increasingly catalysed each other over the course of 2016, connections have been especially explicit in the iconography and wordplay of the #Repealthe8th movement, which have utilised images and slogans such as 'Rise and Repeal' in connecting their struggle to the historic women's movement (e.g. O'Sullivan 2016). In Northern Ireland, there has been a less notable focus on women's roles in the predominantly unionist commemorations of the Battle of the Somme. However, there has been an attempt to articulate the importance of Northern women in the smaller-scale nationalist commemoration of the Easter Rising, especially in Belfast, with the emphasis on the hitherto obscure Corr sisters in public talks, murals and commemorative posters (Monaghan 2016; Morrison 2016). The greater focus on male experiences of the Somme is perhaps understandable, given the different forms of warfare being commemorated (with the mono-focus on the Battle of the Somme making the inclusion of women more difficult, despite their various roles during the war, including as munitions workers and nurses; see Peatfield 2016), but it also clearly follows a long-standing trend to prioritise remembering male experiences of the past over women's in loyalist communities. With regard to these salient issues of memory-making and gender this chapter will mainly focus on case studies from two loyalist communities in Belfast.

Urban planning, 'peace walls' and the enduring materiality of division in Northern Ireland

To understand the role and importance of commemorative landscapes in Northern Ireland – and particularly in Belfast – one needs to understand the significance of urban planning, peace walls and materialised sectarian divisions in how the city functions on a practical level and imagined basis. In the context of the Troubles, monumental walls – called 'peace walls' – were created to essentially control access, use of space and create a sense of security and belonging – or insecurity and exclusion – in the urban environment (see McAtackney 2011). Over time they have played both positive and negative roles, but they do not simply exist; they carry the weight of intention and fear of the unknown, and materialise the residues of previous violence and even death that have occurred around them. They are both physical and psychic, and can be monumental structures that are designed to separate and allow only sporadic and controlled physical interactions, especially in areas of social housing, whilst simultaneously remaining relatively absent from city centres, middle-class areas and even official maps. Whilst walls play a significant role in directing the physical experiences of any city, they are particularly important in socially and politically divided cities such as Belfast, where security and belonging have heightened importance and where walls have ideological meanings connected to identity (see McAtackney and McGuire 2018: introduction). In a normative society walls define property, boundaries and barriers, and despite the fact that they often materialise inequality, their ubiquity ensures that they are considered a mundane and commonplace phenomenon that is generally unremarked on and naturalised. However, walls in divided cities fundamentally act as barriers that create distinctive enclaves; they shape access to space, and they can play a heightened role during conflict as they can have multiple and often contradictory meanings. They can prohibit movement, maintain difference and facilitate the focussing of tensions at interfaces (see Jarman and O'Halloran 2001). However, they can also have unforeseen and even creative roles: they can act as canvases to communicate opinion, direct and maintain identity (especially through graffiti and Belfast's famed wall murals [see McCormick and Jarman 2005]), and act as backdrops to commemorative landscapes or memorials that communicate meaning largely unchallenged to the still fundamentally homogeneous communities that walls in divided societies create.

So-called peace walls in Belfast are famously the only security manifestation associated with the Troubles that have continued to expand since the conflict ended, but they are increasingly becoming the focus of initiatives to enable their removal (including McDonald 2017). Whilst quantifying the numbers of peace lines is difficult, disputed figures from the Community Relations Council (CRC) state that there were eighteen barriers in the early 1990s, and this reached eighty-eight by 2009 (c.2009: 3). In a place where language matters, these separation barriers have had many different names – 'peace lines', 'peace walls', 'environmental barriers' (Boal 2002: 692), 'security walls' (Birrell 1994: 113) and 'interface barriers' (CRC c.2009: 3) – but are most commonly known as 'peace walls'. The use of the word 'peace' acts to justify their existence by associating their construction with ensuring peace through separation rather than acknowledging them as mechanisms they are inherently based in conflict. Indeed the assumption that walls maintain peace is contradicted by evidence, including from Neil Jarman and Chris O'Halloran, who have argued that walls channel rather than prevent violent confrontation (2001). There is also a notable absence of engagement with materiality, timelessness and placelessness in public discourse around these barriers that ignores changing community forms and shapes, and how the enduring materiality of monumental walls tends to solidify community relations at a low point.

Likewise there is a need to engage with the use of 'walls'. Although 'peace walls' is in some respects preferable to 'peace lines', which ultimately denies the material nature of many of the barriers, the peace walls in Belfast are not normative. This term does not represent decorative or symbolic property walls, marking boundaries or even gable walls, where many monumental murals are placed; they are ideological walls built to ensure almost complete separation from the other side. Frequently, they are monumental in the real sense of the world, towering over their surroundings. However, the use of 'lines' should not be completely discarded. Barriers in a long-divided city like Belfast are often psychic as well as physical and ethnic; political, religious and even socio-economic divisions are not simply mirrored in monumental constructions. Dividing walls are infrequently complete, with room for expansion at either end, and most have doorways or openings (official or unofficial) that allow movement – albeit controlled – at particular points, thus allowing them to be permeated or transgressed. They are not static, and they are not impenetrable. They do not affect everyone who physically experiences them equally; one has to come from the communities who live alongside them to know what the rules are to abide by or defy them. Due to the ambiguities surrounding them they as often evoke fear as security and have ensured that generations have grown up with, what Bryonie Reid has called, 'a psychology of spatial confinement' (2005: 489). Whilst they were created to control social interaction they are not always obeyed, and, indeed, they can invite active defiance by channelling violence to flashpoint areas where one side can confront those who usually live, visually hidden, 'on the other side'. A more insidious impact in the long-term maintenance of walls intended to prevent violent interactions is that they also prohibit the development of knowledge, understanding and empathy between near neighbours. They literally visually block the experiences of similarly disadvantaged and conflict-torn communities from each other, and they facilitate disconnects between those who have been most adversely affected by the Troubles, albeit on opposing sides. Effectively they act to maintain and even strengthen segregation into a post-conflict context. Furthermore, they also negate critiques of their self-created and at times defensive identities that materialise alongside these walls. This ensures that very particular and skewed views of the past can develop; alongside the 'othering' of the community hidden from view this also allows misrepresentations of the past to be propagated within. In this context – of an enduringly materially segregated Belfast twenty years post-Agreement – the proliferation of bottom-up, community memorials that have appeared alongside these walls is an important means of 'reading' how communities engage with, and reproduce, their understandings of their identity and community – and who is included within it – on their side of the peace wall.

Memorialisation, commemoration and gender

Unofficial, community memorials commemorating the Troubles have proliferated in the shadows of walls in post-Agreement Belfast. These memorials are designed and placed by the local communities, or more precisely those who hold power within them, and are most frequently found in working-class, urban areas of Northern Ireland alongside peace walls. This phenomenon has been relatively under-researched in the context of the peace process (although see McDowell 2008; Graham and Whelan 2007; Viggiani 2006); however, it is clear that the proliferation of memorials follows global as well as local trends in materialising memory. Erika Doss, writing about the contemporary US, has noted how memorialisation is increasingly being used to remember a wide variety of people, events and occasions in deeply personal as well as political ways. She argues that these memorials are important because of the potential for multiplicity of meanings and their ability to 'evoke memories, sustain thoughts, constitute political conditions and conjure states of being' (Doss 2010: 71). Whereas McDowell has argued that memorial landscapes tend to emphasize stereotypical gender roles in their focus on war and attempt to articulate the connection of the individual to the nation (2008: 337). They are multifaceted things. From one perspective they are inherently political and reflect the power to materialise memory and the ability to claim certain narratives as representing the places where these memorials are located, but conversely they can be deeply personal because they reflect local emotions, fears and losses. Akin to the American context that Doss describes, community memorials to the Troubles twenty years into a peace process must be examined with shades of nuance as they can be read in multiple ways that cannot be disconnected from their wider societal context. As noted at the start of this chapter, in civic society contentious aspects of 'the past' (often used as a shorthand for 'The Troubles') were deliberately bypassed at a political level in the Agreement, considered too difficult to confront without potentially reigniting conflict and reinforcing divisions (McGrattan 2009: 164). However, this top-down decision to not meaningfully engage with particularly difficult aspects of the past did not result in the past being ignored. In many areas of Belfast, particularly working-class areas, the public have long been disengaged from official heritage and its glossing over of a troubled past that deeply impacted them. This has resulted in bottom-up initiatives to actively and materially remember localised and partial pasts in places that are often particularly meaningful, and one of the most long-standing examples of these initiatives is community memorials. Many of these memorials are placed against peace walls or alongside them, both tacitly confirming their presence and reason for existence. These community memorials are not attempting to articulate a broad or representative history of the Troubles, sanitised for a post-conflict society; rather they aim to present very localised, and often one-sided, readings of the past. In doing this they are actively facilitated by the walls they reference, sustain and demarcate their community from the other side.

Clearly their spatial setting is important. Their placement is not only determined by mapping onto the people or events being commemorated, but, like murals (McCormick and Jarman 2005), the higher-profile and visually accessible locations hint at hierarchies of who is selected to be remembered, in what form and where. Memorials placed alongside peace walls in Belfast are spatially significant because both the walls and memorials have often been implanted into places that have been replanned and re-landscaped over the course of the conflict and peace process to the extent that the street plan is no longer the same. This means they are materially marking where clashes resulted in conflict, destruction and even death in the past, and in some cases historic photographic images are used as backdrops to ensure that the memory of those events is reinvigorated and acts to subvert the urban planning that aimed to displace them (for example, see the memorial at Bombay Street in West Belfast). Community memorials can be poignant markers that reinforce and implicitly sustain the continued existence of peace walls, especially as the latter are increasingly under threat due to pressure by political and civic elites to materially 'normalise' the city. In this respect peace walls and their associated memorials can reveal a disjuncture between the lived experiences of many communities beside peace lines who are reticent to completely remove them and those who reside in city centres or middle-class suburbs who wish them to be gone. Whilst the liberal media may deride their continued existence from the safety of their broadsheet newspapers (including Geoghegan 2015) those who live beside peace walls can have different relationships with them including as a perceived form of protection from a still feared other.

However, community memorials, whether against peace walls or at the core of the community, reflect a complicated array of experiences and understandings of the past and how it is retained in the present. Whilst they mainly concentrate on the communal experiences and repercussions of sectarian conflict and segregation they also implicitly reference wider social phenomena, including the impact of deindustrialisation, age and gender. When discussed at all their multifaceted nature is often overlooked in the analysis of post-Agreement Belfast due to the emphasis placed on them being read as straightforward reflections of community experiences of the Troubles without taking into consideration their landscape setting, who constructed them, when, why, who is excluded and how they may have evolved in form and meaning since construction. This has ensured that academic analysis tends to focus on places most linked to sectarian conflict, especially nationalist West Belfast (see Viggiana 2006 and McAtackney 2011), and on the explicit narratives constructed by those who created them. The latter is especially problematic as these narratives are often androcentric in maintaining the idea that the most important community experience of the conflict was that of the combatants (and in doing so frequently forgetting about the many victims, especially women and children, see Muldoon 2004).

Furthermore, often memorials are read hierarchically – with most attention given to the biggest, most pronounced and strategically placed examples – as articulating the most significant claims of victimhood and/or victories. What is implicitly being claimed, what is deliberately or unconsciously omitted, the link of historic grievances to contemporary conditions and the subtle interplay of the many and varied constituent parts of the memori-alscape often remains unanalysed.

A close examination of community memorialisation practices in contem-porary Belfast reveals complex and entangled narratives of place, identity and conflict continue to exist twenty years post-Agreement. For example, the myriad elements contributing to place identity in East Belfast are par-ticularly varied, as evidenced in a recent report on the role of curbstones, flags and emblems in place-making and how they are read by the wider public (Bryan et al. 2010). However, the focus of the report on paramilitary or re-imaged murals and flags did not venture into exploring how commu-nity memorials and council-funded public art contribute to place-making, despite their evident roles in creating, subverting or channelling the pro-jected 'identity' of the area. A more holistic investigation of these facets of identity in East Belfast reveals the importance of industrialisation as well as the experiences of the recent conflict, with understandings of both these experiences being almost completely androcentric (see McAtackney 2017). Female experiences and contributions to the area are excluded from the materialised public memory of East Belfast with the focus firmly connected to a paternalistic view of men working in and protecting the area. The rest of the chapter will focus on two case studies – from loyalist East and South Belfast – in order to examine the role and place of the memory of women in the post-Agreement context.

Gender and memorial practices in contemporary Belfast

East Belfast

I have previously argued that the long-established sectarian geographies of Belfast combined with both positive and negative aspects of cycles of industrialisation and deindustrialisation to have differential impacts on the place identity of the divided city of Belfast (McAtackney 2017). This con-clusion was supported by analysing the interplay between graffiti, flags, memorials, public art and murals in East Belfast as a means of explaining how its place identity differed from elsewhere in the city due, in part, to its long-term connections to a maritime, industrial past. I argued that the dominance of paramilitary murals and memorials existing alongside in-termittent shipbuilding-inspired public art commissioned by Belfast City Council (with the '*Ship of Dreams*' motif aiming to tie in with the cente-nary of the sinking of the Titanic) was problematic. This was not just be-cause of the ambiguous messages communicated through the intermixing of militaristic, aggressive paramilitary imagery with manifestations of a ship that tragically sank on its maiden voyage but also the more subtle issues of choosing to represent shipbuilding solely by focussing on its golden age and ignoring the societal strains of deindustrialisation in shaping the contemporary identity of the area. I extend this argument here to claim the public art interventions relating to the *Ship of Dreams* implicitly sustain and reinforce the androcentric public memory already entrenched through the pre-existing paramilitary images in East Belfast by focussing solely on men. Taken collectively these various official and unofficial interventions have created a streetscape that almost completely ignores the female experiences, roles and identities in East Belfast by instead focussing on the ideas, experiences and memories of men from the area across both time and space.

Paramilitary murals take many forms in East Belfast, but those that include figurative representations are almost always men with guns. At times the guns are placed alongside the men, passive but a latent threat; however, a number of paramilitary murals in the vicinity of the Newtownards Road in East Belfast depict more aggressive stances. On a gable end wall close to many of the Titanic re-imaged murals and public art and abutting the Lower Newtownards Road (the main thoroughfare from the city centre) a collection of murals commemorates *Ulster's Past Defenders* and *Ulster's Present Day Defenders* (see Figure 10.1). Both murals are triptychs with

Figure 10.1 Mural East Belfast commemorating *Ulster's Past Defenders* and *Ulster's Present Day Defenders*. Photograph by Laura McAtackney.

an insignia in the centre (for 'Ulster's Present Day Defenders' this is the paramilitary group 'UDA' [Ulster Defence Association]) with either side displaying uniformed men. On the left is a full-length, frontal representation of a man wearing sunglasses – a common representation of a loyalist paramilitary from the early Troubles of the 1970s – holding a book entitled 'members', and on the right is a full-length, frontally orientated, camouflaged figure wearing a balaclava and holding a semi-automatic gun pointing out of the image. The overt aggression of a gun pointing from a mural was a relatively rare mural image immediately post-Agreement in Northern Ireland. However, alongside the re-emergence of explicitly paramilitary murals since 2010, such militaristic images are becoming more common as uncertainties grow about the real benefits, and beneficiaries, of the peace process (Bryan et al. 2010: 41). Compounding the aggressive and masculine tone of these monumental murals community memorials to the Troubles, which have proliferated post-Agreement, continue the tradition of focussing on male combatants from the Troubles. Of those memorials placed on or alongside the Lower Newtownards Road (including on peace walls) the vast majority only name and remember those who died in active service or whilst members of named paramilitary organisations. Reaffirming what McDowell recorded ten years ago, these memorials contribute to an androcentric landscape through their number, location and focus on named men (as few as four) listed on sparse plaques (in comparison many of the community memorials in nationalist areas remember civilians, including women and children, who died during the conflict [see McAtackney 2015]). To add to their exclusive nature these memorials are visually accessible but are contained behind locked gates with only keyholders able to enter. Clearly, the growth in the number of these community memorials indicates they are in some ways meaningful to the community. However, they are also indicative of a memory race between paramilitary groups in the locale and are problematic in a broader sense in focussing community memory in East Belfast on a 'Troubles' that is almost exclusively the preserve of male combatants, with little acknowledgement of the experiences of others.

In the post-Agreement context the city council has not been passive in engaging with the identity of places associated with conflict during the Troubles. Two of their more proactive attempts to transition communities from negative to positive places are through reimaging previously paramilitary murals and dedicating public art (see Crowley 2011). In East Belfast an initiative to commemorate the centenary of the sinking of the Titanic in 2012 has been used an opportunity to engage with the community to ensure murals were re-imaged and public art was unveiled. Whilst the much-publicised and celebratory unveiling of bronzes to workmen have focussed on cross-community political support for the initiative (Belfast Telegraph 2012) the singular focus on the experiences of men compounds the highly gendered nature of this space. There are no women present – whether one considers the trio of 'Titanic Yardmen 401' statuary bronzes or '*Ship of Dreams*' murals that exhibit a range of images including the ship, motif, architect, shipyard workmen and captain. There are no women depicted in either the construction, sailing or sinking of the ship or the industrial heritage of the area. Whilst the replacement of paramilitary images with those of a ship is celebrated as a welcome change the almost complete exclusion of women from the various high-profile visual markers of place identity around the main thoroughfare of East Belfast goes undiscussed. Akin to the paramilitary murals that remain the exclusion of women from the iconography of East Belfast is not a post-Agreement phenomenon but is a continuation from the Troubles. Previously, Bryonie Reid has examined how a female artist has engaged with the androcentric nature of this area in 1994 (2005). She described how Sandra Johnson created two performances as a means of reacting against the marginalisation and vulnerability she felt as a woman living in the area after she experienced assault and intimidation (Reid 2005). In this context the appearance of community memorials and *Ship of Dreams* street and public art in the post-Agreement context are new developments (and the latter may be considered a welcome change from explicitly paramilitary murals). However, their lack of redefining 'the community' beyond the confines of pre-existing foci only compounds the idea that public space in East Belfast continues to be inherently male. The changes that have occurred merely add a new facet to the maleness of the place identity, and in some respects the appearance of community memorials to dead paramilitaries negates the positive move of introducing industrial heritage as a facet of identity. However, since the tenth anniversary of the Agreement there have been more recent interventions in loyalist areas that have attempted to address the deficit of women and so this chapter will move to Sandy Row, a loyalist community in the inner city of South Belfast.

South Belfast

In her article of 2008 McDowell described a 'celebration of loyalist culture' that included the creation and unveiling of thirteen murals in the Lower Shankill area of West Belfast initiated by the loyalist paramilitary organisations UDA/UFF (Ulster Freedom Fighters) in 2000. She noted that all but one of the murals were 'militant' and commemorated men or male-orientated events connected to loyalist identity and history. The one exception was a mural of Princess Diana, which she reported the local women she interviewed considered tokenistic (2008: 341). McDowell also noted that the militaristic and aggressive nature of the majority of the murals' themes and stylistic representations were mirrored in the aggressive commemorative events that marked their unveiling (which included the firing of volleys at each mural) (ibid). She noted through her experiences of unveilings and commemorations that the aggressive mixture of murals, memorials and public art acted as a catalysing backdrop to the aggressive nature of loyalist commemorations that were led by men and for which women's only roles were to be supportive and passive onlookers (McDowell 2008: 340–343). In this respect her findings for loyalist place identity across Belfast in 2008 reinforced Reid's discussions of Sandra Johnson's experiences and performances in East Belfast in 1994 (Reid 2005). The city council has increasingly acknowledged the need to address loyalist place identity post-Agreement (especially in comparison with nationalist areas, which tended to transition away from militaristic street art and murals voluntarily [Bryan et al. 2010: 41]) and has responded by funding many public art initiatives, such as those previously discussed in East Belfast. Whilst the use of public art to gentrify and aestheticise the transitional city is not unique to post-Agreement Belfast the form and means of implementing these policies does seem to recognise that place identity associated with conflict is also largely androcentric. This may explain why many examples of post-Agreement public art take a female or gender-neutral form. Whilst the majority of these artworks have been located in neutral, city centre locations – including the 'Beacon of Hope', which was created by Andy Scott and installed in Thanksgiving Square in Belfast in 2006 and 'Monument to the Unknown Woman Worker', which was created by Louise Walker and installed on Great Victoria Street (GVS) in Belfast in 1992 – others have been placed in loyalist areas. One of the most recent female-focussed pieces of public art was unveiled on the margins of the loyalist community of Sandy Row in South Belfast in 2010. Again, placement is important – Sandy Row is a working-class, loyalist area centrally located on the edge of Belfast central business district. It has in some ways been a troubling remnant of the past for a city that is increasingly trying to attract international tourists particularly due to its continued display of paramilitary murals. Perhaps most notable was the existence until 2010 of a paramilitary mural that communicated from a large, gable wall towards the city's main bus and train station on 'GVS'.

From 2003 to 2010 the gable wall that faced GVS transport hub contained a paramilitary mural composed of paramilitary-related text and a hooded, paramilitary gunman. Referencing the famous 'You are now entering Free Derry' wall mural it stated, 'You / Are now / Entering / Loyalist Sandy Row / Heartland of South Belfast / Ulster Freedom Fighters'. This mural was created during the peace process and was retained at a highly strategic location between 2003 and 2010. In 2010, after extensive negotiations with the local community, a new re-imaged mural was put in place that 'transformed' the previous overtly loyalist mural to a representation of the loyalist figurehead King William of Orange (BBC 2012). William holds a heightened place in public memory in Northern Ireland as his victory over his father-in-law, the catholic King James, at the Battle of the Boyne in 1690 is central to loyalist identity and is therefore a hugely popular mural theme (Rolston 1992). Therefore, whilst the wall no longer projects out a hooded gunman the change of focus to King William is only slightly less problematic. Despite him meaning little to foreign visitors who may be using the bus/train station the depiction is still focussed on a male military figure and is exclusionary to the nationalists living in the city. Therefore, further attempts to neutralise the long association of this corner with loyalist paramilitary men were attempted with the placement of the sculpture *Mother, Daughter, Sister*, which was unveiled in June 2015 at the corner directly in front of the mural (see Figure 10.2). At the

Figure 10.2 Sculpture *Mother, Daughter, Sister,* unveiled in June 2015. Photograph by Laura McAtackney.

time the sculpture was articulated by the Arts Council Northern Ireland (ACNI) as a means of adding women to public space, but it was also clearly a means of reconfiguring place identity as part of a wider re-imaging initiative (ACNI 2015). At the time of the unveiling, which included women from the community as well as the current First Minister Arlene Foster, the Chairman of Belfast South Community resources claimed, 'Women have long been the rod of steel that runs through and supports our community. Together with artist Ross Wilson, women of all ages from Sandy Row, took part in workshops exploring themes of identity, reconciliation and peace' (ACNI 2015). Whilst it was evident that the women of the community played a central role in conceiving the sculpture, much like discussions of East Belfast, one does need to examine the final product and its context together.

The sculpture is life-sized, on a plinth and placed close to the roadside. It is figurative in form and is largely symbolic in its representation as a young, contemporary woman who is anonymous rather than commemorating by an individual. The artist claimed the sculpture was inspired by older women and their memories, it was noted the words 'Que Sera Sera' were added to the base as many of the women liked this Doris Day song from the 1950s (ACNI 2015). The title of the sculpture – *Mother, Sister, Daughter* – reinforces her anonymity as she is essentially understood through her relationship to others. Whilst it is difficult to meaningfully represent a cross section of women from the area in figurative sculpture this piece follows a noticeable trajectory in representing women in conflict in a way that elides their experiences and roles (McDowell 2008: 337) and this is most effectively done when representing them as symbolic and anonymous. This representation is particularly ambiguous when one takes into account that the representation is of a young woman inspired by old women that claims to include the memories of the latter whilst simultaneously being 'forward-looking' (ACNI 2015). Likewise, the claim that it reinserts women and their experiences into the public space appear disingenuous when its setting is considered. The sculpture is placed on the margins of Sandy Row, at a psychic boundary between the community and the more neutral space of the transport hub at GVS. It is placed directly in front of a monumental mural commemorating the loaded historical figure of King William with the residual memory of a long-standing paramilitary mural just a few layers of paint underneath. Such a setting means the mural is effectively the frame and backdrop to the sculpture and as such can only undercut the latter's role and intended meaning. Following from earlier discussions on place identity (including Bryan et al. 2010) clearly this singular statue may tick a gender box, but one has to question whether the experiences of women are being materialised in Sandy Row because it is meaningful or simply to try to neutralise the pre-existing place meaning?

Conclusions

Looking back and attempting to assess how Northern Ireland has moved forward as a society in the twenty years post-Agreement gives us many heritage-related vantage points including how the past is remembered (both top-down and bottom-up), how contemporary identities are represented and have evolved, what aspects of contemporary Northern Ireland are meaningful changing and how the challenges or remembering whilst moving forward have been taken up by various communities. Perhaps unforeseen at the time, in the twenty years since the Agreement heritage has been used an important tool for attempting to allow society to move on whilst retaining some link to the past and particularly in terms of productively engaging with identity and history to attempt to transform places and communities associated with conflict. Hitherto, attempts to assess how far Northern Ireland has transitioned to a 'normal' society post-Agreement has focussed on the transformation of conflict-related problems such as sectarianism and enduring paramilitarism without considering other, perhaps more insidious issues and how a variety of factors may result in very different transitions. This need to look beyond conflict and explore what is forgotten as well as what is remembered prompted this chapter to focus on the role (or absence) of gender in exploring official and unofficial attempts at place-making in loyalist areas of Belfast.

The focus of this chapter on loyalist communities in East Belfast does not mean that nationalist areas are above critique. Whilst the dual commemorations of the Battle of the Somme and the Easter Rising in 2016 provided both communities with opportunities to reformulate and repackage their well-worn tropes and symbols for a post-Agreement context, the opportunities to do so were constrained by both source material, circumstances and possibly will. Nationalist, perhaps taking a lead from the focus on women that accompanied the Easter Rising commemorations in Dublin, located some local heroines, including the Corr sisters (see Morrison 2016) and Winifred Carney (McCormack 2016), but there were few new inclusions alongside the mass of anonymous women depicted in murals and long-term token individual, Countess Markievicz. Loyalist communities had less opportunity to explore female figures for the Battle of the Somme, even if the will was there to do so, and the maintenance of tradition may be all that could be expected against a backdrop of uncertainties with the spectra of Brexit and a redundant Stormont lingering throughout the year. This wider context is important to recognise as commemorations are determined by their contemporary context as much as by the past that is being marked (Daly and O'Callaghan 2007), and this chapter has shown there is a long-term and more insidious background to the lack of female inclusion in the public memory of loyalist communities in Belfast and so it was selected as the focus.

Using two case studies – the Newtownards Road in East Belfast and Sandy Row in South Belfast – this chapter was inspired by Sara McDowell's study of the androcentric nature of commemoration and memorialisation in Northern Ireland ten years after the Agreement (2008) and it intended to be a brief update moving ten years on. What it found was that whilst changes have occurred – community memorials have proliferated and public art has been used to attempt to reconfigure place identity – underlying continuities remain fairly similar. This is especially regarding the need to not only consider the role of women and women's memories but also meaningfully insert them into public space. In East Belfast it is clear that spatially significant spaces are still dominated by the images, militarism and aggression of male, combatants from the Troubles. Whilst there has been an intention to dilute this by inserting murals and statues connected to historic shipbuilding this has been problematic in not allowing any room for women. Likewise the proliferation of community memorials since 1998 reveals that these exclusive and modest structures that have appeared around the main thoroughfare and alongside peace walls in East Belfast are not intended to commemorate the community but only paramilitary (male) combatants. In the ten years since McDowell's article the place identity of this part of East Belfast remains tied to overt displays of military strength by paramilitaries and an opportunity to de-masculinise the space was lost in the decision to focus on the Titanic as a non-sectarian (but female-free) symbol for the community. In some ways Sandy Row in South Belfast has fared slightly better in terms of female representation in public space with the erection of *Mother, Daughter, Sister* in 2015. This bronze sculpture of a young, female standing at a prominent corner on the margins of Sandy Row is superficially a meaningful inclusion of female memory into the areas as it was created after consultation with women of the area. However, an investigation of its context reveals how a prominent re-imaged mural of King William of Orange acting as its backdrop overwhelms the life-sized sculpture. Taken together as a meaningful landscape they lack coherence and as such they can only be in competition with each other in terms of directing place identity: a competition the smaller bronze inevitably loses. Regardless of the undoubtedly honourable intentions of this commission it clearly maintains the tradition of women subsidiary, passive and tokenistic in the public space of loyalist community (cf McDowell 2008: 343; Reid 2005). Now that we are twenty years post-Agreement in Northern Ireland it is clearly time to move away from a mono-focus on sectarian conflict and to think more intersectionally about what a normalised society should look like – one that aspires to give voice to the enduringly silenced women.

Bibliography

Arts Council Northern Ireland. (2015). New Artwork Celebrates the Women of Sandy Row. [online] 15 June 2015. Available at: http://artscouncil-ni.org/news/new-artwork-celebrates-the-women-of-sandy-row [Accessed December 2017].

BBC. (2012). King Billy Portrait Replaces UFF Mural on Sandy Row. *BBC News* 2 July. Available at: www.bbc.com/news/uk-northern-ireland-18672651 [Accessed 18 December 2017].

Belfast Agreement. (1998). Agreement Between the Government of the United Kingdom of Great Britain and Northern Ireland and the Government of Ireland.

Belfast Telegraph. (2012). Titanic Workers Sculpture Unveiled. 28 March 2012. Available at: www.belfasttelegraph.co.uk/news/local-national/northern-ireland/titanic-workers-sculpture-unveiled-28731593.html [Accessed 7 May 2014].

Birrell, D. (1994) Social Policy Responses to Urban Violence in Northern Ireland. In: Dunn, S. ed. *Managing Divided Cities*. Keele: Keele University Press. pp. 105–118.

Boal, F.W. (2002) Belfast: Walls Within. *Political Geography*, 21(5), pp. 687–694.

Bryan, D., Stevenson, C., Gillespie, G. and Bell, J. (2010). Public Display of Flags and Emblems in Northern Ireland 2006–2009. Belfast: Institute of Irish Studies.

Byrne, S., Thiessen, C., Fissuh, E., Irvin, C. and Hawranik, M. (2008). Economic Assistance, Development and Peacebuilding: The Role of the IFI and EU Peace II Fund in Northern Ireland. *Civil Wars*, 10(2), pp. 106–124.

Community Relations Council (CRC). c.2009. *Towards Sustainable Security: Interface Barriers and the Legacy of Segregation in Belfast*. Belfast: Community Relations Council.

Concubhar. (2017). Ulster Scots, Ulster Irish, Irish Scots, Ulster Gaelic, Gaelige Uladh. [online] Slugger O'Toole 20 July 2017. Available at: https://sluggerotoole.com/2017/07/20/ulster-scots-ulster-irish-irish-scots-ulster-gaelic-gaeilge-uladh/ [Accessed 18 December 2017].

Crooke, E. (2010). The Politics of Community Heritage: Motivations, Authority and Control. *International Journal of Heritage Studies*, 16(1–2), pp. 16–29.

Crowley, T. (2011). The Art of Memory: The Murals of Northern Ireland and the Management of History. *Field Day Review* (7), pp. 22–49.

Daly, M. and O'Callaghan, M. (2007). 1916 in 1966: Commemorating the Easter Rising. Dublin: Royal Irish Academy.

Department of Culture, Heritage and Gaeltacht. (2017). *Decade of Commemorations* [online]. Available at: www.decadeofcentenaries.com [Accessed 19 December 2017].

Doss, E. (2010). *Memorial Mania: Public Feeling in America*. London: University of Chicago Press.

Geoghegan, P. (2015). Will Belfast Ever Have a Berlin Wall Moment and Tear Down Its 'Peace Walls'? [online] *The Guardian* 29 September 2015. Available at: www.theguardian.com/cities/2015/sep/29/belfast-berlin-wall-moment-permanent-peace-walls [Accessed 20 December 2017].

Graham, B. and Whelan, Y. (2007). The Legacies of the Dead: Commemorating the Troubles in Northern Ireland. *Environment and Planning D: Society and Space*, 24(3), pp. 476–495.

Hain, P. (2017). Paralysis Has Gripped Northern Ireland but Politicians Just Look Blithely On. [online] *The Guardian* 14 November 2017. Available at: www.theguardian.com/commentisfree/2017/nov/14/northern-ireland-politicians-sinnfein-dup-stormont-theresa-may [Accessed 18 December 2017].

Hayward, K. (2017). The DUP Was Painted into a Corner by Brexiter's Hyperbole, but a Solution is Possible. [online] *The Guardian* 6 December 2017. Available at: www.theguardian.com/commentisfree/2017/dec/06/dup-brexiters-northern-ireland-brexit [Accessed 18 December 2017].

Holtorf, C. and Høgberg, A. (2015). Contemporary Heritage and the Future. In: Waterton, E. and Watson, S. eds. *The* Palgrave *Handbook of Contemporary Heritage Research*. Palgrave: Manchester, pp. 509–523.

Jarman, N. and O'Halloran, C. (2001). Recreational Rioting: Young People, Interface Areas and Violence. *Childcare in Practice*, 7(1), pp. 2–16.

McAtackney, L. (2011). Peace Maintenance and Political Messages: The Significance of Walls During and After the 'Troubles' in Northern Ireland. *Journal of Social Archaeology*, 11(1), pp. 77–98.

McAtackney, L. (2014). *An Archaeology of the Troubles: The Dark Heritage of Long Kesh/Maze Prison*. Oxford: Oxford University Press.

McAtackney, L. (2015). Memorials and Marching: Archaeological Insights into Segregated Tradition in Northern Ireland. In Northern Worlds Special Edition of *Historical Archaeology*, 49(3), pp. 110–125.

McAtackney, L. (2017). Repercussions of Differential Deindustrialization in the City: Memory and Identity in Contemporary East Belfast. In: McAtackney, L. and Ryzewski, K. eds. Contemporary Archaeology and the City: Creativity, Ruination and Political Action. Oxford: Oxford University Press. pp. 190–210.

McAtackney, L. and McGuire, R., eds. (2018). *Living in a World of Walls*. Albuquerque: University of New Mexico Press.

McCormack, J. (2016). Easter Rising 1916: How Winifred Carney became James Connolly's confidant. [online] 27 Mar 2016. www.bbc.com/news/uk-northern-ireland-35849250 [Accessed 19 December 2017].

McCormick, J. and Jarman, N. (2005). Death of a Mural. *Journal of Material Culture Studies*. 10(1), pp. 49–71.

McDonald, H. (2017). Belfast 'Peace Wall' Between Communities Felled After 30 Years. *The Guardian* 20 September 2017. www.theguardian.com/uk-news/2017/sep/20/belfast-peace-wall-between-communities-felled-after-30-years [Accessed 8 December 2017].

McDowell, S. (2008). Commemorating Dead 'Men': Gendering the Past and Present in Post-conflict Northern Ireland. *Gender, Place and Culture*, 15(4), pp. 335–354.

McGrattan, C. (2009). 'Order Out of Chaos': The Politics of Transitional Justice. *Politics*, 29(3), pp. 164–172.

Monaghan, J. (2016). Housing Executive Provides Funds to Commemoration Family Divided by Rising and Somme. 31 March 2016. Available at: www.bbc.com/news/uk-northern-ireland-35862231 [Accessed 8 December 2017].

Morrison, C. (2016). A Belfast Family Took Part in the Rising and the Somme. 22 March 2016. Available at: www.bbc.com/news/uk-northern-ireland-35862231 [Accessed December 2017].

Muldoon, O.T. (2004). Children of the Troubles: The Impact of Political Violence in Northern Ireland. *Journal of Social Issues*, 60(3), pp. 453–468.

Mullally, U. (2016). Why Women Have Risen to the Top in 1916 Lore. Available at: www.irishtimes.com/opinion/una-mullally-why-women-have-risen-to-the-top-in-1916-lore-1.2588986 [Accessed 9 July 2017].

O'Sullivan, J. (2016). Press Release from Abortion Rights Campaign: Huge Cross-Party Show of Support for Repeal of 8th Amendment as Politicians Pledge to Secure Abortion Rights. [online] 20 September 2016. www.abortionrightscampaign.ie/2016/09/20/press-release-from-abortion-rights-campaign-huge-cross-party-show-of-support-for-repeal-of-8th-amendment-as-politicians-pledge-to-secure-abortion-rights-in-ireland/ [Accessed 17 December 2017].

Parr, C. and Burke, E. (2017). Brexit: What are the Issues Surrounding Northern Ireland's Border and Could Scupper UK's EU Withdrawal. [online] *The Independent* 17 December 2017. Available at: www.independent.co.uk/news/uk/politics/brexit-latest-northern-ireland-border-republic-dup-arlene-foster-theresa-may-david-davis-eu-a8093171.html [Accessed 7 December 2017].

Peatfield, L. (2016). Ireland's Role in the First World War [online]. Available at: www.iwm.org.uk/history/irelands-role-in-the-first-world-war [Accessed 17 December 2017].

Reid, B. (2005). 'A Profound Edge': Performative Negotiations of Belfast. *Cultural Geographies*, 12(4), pp. 485–506.

Rolston, B. (1992). Drawing Support: Murals in the Northern of Ireland. Belfast: Beyond the Pale Publications.

Viggiani, E. (2006). Public Forms of Memorialisation to the 'Victims of the Northern Irish Troubles' in the City of Belfast. MA Thesis, Queen's University of Belfast.

Index